Addie Joss on Baseball

THE MCFARLAND HISTORICAL BASEBALL LIBRARY

1. Cobb, Ty. *Busting 'Em and Other Big League Stories* (1914). 2003

2. Axelson, G.W. *"Commy": The Life Story of Charles A. Comiskey* (1919). 2003

3. Ellard, Harry. *Base Ball in Cincinnati: A History* (1907). 2004

4. Richter, Francis C. *Richter's History and Records of Base Ball, the American Nation's Chief Sport* (1914). 2005

5. Lanigan, Ernest J. *Baseball Cyclopedia* (1922). 2005

6. Evers, John J., and Hugh S. Fullerton. *Touching Second* (1910). 2005

7. Rice, Grantland. *Base-Ball Ballads* (1910). 2005

8. Claudy, C.H. *The Battle of Base-Ball* (1912). 2005

9. Kelly, Mike "King." *"Play Ball": Stories from the Diamond Field and Other Historical Writings about the 19th Century Hall of Famer* (1888). 2006.

10. Anonymous and Noah Brooks. *The Great Match* [1877] *and Our Base Ball Club* [1884]*: Two Novels from the Early Days of Base Ball,* volume editors Trey Strecker *and* Geri Strecker. 2010

11. Green, Guy W. *The Nebraska Indians* [1900] *and Fun and Frolic with an Indian Ball Team* [1907]*: Two Accounts of Baseball Barnstorming at the Turn of the Twentieth Century,* volume editor Jeffrey P. Beck. 2010

12. Salsinger, H.G. *Ty Cobb: Two Biographies—"Our Ty: Ty Cobb's Life Story" (1924) and "Which Was Greatest: Ty Cobb or Babe Ruth?" (1951),* volume editor William R. Cobb. 2012

13. Joss, Addie. *Addie Joss on Baseball: Collected Newspaper Columns and World Series Reports, 1907–1909,* compiled and annotated by Rich Blevins. 2012

Addie Joss on Baseball

Collected Newspaper Columns and World Series Reports, 1907–1909

Compiled and Annotated by
RICH BLEVINS

McFarland Historical Baseball Library, 13
Gary Mitchem *and* Mark Durr, *Editors*

McFarland & Company, Inc., Publishers
Jefferson, North Carolina, and London

Library of Congress Cataloguing-in-Publication Data

Joss, Addie, 1880–1911.
Addie Joss on baseball : collected newspaper columns and world series reports, 1907–1909 / Compiled and Annotated by Rich Blevins.
p. cm. — (McFarland historical baseball library ; 13)
[Gary Mitchem and Mark Durr, series editors]
Includes bibliographical references and index.

ISBN 978-0-7864-6356-5
softcover : acid free paper ∞

1. Baseball — United States — History — 20th century.
2. Baseball — Press coverage — United States — History — 20th century.
3 Sports journalism — United States — History — 20th century.
4. Newspapers — United States — Sections, columns, etc.
I. Blevins, Rich, 1950– II. Title.
GV863.A1J67 2012
796.357'64097309041—dc23 2012014173

British Library cataloguing data are available

On the cover: Cleveland pitcher Addie Joss (Cleveland Public Library)

Manufactured in the United States of America

McFarland & Company, Inc., Publishers
Box 611, Jefferson, North Carolina 28640
www.mcfarlandpub.com

To Cy Voorhees
AND
Jim Lowell

Acknowledgments

I have found that talking about baseball tends to bring out the best in people. And baseball people are unfailingly helpful. The Mud Hens' John Husman supported my project from its nice-idea stages, and he even hosted me at the ballpark. I came to rely on librarian and editor Donna Christian, at the Toledo-Lucas County Public Library, and Lynn M. Duchez Bycko, at Cleveland State's Michael Schwartz Library. The previously unpublished Sacred Heart College team photograph is reproduced by permission of David Stalker, from Watertown, Wisconsin. John, Donna, and David work in the great American tradition of the local historian I first encountered, growing up in Seville, Ohio, in Lee Cavin and later recognized in the work of Charles Olson. At the University of Pittsburgh at Greensburg, my chairman, Bill Rued, twice directed travel funding my way. Secretary Valerie Kubenko was a cheerful supporter. And faculty secretary Linda Szypulski took a special interest in the Joss microfilm. My friend, the poet Tom Kryss, is my guide to Cleveland past and present. Tom's collection of over 15,000 photographs, most of them Cleveland baseball, was a source and an inspiration. Librarian Patrice Hamiter kindly searched the Sports Collection of the Cleveland Public Library for Joss materials. Jim Vikartosky (Pitt-Greensburg), Deb Jayne (SABR)), and Freddy Berowski (National Baseball Hall of Fame) made the Appendix possible.

I save my biggest thanks for my wife, Martha. Like spring training, she makes all things seem possible again.

— Rich Blevins.

Table of Contents

"Addie was one of us: an off-season newspaper bloke whose efforts were good enough that he could have made a career writing about the game."—Bob Broeg

"To be a pitcher! ... A pitcher, standing at the axis of event."—Eric Rolfe Greenberg

"The universe is made of stories, not atoms."—Muriel Rukeyser

"Pitching is a large subject."— Marianne Moore

Preface

Toledo newspaper mogul Nigel D. Cochran was a winner, and he had just won again. Within a few months, Cochran's gamble to hire the popular 27-year-old baseball player had already proved a wild success with readers of his *News-Bee.* He recently had to order the press run increased to 12,000 copies, and install a direct telephone line for all the calls to his new sports editor's desk.[1]

The move had been risky on two counts. Cochran was counting on Addie Joss, the young man without portfolio in sports journalism (or experience in writing of any kind), to edit and largely write two full pages for a new, and untested, 24-page Sunday edition.[2] Nigel Cochran was a great one for innovations. In Chicago, he would experiment with an ad-free newspaper, named the *Day Book.* But this wasn't Chicago, and the *News-Bee* had to share the smaller Toledo market with a well-ensconced rival paper, the *Blade.* Nigel Cochran was ever the civic-minded journalist, wherever he worked. The idea of the direct phone line would have come naturally to a man like him. Plus, it appealed to the users of the era's new technology, much in the way we are drawn to sports talk shows and baseball players' blogs today. When Addie became sports editor, the *News-Bee* was routinely inviting its subscribers to "Telephone YOUR WANT AD to The News-Bee and reach 90% of all Toledo."

Albeit new to journalism, Addie would have come to Cochran highly recommended by Samuel Hopkins, a Cleveland connection of his own. Addie had been partners with the prominent businessman. Hopkins was a big baseball fan, and he liked to work out with the Naps. In turn, Cochran would have recommended Addie to R.F. Paine, who hired the pitcher-turned-writer to cover three World Series as a syndicated reporter for the Scripps newspaper chain and its flagship, the Cleveland *Press.*[3]

Cochran's decision was boldly announced to readers by the cartoon on the front page of their January 19, 1907, newspaper. "Addie Has 'Control' of the Copy" it read, above an artist's rendition of the new sports editor throwing copy to the newsroom catcher. By February, Joss was also contributing weekday stories. Over the next two off-seasons — from the end of the Cleveland Naps' regular season each fall, right up to the week in early spring when he took the train south for spring training — Addie wrote about the game he loved. He filled the empty winter months, already known as the Hot Stove League, with his stories about the game he knew firsthand, its characters, its greatest plays, and how it should be played. Beginning in 1908, Addie's column was called "Winter Baseball." Readers could easily locate it beneath the dingbat of men warming themselves by a pot-bellied stove. And then, with the publication of "Addie Joss' Farewell Story," on February 22, 1909, Addie's tenure at the *News-Bee* was over. In the two off-seasons left in his short life, Addie would join some White Sox friends on the winter vaudeville tour and operate a pool hall in downtown Toledo. He continued to be a welcome visitor to the *News-Bee*'s offices, a short streetcar ride from his house.

Addie also contributed a series of feature articles to the Cleveland *Press*, during the off-season of 1907-1908, and for two months after the World Series of 1908. His earliest stories for the *Press* were also syndicated by the Newspaper Enterprise Association and reached a wide readership; eventually, he became a regular columnist for the Monday edition. During Addie's playing career, the *Press* was Cleveland's big-circulation afternoon daily, serving a robust city of 381,768 (ranked seventh-largest city in the 1900 census). His game-day reports of three World Series (1907, 1908, and 1909) were syndicated by the *Press* and printed in many newspapers.[4]

Sometime before Christmas in 1906, Addie must have been pleased to accept Cochran's offer of a job. Salaries for a major league player during the Deadball Era made off-season jobs and barnstorming tours a necessary supplement to his modest income. Besides, Addie's standard contract with the Naps meant a paycheck only during the baseball season. There was the mortgage on the house to pay every month, and the Joss household was now up to four members, counting a toddler daughter.

Addie was a star ball player and a student of the sport, but as a sports writer he was a yannigan, a rookie. True, over the long Toledo winters, he had enjoyed the easy camaraderie of reporters and staff at 328 St. Clair Street.

***The January 19, 1907,* News-Bee *cartoon heralding the start of Joss' writing career* (courtesy Toledo–Lucas County Public Library, obtained from http://images2.toledolibrary.org/).**

But now that Addie was a professional newspaper man, starting his career at the age of 27, it's a good bet that he ran his copy by veteran Toledo baseball reporter Dick Meade. (Meade's contribution to the success of the Mud Hens in the city was so great that he appears in the 1905 team photograph, and he would serve as team president in the 1920s.) His influence on Addie's writing must have been profound.

Addie proved himself a natural in the newsroom. He possessed an inventive mind to complement his newest employer's. Addie was required to review a wide range of sports in his job as sports editor. I have made no attempt to estimate, much less reprint, all of the work in this vein that he must have written, sans byline, in his years at the *News-Bee*. I have omitted enough material for a small book of stories on college football, tournament bowling, horse racing, professional boxing, 100-yard sprint competitions, and even international boat racing. Baseball pitchers Otto Hess and Nick Altrock, he informs us, are great bowlers. A biographical sketch he wrote for the Cleveland *Press,* in his best Horatio Alger style, assures his readers that the young professional pool player is a model around kids.

Just who did read Addie Joss' articles on baseball and diverse sports topics? Writing about Billy Sunday's eulogy for Addie, a *News-Bee* reporter inadvertently identifies the beloved Joss' audience for us. Addie's readership encompassed "all Toledo ... the mayor ... all the city officials and the county officials ... the firemen and policemen ... the lawyers ... the physicians; the business men, the bankers, tradesmen and artisans; the staffs and employees of the Toledo newspapers ... hotel employees, from proprietor to bell-hop; the men in the shops, railroad men, street car men, post office employees." Before he was a baseball writer, and well before he became a sports star in Cleveland, Addie was first a Toledo celebrity, when he pitched for the Mud Hens. He had married a local girl, and was raising a family in the city. A *News-Bee* headline saw fit to inform those readers when "Joss Leaves for Spring Training Trip," the year before Addie hired on as sports editor. Of course, his syndicated Cleveland *Press* reports on the World Series briefly reached a national readership.

I like to think of Addie's baseball writing as our own direct line to one of Cooperstown's most disappeared inductees. The extant articles are Addie's first-person observations of the game and its players, many of them baseball immortals and most of them his good friends, from the first decade of the American League.

So little else remains of the man. We have but a handful of photographs of his pitching motion. His autograph is among the rarest for a Hall of Fame member. The places we might most associate with him — League Park and Armory Park, the house on Fulton Street, the *News-Bee* office building, even the Masonic temple where many of the game's star players gathered with the people of Toledo for his funeral — have all been erased from the cityscapes. I failed to turn up a single sample of his newspaper copy, any account of his method of composition or the models he had in mind when he wrote. Adrian Joss went from birth in Woodland, Wisconsin, to burial in Woodlawn Cemetery, Toledo, in the blur that was 30 years. Addie died before the Cleveland

Indians or radio broadcasts or the Cy Young Award or the *state* of Arizona (much less the D-Backs or Firestone Park). Nearly 30 years have passed since David Fleitz interviewed the last surviving member of the Joss family, Arlene (a daughter-in-law Addie did not live to meet). No Joss could attend the ceremonies in Cooperstown, when Addie was at last inducted, almost like an afterthought. Surely, no one is alive who saw Addie Joss pitch.[5] He is so little remembered that it took 87 years for his only full-length biography to appear in print.

I wanted to find Addie Joss. Growing up an Indians fan, I had encountered Addie Joss' old-fashioned name and some impressive statistics, but little else.[6] After I read and reread *Addie Joss: King of the Pitchers,* I wanted more of the tantalizing newspaper articles that Scott Longert excerpts. I was soon amazed to discover that no one had bothered to edit a collection of Addie's baseball writing. Furthermore, the scope of Addie's writing for the Cleveland *Press* has been forgotten and, until now, uninvestigated in our era.

The contents of this book, found in Toledo and Cleveland on the old *News-Bee* and *Press* microfilms, might be thought of as Addie Joss' accidental memoir. The voice I hear speak from Addie's book is compelling, like he was said to be in person. At a certain point, as I was retyping these century-old stories, I felt involved not so much in a writing project as in a listening one.

For a passing moment, it seemed that I had tapped the direct line. As in all good conversations, this talk between two people inevitably opened up, to include a world of people, places, and popular culture.

A Note on the Text

Of course, Joss's columns were never intended to be published in book form. Minor proofreading errors in the typesetters' original texts have been silently corrected, whenever they do not affect the meaning of Joss' sentences. To afford the close reader a sense of Addie's development as a writer — or improvements in his copy editors! — and for the more casual reader, a flavor of vintage sports writing, neither syntax nor usage has been strictly regularized. (An exception is in the spelling of the twentieth-century word "baseball"; while the Cleveland sports pages stubbornly retain the throw-back "base ball," I make the distinction between eras.) Sometimes, when the condition of the microfilm makes it difficult to impossible to read, passages have been reconstructed within brackets. When an article appears in both the Toledo *News-Bee* and the Cleveland *Press*, only the original is reprinted here, unless Joss has made significant changes.

Not all of Addie's *News-Bee* articles have survived the decades since the newspaper ceased operations, on August 2, 1938. This volume is necessarily a selection from his baseball writing (a bit like trying to gather the limbs of Osiris) because, I believe, no complete edition can be compiled at this time. Nigel Cochran sold the defunct newspapers' morgue and files to the *Blade*, which would eventually microfilm the old newspapers minus an entire run of Sunday editions going back to Addie's second year of writing. The Cleveland *Press* was in business until 1982. Its microfilms are complete; but this daily printed no Sunday edition, so Addie's reports from the World Series are incomplete. If readers of this book have copies of the old newspapers that fill in the missing pages, they are urged to contact me at rblevins@pitt.edu.

In addition to Addie Joss' regular columns and World Series reports, his work sometimes appeared in *The Sporting News*, the *Washington Post*, and *The Baseball Magazine*. Occasional pieces are located in the Appendix.

I'm a lifelong Cleveland Indians fan, not a historian, nor a sociologist or a journalist. So I've compiled a book, above all, about early baseball in Cleveland and Toledo, with my fellow northern Ohio baseball devotees in mind.

Abbreviations used are TNB (Toledo *News-Bee*) and CP (Cleveland *Press*).

— Rich Blevins.

A Brief Biography

Toledo Mud Hens, 1900–1901
Cleveland Bronchos, 1902
Cleveland Naps, 1903–1911

Addie Joss' 160 wins were the most by a Cleveland pitcher in the Deadball Era. His 1.89 career ERA is second lowest among Hall of Famers. He remains the only pitcher with a lifetime WHIP below 1.00 (.968). His record includes 234 complete games in 260 starts, 45 shutouts, and seven one-hit performances. He is one of 30 elect pitchers in history to fashion two no-hitters. His perfect game was accomplished under the pressure of the last week of Cleveland's memorable race for the 1908 American League pennant. Also an accomplished fielder, Joss' 3.0 assists per game rank first all time among pitchers.

During Addie's short lifetime, baseball—and the role of the pitcher—changed into a game recognizable by today's fans. But in the year of Addie's birth, the "twirler" still offered underhand throws from a "box" only 45 feet from a diamond-shaped home base. The batter called for a high, low, or fair pitch—with two strikes, he was given a "good ball" warning by the umpire—and a walk took eight balls. Jim McCormick toiled over 657 innings that season, winning 45 of Cleveland's 47 victories. Worcester's John Lee Richmond recorded baseball's first perfect game (over Cleveland). The name of the game was "base ball," two words.

Adrian Joss is born, on April 12, 1880, in Woodland, Wisconsin, the only child of Jacob Joss, a Swiss emigrant cheese maker and local politician, and Theresa Staudenmayer, the daughter of a German emigrant father. When Addie is 10 years old, his father dies, from the effects of alcoholism, and his mother goes to work as a milliner.

In 1899, after a year at the Wayland Academy, Joss played for Sacred Heart College. Here he poses (back row, middle) with his teammates, among them his catcher, John "Red" Kleinow (seated, third from right), who had an eight-year career in the major leagues **(David Stalker).**

High school (Juneau, Wisconsin, class of 1896) prepares Addie for a teaching career. He also plays right tackle on the championship football squad and second base for the baseball team. Still a teenager himself, Addie is a schoolmaster for two years, in nearby Horicon and Herman. He also pitches his first game, in the summer of 1897, for the Horicon town team against Beaver Dam. Addie's college career begins in spring 1898, when he is recruited to pitch for Wayland Academy (Beaver Dam). He wins seven of nine decisions, hits .325, and steals 12 bases, for this branch campus of the University of Chicago. After the close of the college season, Addie pitches for the Juneau town team, throwing his first no-hit game, against Hartford. In the fall, he is recruited to play baseball for Sacred Heart College (Watertown), possibly without enrolling in classes. His team will claim the Wisconsin collegiate baseball championship for 1899. As a result of playing for

Watertown's town team in an exhibition game against Charles Comiskey's Western League St. Paul Apostles, Connie Mack hears about Joss and offers him a professional contract to pitch for the newly formed Albany Senators (a class C club in the New York State League), with the promise of a promotion to his Milwaukee club. Reluctant to leave central Wisconsin, he refuses to sign. Instead, he winds up his amateur career by pitching and playing second base for Oshkosh and Manitowoc. By season's end, Addie is ready to sign with Charles J. Strobel's Toledo club, then in the Inter-State League, for the 1900 season.

His years in Toledo are formative for Addie. In two seasons with the Mud Hens (playing in the Western Association in 1901), Addie wins 46 games and learns the pro game from team captain and former Cleveland Spider Bobby Gilks. When he makes his first professional start, on April 28, 1900, in Armory Park, his future wife, Lillian Shinavar, is in attendance. After the season, they marry and he adopts his wife's Toledo for his own hometown. In 1905, the Joss family moves into the only house he will ever own, at 2440 Fulton Street (now demolished). By 1908, when Addie is the sports editor for a rival city newspaper, the Toledo *Blade* claims: "Addie Joss has more friends in this city than any other man."

After two years in the minor leagues, Addie signs with Cleveland for the American League's second season of play. In 1902, Charles W. Somers's club has a new nickname, the Bronchos, and a new manager. Bill Armour is field manager for most of Addie's first three big league seasons, and his importance as a mentor in the young man's life continues when Armour directs the local Mud Hens. Addie is a success right out of spring training in New Orleans. On April 26, he tosses a one-hitter in his major league debut, a win over the Browns. In his third start, on May 4, he no-hits the Tigers into the ninth inning. By June, Napoleon Lajoie joins his ex–Philadelphia Athletics' teammate Elmer Flick on a much-improved Cleveland team.[1] The rookie pitcher posts a 17–13 record, along with a 2.77 ERA, in 269⅓ innings. It will be Addie's career-worst ERA for a season, but his five shutouts lead the league. This year, he is also initiated into fatherhood, when his son Norman is born.

Starting in 1903, the Cleveland team calls itself the Naps, after its star second baseman, Napoleon Lajoie. Addie's pitching is significantly improved in his sophomore year — more complete games, innings, and strikeouts, fewer walks, an ERA of 2.19 — but he wins only one more game (18–13). This year is a challenge for Addie off the field, as well. Before the regular season opens, his friend Win Mercer commits suicide at the end of a three-month barnstorming tour of the West, and Addie accompanies the pitcher's body back to Ohio for burial. In the early morning hours of August 29, five days after he fashions a one-hitter against Philadelphia, Addie and his teammates survive the derailment of their train, west of Toledo. This off-season, Addie's and Roger Bresnahan's offer to buy the Mud Hens franchise is turned down.

More personal problems dog Addie into the 1904 campaign. The veteran lowers his ERA for the second straight year (to a league-best 1.59), but he manages only 14 wins against 10 losses when a lingering fever limits him to 24 starts. By September, his mentor Bill Armour is forced to resign, in favor of new playing manager Lajoie.

In 1905, Addie becomes a 20-game winner, which earns him a $500 bonus. (He will win at least 20 games for four consecutive seasons.) His 132 strikeouts mark a career high. Addie, Lillian, and Norman move into the frame house on Fulton Street, in Toledo.

Addie's 21-win effort for 1906 (against only nine losses) qualifies him for another $500 bonus. His ERA is 1.72. This fall, Addie plays in the outfield for Bill Bradley's Boo Gang, a barnstorming team that includes Rube Marquard and four of Cleveland, Ohio's Delahanty brothers. The Joss' daughter Ruth is born.

In January 1907, Addie is hired as sports editor for the new Sunday edition of the Toledo *Times-Bee.* He writes for the newspaper, soon to be renamed the *News-Bee,* over three straight off-seasons. When this year's $500 bonus is not forthcoming, Addie holds out into March, for a salary increase to $4,000 for the upcoming season.

Addie wins his first 10 starts of 1907. He will post 27 victories (a tie for most in the league, and his personal best) and throw three one-hitters, while pitching over 300 innings for the first time. Charles Somers sends Bill Armour to manage in Toledo, as the Mud Hens become an important part of the first farm system. Addie covers his first of three consecutive World Series, as a syndicated reporter for the Cleveland *Press.* Addie is also a regular contributor of feature articles to the Cleveland weekly, from December 1907 through February 1908.

The 1908 season begins inauspiciously when, on March 7 (near Lexington, Kentucky), two bricks shatter a window in the Naps' train bound for spring training, at a Macon, Georgia camp. Teammates Bill Bradley and Harry Bay are cut by flying glass. This year, Addie enjoys his greatest season in baseball, yet the team finishes a frustrating second in the final standings. He goes 24–11, his fourth straight 20-win season, and lands his second ERA title, with a career low 1.16. Addie walks only 30 batters all year, and surrenders 232 base hits, in 325 innings. On October 2, he crafts a 74-pitch perfect game in the final week of Cleveland's pennant race. Losing White Sox pitcher Ed Walsh strikes out 15 Naps in baseball's greatest pitching duel with playoff significance. Cleveland finishes a mere .004 winning percentage behind Detroit, who plays three fewer games in an unbalanced schedule.

Over the off-season, Addie engineers and markets the Joss Indicator, an electronic score-keeping device for the scoreboard at League Park (now demolished).[2] He's back writing features for the Cleveland *Press*, after the 1908 World Series and into December. In February 1909, Addie Joss writes what will be his final columns for the Toledo *News-Bee*.

On the strength of the previous season, Cleveland goes into 1909 as a contender for the American League pennant — only to disappoint, finishing 11 games under .500. Addie's record is a mediocre 14–13. His 1.71 ERA is club best, and his 1.15 walks per game leads the league for a second consecutive season; but 42-year-old Cy Young leads the Naps in wins. After 114 games, Lajoie resigns as manager, but continues to play in the field. This off-season, Addie joins a touring team of major league all-stars, which plays December dates in Cuba, against Rube Foster and John Henry Lloyd.

April 20, 1910, just weeks after the grand opening of Somers' rebuilt League Park, Addie no-hits the White Sox (recording 10 assists). However, a ligament tear in his pitching elbow sidelines him for all but 12 starts in what turns out to be Addie's last regular season. At one point, the Cleveland club sends him to recuperate on the beach at Sandusky, Ohio. His friend Cy Young notches his five hundredth win, on July 19; five days later, Addie lasts five innings, versus the Athletics, in his final regular season game. Even while Addie is fading from competition, he enjoys a star's reputation. Alfred H. Spink, in *The National Game*, names Joss "the brainiest pitcher in the American League." The Cleveland *Press* refers to him as "the world's greatest pitcher."

For the 1910-11 off-season, Addie sings bass in pitcher-turned-songwriter "Doc" White's vaudeville quartet. When he's in Toledo, he operates his pool hall in the downtown St. Paul building (demolished). As late as February 1911, his pitching arm is in a plaster cast.

Addie sees no action with an otherwise promising spring training club, which breaks camp (Alexandria, Louisiana) with new Naps Joe Jackson and Vean Gregg on its roster. On April 3, 1911, Addie collapses on the Naps' bench at a game at Engels Field, in Chattanooga, Tennessee, a barn-storming stop on the trip north. He returns home to Fulton Street, while his team plays exhibition baseball a few blocks from his sick bed.

Addie Joss dies, from tubercular meningitis, on April 14 (Opening Day), two days after his 31st birthday. Ballplayer-turned-evangelist Billy Sunday preaches the eulogy, three days later, in Toledo's Masonic Temple (now demolished). The funeral is the second largest in the city's history, after mayor and Sunday-baseball advocate Samuel "Golden Rule" Jones. Burial is in Woodlawn Cemetery.

On July 24, at League Park, a team of American League all stars plays the Naps in a benefit exhibition, often called baseball's first All-Star Game. Ticket sales raises $12,914.60 (about $260,000 today) for the Joss family.

*In 1951, Addie Joss is inducted into the Wisconsin Athletic Hall of Fame, with his family and Cy Young in attendance. He is also enshrined in the Cleveland Indians Hall of Fame. Since Addie played before players wore numbers, the franchise never retires his uniform number. (He would have requested his favorite, 13.) By the time the Veterans Committee selects Addie for the National Baseball Hall of Fame, in January 1978, no member of the Joss family is alive to accept the honor.**

**Passages in italics hereafter are by the editor.*

1

"I Have Not Had Better Friends"

Players, Great Players and All the Rest

Let's suspend chronological order for now and open this section of Addie Joss' mostly eyewitness accounts of baseball men, famous and forgotten, with his story of how he broke into the Big Leagues five years before (to start with his first start). Addie wrote this piece on the eve of spring training, probably always a nostalgic time of year for him. As he tells it, the tale approaches allegory, from fearful intimidation to handshake initiation. The ugly hazing he recalls is typical for the game that was still evolving, according to Ban Johnson's vision of a national pastime, away from the rowdy style practiced with great success in the previous decade by the Spiders' Patsy Tebeau[1] *and the Orioles' John McGraw. Although he's too modest to remind us, Addie's first game for Cleveland was a one-hitter. It would be the first of seven he would throw, mixed in with two no-hit games, in his abbreviated career. Long-time Cleveland Spiders star Jesse Burkett, now late in a Hall of Fame career, got the only hit this afternoon—a hotly disputed one—in the sixth inning.*

(March 10, 1907, TNB)

I suppose all young players feel shaky when they play their first game in a major league, but I don't know any youngster whose league baptism could be more severe than the one handed me.

Bill Armour arranged for my debut at St. Louis, and what I went through that day no one but Addie knows. Imagine sending a kid into his first tryout against a gang composed of Jack O'Connor, Jack Powell, Emmet Heidrick, Bobby Wallace and Jesse Burkett, to say nothing of Davy Jones, Jim McAleer and a few others.

They didn't pay too much attention to me until along about the third inning, and as I was getting away with the game I had discovered that my confidence was not lost after all. But it began to warm up soon enough.

Along about the fourth, Burkett took a position at one corner of the diamond, Jack O'Connor stationed himself at the other, and the stuff shot at me was enough to make me dizzy. They would not talk to me, but would shout nice, pleasant things at each other, which, as I was half way between them, did not get past without being heard.

"So you are the guy that came up from Toledo to show us how to play ball, are you, Jack?" Burkett sung out.

"Yes, I'm it. I broke that Inter-State [League] all to pieces, and thought I'd come up and show you mugs how to pitch," Jack shot back.

"Well, well, you long legged toothpick, if you don't stop working so hard you'll lose your bonnet," was another.

"Oh, no, I won't. It's pinned to my curly locks," O'Connor replied, just loud enough for me to hear.

This was kept up until they saw that I was not worried by their talk. Then they changed their tactics and instead of handing me verbal bon mots, lined up when we changed places, and the looks they gave me, sizing me up from shoes to cap, would have made a saint want to fight.

That evening at the dinner table we found an immense bunch of carnations at our table and the head waiter handed me one as I sat down. I pinned the flower in my buttonhole and later, as I entered the office, Heidrick was turning in his key.

"Huh! Think so well of yourself you wear flowers, do you?" he asked. "It's a nice, wise guy you are. Sort of swelled up over your dinky one-hit game, I guess, aren't you? Wait until we get at you again, you human sign post, and what we'll do to you will make you long for the bushes."

Just then he handed in his key and turning around stuck out his hand with a grin, saying: "Shake hands, kid; you deserve all the credit in the world. You pitched a great game." And from that day to this I have not had better friends than that same bunch of ball players, the St. Louis Browns.

Opposite page: ***Cleveland newspaper ad for the upcoming Naps season, Joss' second. Napoleon Lajoie is identified as Bill Armour's team captain*** **(Cleveland State University Library Cleveland Press Collection).**

The Cleveland Base Ball Team
1903.
W.R. Armour
MANAGER
Napoleon Lajoie
CAPTAIN & 2nd BASEMAN
THE CLEVELAND PRESS
A LIVE NEWSPAPER
BASE BALL AND SPORTING EDITION
IMMEDIATELY AFTER THE GAME
AT HOME.
April 28, 29, 30th and May 1st ... ST. LOUIS.
May 7, 8 and 9th ... DETROIT.
May 11, 12, 13 and 14th ... BOSTON.
May 15, 16, 17 and 18th ... NEW YORK.
May 19, 20, 21 and 22nd ... WASHINGTON.
May 23, 25 and 26 ... PHILADELPHIA.
May 27, 28 and 30th ... CHICAGO.
June 18, 19, 20 and 21st ... BOSTON.
June 22, 23 and 24th ... NEW YORK.
June 25, 26 and 27th ... WASHINGTON.
June 29, 30 and July 1 and 2nd, PHILADELPHIA.
July 23, 24 and 25th ... ST. LOUIS.
August 4, 5, 6 and 8th ... DETROIT.
August 10, 11 and 12th ... CHICAGO.
August 13, 14 and 15th ... NEW YORK.
August 17 and 18th ... BOSTON.
August 19, 20 and 21st ... WASHINGTON.
August 22, 24 and 25th ... PHILADELPHIA.
August 26, 27 and 28th ... ST. LOUIS.
September 7 and 8th ... CHICAGO.
September 10, 11 and 12th ... DETROIT.
YOU CAN'T AFFORD TO MISS IT
ABROAD.
April 22, 23, 25 and 26th ... DETROIT.
May 2 and 3rd ... CHICAGO.
May 4, 5 and 6th ... ST. LOUIS.
May 10th ... DETROIT.
May 31 and June 1 and 2nd ... CHICAGO.
June 4, 5 and 6th ... NEW YORK.
June 8, 9 and 10th ... WASHINGTON.
June 11, 12 and 13th ... PHILADELPHIA.
June 15, 16 and 17th ... BOSTON.
July 4, 6 and 7th ... WASHINGTON.
July 8, 9, 10 and 11th ... PHILADELPHIA.
July 13, 14 and 15th ... BOSTON.
July 17, 18, 20 and 21st ... NEW YORK.
July 26, 27 and 28th ... ST. LOUIS.
July 30 and August 1 and 2nd ... CHICAGO.
August 9th ... DETROIT.
August 29, 30, 31 and September 1st, ST. LOUIS.
September 2, 3 and 4th ... DETROIT.
September 5 and 6th ... CHICAGO.
September 13th ... DETROIT.
September 16, 17 and 18th ... BOSTON.
September 19, 21 and 22nd ... NEW YORK.
September 23, 24 and 25th ... WASHINGTON.
September 26, 28 and 29th ... PHILADELPHIA.

The nicknames stuck with Addie, and photographs show them to be accurate descriptors of the preternaturally long-armed slinger, his unruly curls of hair escaping from beneath the beanie-fit caps of that era. And the good-natured Joss harbored no ill feelings toward Burkett, nicknamed the "Crab," for either the hit or the ribbing. Joss liked to portray himself as a member of what he called "the brotherhood" of baseball players.

Early baseball teams didn't employ professional base coaches, so players like O'Connor and Burkett filled in, more to heckle the opposing pitcher than to coach. Christy Mathewson writes in Pitching in a Pinch, *"For many years the two men who stood at first and third bases were stationed there merely to bullyrag and abuse the pitchers, often using language that was a disgrace to a ball field." Both "Rowdy" Jack O'Connor and "Snags" Heidrick had played with the Cleveland Spiders. O'Connor caught and chattered for 21 major league seasons. He was also called "Peach Pie," but not for a sunny disposition: it was his habit to indulge in three pieces of pie after team meals. Heidrick, a standout center fielder, hit .300 lifetime. Ohio natives Bill Armour and Jimmy McAleer were important friends, and mentors, to Joss, and their names are encountered many times in his columns. Armour, Addie's first major league manager, was replaced by Napoleon Lajoie by September 1904 only to land in Toledo, in 1907, where he reinvented himself as the minor league Mud Hens' owner and manager.[2] McAleer had managed the Cleveland Blues just the season before Addie arrived in the city. As a brilliant young center fielder (Bill James rates him the best defensive outfielder of the 1890s), he had played for the old Spiders on teams with Bobby Wallace and Jesse Burkett. But McAleer couldn't hit, unlike the rest of the lineup Addie faced in his first game. (It was McAleer who managed a team of American League All-Stars in the Joss benefit game, July 24, 1911, at League Park.)*

(January 20, 1907, TNB)

I read last week that John I. Taylor, president of the Boston Americans, had signed "Cy" Young, that grand old twirler, to a 1907 contract.

If ever there was a player who was a credit to the national game that man is certainly the famous "Rail Splitter from Tuscarawas County." Coming to the Major League in Cleveland 17 seasons ago, he stands today the grandest old twirler the game has ever produced.

Some people are under the impression that Denton has about outlived his usefulness, but should anyone with this impression happen to be at the plate sometime next July and see him whipping them through with that same old cannon ball speed, and accuracy for which he is noted, most likely he would change his opinion.

Last season he missed the services of his old running mate, Louis Criger, that great catcher, and was correspondingly handicapped.

Control was always "Cy's" forte, and in 44 games last season he gave just 2 bases on balls, and still they say he is going back.

I well remember the first game I ever pitched against the great "Cy." It was in Cleveland early in the season of 1902. We had Boston beaten 1 to 0 up to the eighth inning, with two out and Criger on first. "Cy" came to bat and hit a short single to right field.

Our score board was along the right field foul line and in some unaccountable way a small hole had been dug under the end nearest the foul line.

Well, that ball rolled in that hole and by the time [Elmer] Flick dug it out both Criger and Young had scored and we were beaten 2 to 1.

You have to wonder whether the excavation under that fence wasn't the handiwork of knot-hole gang kids, who hung out along Lexington Avenue outside the short right-field wall. Ground rules of the day called a ball in a hole, or one rolling underneath a spectator's carriage parked along foul lines, to be in play. "Cyclone" Young had been on a pitching tear, through April and May of 1902, when he beat the likes of Eddie Plank, Clark Griffith, and Joss. But he must not have considered himself much of a hitter: a photograph from the Hall of Fame shows him at bat, in a Boston uniform, with his fielder's glove in his belt.

The game Addie remembers was played on June 5. Baseball historians always have Cy's inside-the-park home run ball rolling past Charley Hickman and under the left-field fence. Naturally, Addie's account is accurate—Flick was the rattled right fielder.[3] And in his 102 games with the Broncs, Hickman played first base, a little second, and even pitched. The slugger was a bat in search of a position, all his career. (Christy Mathewson also complains that Hickman clogged up the bases as a runner.) Guess who will hit the first home run at Toledo's Swayne Field—and on Opening Day, July 3, 1909—in the park that Bill Armour built? It was "Piano Legs" himself. Denton True Young and Joss became dear friends, and they were united on the Naps staff in 1909, the last good season for both Hall of Famers.

(JANUARY 20, 1907, TNB)

There have been some rumors to the effect that Charles Hickman, the hard-hitting Washington player, is to go to Minneapolis for the coming season. While it appears that there is no foundation for the yarns, a few American league pitchers would be satisfied should "Cheerful Charley" decide to play in the American association, among them being the writer. Not for personal grievance, for, be it remembered, Charley is as popular a player as ever wore a pair of spiked shoes.

No player is more likely to break up a game than that same Charley Hickman. He hits more balls through the box than any other player, with the possible exception of Lave Cross, and with such force that, should he hit one on any part of the body, it would no doubt prove dangerous.

The writer has had some experience with "Cheerful Charley." One day, in 1905, "Hick" hit one that struck me on the arm, rendering that member useless for a few seconds, and when the ball was relayed back Charley was resting on second.

[Washington Senators manager] Joe Cantillon can send "Hick" to Minneapolis just as soon as he wants to, and make a few pitchers I know breathe a little easier.

It may well be that Joss' recommendation reached the ears of the Cleveland front office: Both players he promotes in his first articles for the News-Bee *would ultimately become his teammates. Naps general manager Ernest S. Barnard is Addie's most likely contact. While John Kilfoyl worried himself into ill health and Charles Somers was busy redesigning the new League Park in his image, it was Bernie Barnard who oversaw the club's first farm teams, and Toledo was among them. Further, Barnard's background in baseball would have attracted Addie. Barnard had been a newspaper journalist and business manager for the minor league club in Columbus, Ohio. In later years, Barnard would become the second president of the American League. "Pongo" Joe Cantillon, a most remarkable character, was an umpire in the majors before managing the Senators. (He umpired the first Cleveland Americans game, in 1900.) Once, scouting for the club, Cantillon passed on signing Joe Jackson. Records now show 25 walks for Young in 1906, against 140 strikeouts, still an impressive control figure. Joss was prescient— Young would bounce back from his worst season, in 1906, to average better than 20 wins over his next three years.*

(JANUARY 20, 1907, TNB)

Umpire [Hank] O'Day gives reason for the failure of so many "phenom" pitchers to make good in the major leagues. "A big grist of the undeveloped [Christy] Mathewsons come into the major leagues every year and a small percentage of them make good," said O'Day. "Their friends from the small towns wonder why their pets fail to cause the same stir in the big leagues they did in the 'bush' organizations. The reason is that the reputations made by those 'phenoms' were helped along by the poor batsmen.

"The batsmen in some of the minors hit at everything served, and naturally a pitcher gets a name for big strikeout lists and holding teams to a few scattered hits. Well, when they get into the majors these pitchers are just as good as ever, but the batsmen are a different proposition. They make a pitcher stick the ball over the plate or they let it go by and take a base on balls. In the big leagues the pitcher must have control or he isn't a pitcher.

"I can name thirty big league men of the Willie Keeler class who don't hit at half a dozen poor balls in a season. Against those men these new pitchers are up against it, and they can't keep up the no-hit games they were pitching in the minor leagues.

"After years of experience in pitching and umpiring my advice to a young pitcher would be to develop good control of a fast ball. I claim it's the speed that counts. You don't see these fast pitchers hammered very hard when they are showing good control of their steam. I've looked them all over and noticed that the boys with the speedy delivery and the control are doing pretty well."

Henry F. O'Day was an umpire for 30 seasons (1895–1911, 1913, 1915–1927) and worked the first World Series. He got his start in major league baseball as a pitcher for the American Association Toledo Blue Stockings, where his catcher was Moses Fleetwood Walker. His battery mate with the Washington Nationals (1887–1889) was Connie Mack. He also managed for parts of three seasons. But he is best remembered for his Merkle's Boner call from home plate, on September 23, 1908, still one of baseball's most controversial plays. Cait Murphy, in Crazy '08, *finds O'Day's decision "perhaps the single most courageous act a baseball umpire ever commits on the field of play." The umpire brings out some of Christy Mathewson's (Fred Merkle's teammate) most colorful language in* Pitching in a Pinch*: "O'Day cannot be reasoned* *with. It is as dangerous to argue with him as it is to try to ascertain how much gasoline is in the tank of an automobile by sticking down the lighted end of a cigar or a cigarette." Off the field, O'Day was famously laconic, as private and reserved as fellow umpire Tim Hurst was social and expansive, as we'll see in the next chapter, on baseball humor.*

(JANUARY 27, 1907, TNB)

In Saturday's *News-Bee* the old sport said he would like to know something about George Stone, who tied Nig Clarke as the leading hitter of the American League last season, giving as his reason that he thought this would be particularly interesting to Toledo fans on account of Stone being a member of the American Association prior to his American League engagement.

Much has been said about Stone and his remarkable hitting last season, and it will be hard for me to say anything that has not been told. In the first place Stone assumes an extremely awkward position at the bat and for that reason is hard to pitch to. He stands with feet spread far apart, close to the plate, crouching low and holding his bat over his shoulders in rather a careless manner.

When hitting he steps directly forward, in this way getting all the force of his body in the swing.

Stone is what is termed a "free hitter." By this I mean he hits in any field and is just as liable to hit for three bases as for a single.

Another point in his favor is his remarkable speed going to first base. This helps his batting average considerably, as he beats out many a slow infield hit which for a slower man would mean a put out.

Stone apparently has no weakness at bat[;] still I have heard American league pitchers say he can't hit a low ball on the outside.

As he made nine hits in 15 trips to the plate on me last summer I couldn't have put many in that spot.

Stone is very effective against left-handed pitchers, something rare for a left-handed batter.

[Type is unreadable here] the form he showed last season, Stone should be one of the real contenders for the batting honors next season. One strong factor in his favor is the fact that he is a player of exemplary habits and can always be relied upon to give the club he is working for his best effort.

The News-Bee *printed a regular sports column, when Addie was sports editor, under the byline "The Old Sport."*[4] *The column was clearly not written by Joss himself: you can tell by the differences in styles and attitudes. "Silent" (as a) Stone was having a remarkable season in the minors with the Milwaukee Brewers in 1904 before his trade to the majors. As a rookie in 1905, George Stone led the American League in at-bats, hits, and total bases. To qualify for the batting championship in Addie's day, a player was only required to appear in at least 100 games in a 154-game schedule. In his career year of 1906, Jay J. "Nig" Clarke played 57 games, hitting .358 (in 179 at-bats, which is what we look at today). Clarke's teammate Nap Lajoie officially came in behind Stone's league-leading .358 mark, at .355.*

(JANUARY 27, 1907, TNB)

No minor league ever attracted the attention in so brief a time as did the old Interstate league, in 1900, when so many pitchers left the organization to go to the majors.

Toledo fans who know the players of those days, may recall with interest some of the men who went from the little organizations to the big ones, to play winning baseball.

In chief, the men who climbed the ladder were Jack Harper, who went from Ft. Wayne in the fall of 1900, to the St. Louis National league [team], but jumped to the American league team in the same city the following year. In 1903 he went to Cincinnati, where he remained until the middle of last season, when he was traded to the Chicago National league team, of which he is still a member. [H. Swaim] Swain and [Henry] Fricken, also members of the Ft. Wayne team, never went any higher, although Swain had pitched for Washington before going to the Indiana city.

Otto Krueger at that time was doing stunts around the short field for Ft. Wayne, and went to St. Louis with Harper.

At Dayton, where Manager [Bill] Armour had charge, the men who did the box work were Earl Moore, Bob Wicker, Doc Watkins, and [George] Gilpatrick. Of this bunch, Moore and Wicker went to Cleveland and St. Louis, respectively. Moore has been a member of the Cleveland team ever since and was the team's mainstay in the box continuously until last season, when an injury kept him out of the game most of the year.

Wicker was sold to the St. Louis National league team that same year. In addition, Wicker has played in Chicago and Cincinnati, and was recently sold to Columbus by Garry Herrmann. His career in the American Association will be watched with interest by the Toledo fans, as no doubt his work in a great measure will determine Columbus' chances in the 1907 race.

At Wheeling, the only man to go to the majors was Eddie Poole, who joined the Pittsburg club, but was later sold to Brooklyn, and is now playing in the Eastern league.

John Skopec, that phenomenal little left-hander, was also doing some great pitching for Pop Lytle's team [Wheeling] that season, as was Al Pardee, who later pitched for Toledo.

Skopec finally got a try-out with the Chicago Americans, but didn't last.

Mansfield had no graduate to the elite, [but] still had four pitchers that were by no means easy to beat, in Tom Irwin, Dick Smith, Eddie Ames, and Elmer Meredith.

New Castle had on its payroll these pitchers: [Frank] Figgemeyer, [Jack] Wadsworth, and "Three Fingered" Clarence Smith.

Of these, Wadsworth was the only one who ever saw major league service, being a member of the Cleveland team during the regime of that scrappy leader, Pat Tebeau. The other two have drifted out of the game.

In Toledo we had Ewing, ["Snake"] Wiltse, [Ike] Butler and myself. [Bob] Ewing went to Cincinnati in 1902, and remained there continuously, but is now said to be slated for the Boston club in the National league.

After Wiltse left he was picked up by Connie Mack and pitched great ball during the season of 1901. The next year he helped the Athletics win the pennant, and in 1903 was a member of [Clark] Griffith's Highlanders, from where he went to Baltimore in the Eastern League, and finally jumped that team to join the York Outlaw club.

Butler was given a trial by Baltimore in 1902, but is now out west, while I have been a member of the Cleveland club since 1902.

Columbus at that time was not such an important factor in the pennant race as at present, but had two good men in [Oscar] Streit and [Lou] Mahaffey. Streit was a member of the Cleveland club in the spring of 1902, but was turned adrift about mid-season, and has been playing in the south since, while Mahaffey will be remembered as the man [J. Ed] Grillo signed for a trial last season on one of the Toledo club's trips to Columbus, but who remained with the team but a few days.

Addie is remembering his first year in the minors and the Inter-State League class of 1900. The founding by Ban Johnson of the eight-team American League, which operated as a high minor league for its 1900 season, was responsible for the promotion of so many pitchers so quickly. It was also why some of the pitchers rushed into service had such miserable records in the majors: Ike Butler went 1–10 for Baltimore in 1902 and Oscar Streit was 0–7 for the Bronchos that season. Wadsworth had a 6–38 career in the majors, and Lewis "Snake" Wiltse went 29–31. On the other hand, Bob Wicker was a 20-game winner with the White Sox in 1903. J. Ed Grillo would become president of the minor league American Association in 1903, its second season.

(FEBRUARY 3, 1907, TNB)

Catcher Ossie Schreckengost [sic] of the Athletics is probably the only pad artist in the game using two gloves to do his backstopping.

The reason for this is explained by "Schrek," when he says, "The glove I use when there are no men on bases is old and worn and has such a large pocket in the center that it is impossible for me to get the ball out quick enough to catch a base runner.

"For that reason I use one that is not so much worn whenever there are men on sacks." Schrek's gloves resemble the top of a piano stool, but at that they are not any too large when he is working behind the "Rube" [Waddell].

Half a century before Johnny Bench, F. Ossee (sometimes spelled "Ossie," as if a nickname) Schrecongost perfected the one-handed catching style. I'm not sure if his catcher's mitt was all that oversized, or it was just that the fielder's gloves players wore in Schrecongost's early playing days were so small, actually glove-like gloves. According to Chuck Rosciam's research, the standard "pillow mitt," designed by Jason F. Draper, was so stiff that it required most Deadball receivers to use both hands. "Schrek" was briefly a catcher with Addie's Bronchos before he made a legendary battery—and roommate—with Rube Waddell. He died mere months after the shock of the pitcher's death. Incredibly, he caught all 28 innings of a game Cy Young eventually lost to Waddell, on the Fourth of July 1905. Schrecongost was behind the plate for the other team for Addie's perfect game, the last game he caught in the majors.

(FEBRUARY 10, 1907, TNB)

Speaking of Nick Altrock's great work in catching runners off first recalls other twirlers who can perform some in this respect.

Toledo fans will recall Lew Wiltse, who pitched for the Toledo Interstate league club. He could make base runners hug the bag some, but the best man I ever saw in this respect is [Harry] Hardy, who was tried out by Washington last fall. He has all the others cheated when it comes to nipping runners.

In a game which Hardy pitched against the Naps last fall, [Terry] Turner, who had been walked, was caught off the bag before he had time to take a step back to safety and as he had been cautioned to watch Hardy closely, he was unmercifully roasted when he returned to the bench.

The man with the most to say was Jimmy Jackson, who offered to bet any of us a bat that Hardy could not catch him. About an inning later the "General" reached first and Lajoie, who was coaching, warned him not to get caught. "Never mind; he won't get me," replied Jackson as he took a step toward second.

Quick as a flash Hardy tossed the ball to [Jake] Stahl and when Jackson woke up [Tom] Connolly had called him out. What the gang on the bench did to Jimmy when he sat down will linger long in my mind.

Talk about Altrock! Why, he isn't a marker for Hardy. All the latter has to do is to get you overbalanced and the fire is out.

Left-hander Lew Wiltse (never to be confused with "Hooks" Wiltze earned the nickname "Snake." Maybe now we know why. He patched together only one full season in the majors, 1902, when he split time between two Junior Circuit clubs. Addie might strike today's reader as about the only sportswriter who ever gave Nick Altrock's pitching a passing mention, but Altrock's work as the baseball clown came later. Addie, who dubbed himself "the sporting editor," would have loved the act had he lived to see it. Altrock first became noted for his antics while coaching on the field for Washington in 1912. His pitching record shows him to have been one of best left-handers pitching in the league as Addie knew it. Amazingly, the minor league Altrock was known to intentionally walk batters—so he could pick them off first. Ohio-born Nicholas Altrock's playing career peaked when he beat Three Finger Brown in the opening game of the 1906 World Series. Steubenville, Ohio's Harry Hardy appeared in eight games for Washington in 1905 and 1906, his only time in the Big Leagues.

(FEBRUARY 10, 1907, TNB)

When sporting writers and baseball critics pick out all-around players or utility men, it is noticeable that the name of Larry Lajoie is always conspicuous — by its absence. Why this fact is hard to imagine, for the big Frenchman is one of the greatest all-around players in the game.

Since his connection with the national game Larry has played every position upon the diamond, save that of the pitcher. How well he has filled them all may be appreciated when the statement is conservatively made that he is as much at home in any position as he is on second base.

Lajoie broke into fast company as a first baseman, from which position he was shifted to the outfield, where with [Roy] Thomas and [Ed] Delahanty he completed as fast an outfield as ever graced the roster of any club.

Since he became a member of the Cleveland club Larry has played all the infield positions, showing in each the grace and dexterity which only he can show and which is so much a part of his work.

Leaving second base out of the argument, Lajoie is more in his element at first, perhaps, than in the other positions. I believe that if he would play the initial corner regularly there would be no question raised regarding the identity of the greatest first sacker in the game.

So it may be seen that when speaking of all-round ball players, Lajoie should not be overlooked.

According to Bill James' analysis, the greatest double play combination in the first decade of the American League is not Tinker and Evers, but Terry Turner and Lajoie. Yet James worries — at length, not in his usual laser-surgery analysis — about whether "Larry" Lajoie was really a great fielder. What is it about Lajoie that he has provoked such general anxiety concerning his statistics, offensive numbers included? (Note the perennial debate over who really won the Chalmers 30 automobile, unpopular Ty Cobb or unlucky "Larry," or the notion that the American League had something like "high minor league pitching" in 1901, when Lajoie hit .426.) Is Addie backhanding a compliment to his close friend and manager when he opines that the second baseman would make a great first baseman? Fact is: Addie's, and Lajoie's, first baseman was George Stovall, a guy so good around the bag that he led American Leaguers at the position in assists three years (1909 through 1911), fielding percentage four times (1908 through 1911), and also three more seasons in most double plays completed (1907 through 1909). It's highly unlikely that Addie meant anything by his article other than to compliment Nap Lajoie's stellar glove work at second. Aman Verjee's BaseballStatistics.com finds that Lajoie led American League second basemen in "range factor" four times; Total Baseball *credits Lajoie with the most "fielding runs" in history.*[5]

(FEBRUARY 10, 1907, TNB)

"Rube" Waddell may be crazy off the field, but when the eccentric one is pitching he is far from being dippy. All sorts of stories regarding the antics indulged in by Waddell are heard, but never a word creeps out about his judgment, shown while in the game.

A great deal of "Rube's" success is due to the way he is handled by his battery partner, Schreckengost, and when that team is at its best no club in the country has any license to beat them.

They say "Rube" doesn't use any judgment. Well, possibly not, but there's no denying that he gets results and that is what counts. The big fellow has something on any pitcher in the business when it comes to striking out men. This can be seen by the fact that he usually leads the league in this respect.

When "Rube" has his curve ball and speed working, it is next to impossible to beat him. He knows the strong and weak points of a batter as well as any pitcher, and the idea that he depends on his natural ability alone is erroneous.

Readers of the News-Bee *sports pages had an insatiable appetite for stories about the zany on-field behavior and many marriages of George Waddell, a local legend, who at the time of this article had yet to face a Big League batter. The other pitching "Rube," Cleveland-born Richard Marquard, was playing in the minors in Ohio. The former Naps bat boy Marquard was nicknamed after his resemblance on the field to Waddell. Of course, both "Rubes" were lefties, only Waddell more so.*

(FEBRUARY 17, 1907, TNB)

"Win" Mercer, who will be remembered as the player who came to such an untimely end in 'Frisco during the winter of 1903, was a pitcher who used as good judgment as any twirler the game has ever seen.

"Win" didn't seem to have much speed or a large break to his curve ball, but nevertheless he was about as hard a man to hit safely as any pitcher that ever faced a batter.

He was a twirler on the Clark Griffith order, a cool, nervy, tantalizing man, especially in a tight place. It was a pleasure to see him work a good hitter, in a pinch. Before pitching he had about a dozen maneuvers he would go through and by the time he did pitch he usually had the batter in such a fever of impatience that he would hit at almost anything.

Talk about control! Mercer certainly had it. He could put the ball wherever he desired. It was a common thing to see him, with a runner on first, waste three balls to give the catcher a clear field for a throw to second to catch the runner, and then put the next three right through the center, using for the last strike a slow ball at which the batter ordinarily would swing three times before it got to him.

Besides being a star twirler, "Win" was a fine fielder, a corking good hitter and about as fast on his feet as they make them. In fact, the rest of the members of his club were willing to lose a good sized pool any time a player could be found to bet him in a hundred yards.

While at his best when a member of the Washington team during the regime of the Wagner Bros., he was the matinee idol of the city and to show the high esteem in which he was held by his employers, the following from one of the Wagners is quoted: "I will sell anything I have with the exception of my family or Mercer." Off the field Mercer's conduct was second only to his ability to be a thorough gentleman in every sense of the word.

When the Grim Reaper took "Win" Mercer into his fold he took with him one of baseball's most precious gems.

And so reads Addie's gentle and generous tribute to one of the baseball's suicides. The February 18, 1909, article (see pages 54 and 55) carries Addie's firsthand account of Win Mercer's mysterious final day. Less sympathetic contemporaries believed that Mercer was attempting to steal the players' money, a pot accumulated by the barnstorming tour organized by Mercer and "Tip" O'Neill which started out in good humor from Chicago three months before.[6] *George Mercer, who won 25 games with the last-place 1896 Senators, was indeed a good hitter. In five of his nine seasons, he hit no lower than .294. He led the league in pinch hits for 1895. Mercer played the outfield and all over the infield. And he ran the bases, too, for 88 career steals. George W. Wagner was president of the Senators beginning in 1892, when the Wagners of Philadelphia were granted a National League franchise. (It was Wagner who signed a young pitching prospect named Roger Bresnahan.)*

(February 24, 1907, TNB)

Editor Interviews the Ball Player

Statement by Addie Joss, Pitcher, to Addie Joss, Editor, on Salary Question.

The editor of the Sunday Times-Bee has commissioned me, as sporting editor, to interview Addie Joss in regard to his controversy with the Cleveland club.

Modesty forbids me to say much, but I can say that what has already been written in the main, covers the matter very well.

My relations with the Cleveland club since becoming a member of that organization, have been pleasant, and the differences which now exist are purely of a monetary nature.

Last season, besides a straight salary, I had an agreement with the club whereby if I won 20 games or more I was to get a certain amount in excess of the straight salary. I won 21 games and was paid the extra sum.

This season a contract was sent me calling for less than I earned last year, and therein lies the trouble, if trouble it be.

This alone constitutes the difference between the club and myself, and I trust, and have every reason to believe, that this will be amicably settled in the near future.

After paying Addie a salary of $2,700, plus a $500 bonus for winning 20 games, Somers and Kilfoyl mailed out a contract to Toledo stipulating their star twirler would be earning $3,100 for the upcoming season. Imagine Addie's shock, then feeling of betrayal, when he opened the envelope. The club was offering a raise of $400 over his base salary, but this time without a word of the incentive pay if Addie won his 20 games in 1907. In effect, if Addie had *another good season he would make $100 less than he had in 1906. There were two kids and a wife to support at the Fulton Street homestead. So Addie held out—he indicated to the Cleveland front office that he'd be pleased to keep his desk job at the* News-Bee, *thank you. Cleveland was offering good money for a turn-of-the-century professional. Perennial holdout Ty Cobb was raised, for the 1907 season, to $2,400; in 1902, Addie's rookie season, the Browns made Bobby Wallace the highest-paid player in baseball, signing him to a five-year no-trade contract for $32,500 plus bonus money; six years later, Honus Wagner would hold out signing for 1908 until Barney Dreyfus doubled his salary to $10,000 to supplant Wallace as the game's highest paid.*[7] *But keep in mind that "Old Hoss" Radburn had contracted to pitch for the Providence Grays for $4,000—way back in 1885. (Mark Twain's reported income for 1907 was $70,000.) Besides, Americans were justifiably worried about the stability of the nation's economy: the stock market would crash, on March 13, only to be followed that fall by the Bankers' Panic of 1907. And President "Teddy" Roosevelt was threatening a federal income tax. Toledo readers followed the progress of their sports editor's holdout up to the announcement, in the pages of the March 9* News-Bee, *that Addie had finally signed for $4,000 (about $80,000 in today's dollars). By 1910, at the end of his career, his salary was up to $5,500.*

(FEBRUARY 24, 1907, TNB)

George Evans, who made folks laugh at the Valentine last week with his inimitable black-face act, is a native of Streator, Ill., which also lays claim to Harry Bay, the fleet-footed Cleveland outfielder, and Billy Meyers, the "Streator Cyclone," who met defeat at the hands of Jack McAuliffe in the memorable fistic carnival at New Orleans, the finale of which witnessed the passing of John L. Sullivan.

During their boyhood Harry Bay and the "Honey Boy" attended the Streator high school and the monologist is naturally interested in the success of his brother actor-ballplayer, for, like Bay, Evans is a devotee of the great national game.

"When Bay was a boy he was noted for his marvelous speed," said Evans Saturday evening, "and in the athletic meets was counted upon as a sure winner in the sprints.

"On the ball field, when Bay reached first, it was a foregone conclusion he would score."

Evans still plays baseball and plays well for a man who does not follow the sport as a profession. Early this winter he spent some time in Miami, Fla., where several major and minor leaguers are sojourning as members of the various teams in the Florida Hotel league.

This Florida baseball thing is becoming the big noise during the winter when the wealthy separate themselves from large bundles of money to inhale the ozone of the east coast.

The hotels have supported ball teams composed of collegians for some years, but each season the game gets faster and this winter some of the best known ball players in the American and National leagues have been enjoying the benefits of the south and at the same time have been well paid for their services.

Shortly after he reached Miami the "Honey Boy" was spotted as a ball player and joined one of the teams, playing until he started north. That he is a good player is evidenced by the fact that he was able to hold down the job as long as he remained.

Elmer Flick, the star fielder of the Cleveland club, and without a doubt the equal if not the superior of any outfielder in the game today, is playing on one of the hotel teams and the execution he is doing with his bat among the orange groves may best be imagined.

During the summer Evans lives in Philadelphia, manufacturing jokes at the expense of his fellow townsmen, and when the Philadelphia Nationals are at home spends the mornings practicing with the team. He says the practice keeps him in physical condition.

"Kid" Gleason and Evans are chums and nothing suits the "Kid" better than to slam short grounders to Evans, trying hard to slap the ball against the shins of the "Honey Boy," whose luck in escaping broken fingers is not Gleason's fault.

Before there was a Caribbean Winter League or an Arizona Fall League or a Dominican or Mexican Winter League—even before something called Hawaii Winter Baseball—there was the Florida Hotel League. In Addie's era, no major league baseball was played south of St. Louis. So here was your chance to see Elmer Flick in action; if you numbered yourself among the privileged few who had the wherewithal and leisure time to book a vacation in one of those new Florida hotels. George Evans was the co-author of "In the Good Old Summer

Time." A loving cup in his name was awarded from 1909 through 1912 to the major league player with the highest batting average. (Only Honus Wagner, in 1909, and Ty Cobb won the trophy in its short history.) John L. Sullivan was the first American sports figure to earn hero status. Sullivan was the last bare-knuckle boxing champion, and the first heavyweight champ of the gloved era. He came out of retirement to defend his title, in New Orleans, on September 7, 1892, against Jim Corbett, the eventual winner in 21 rounds. Addie may well have witnessed Sullivan's last bout, in 1905, a two-round fight in Grand Rapids, Michigan. William Gleason played in nearly 2,000 major league games, mostly at second base, but he is remembered today for managing the 1919 "Black Sox."

(FEBRUARY 24, 1907, TNB)

A.S. Burkhard, owner of the Jackson team in the Michigan state league, who was in the city last week getting talent for his 1907 team, takes credit for discovering "Nig" Clarke, whose wonderful work last season was one of the sensations of the year.

Burkhard formerly managed an independent team in Detroit that was considered the fastest thing in amateur circles about town.

Another organization copped Burkhard's star battery and challenged for a three-game series for the city championship and a good side bet, winner to take all the gate receipts.

Each team won one game and when the last was to be played Burkhard went to Windsor and dug up Clarke. In order to prevent the opposition getting "next" he had "Nig" give a poor exhibition in practice, and when they saw how he performed the other fellows turned away to hide a smile.

Burkhard had "Nig" hitting fourth in the list. The first man up got on and was sacrificed to second. The third walked, and Clarke picked up his war club and advanced to the plate. The pitcher, holding him cheaply, handed over a straight one, and "Nig" met it flush on the nose and started it toward Canada. The last seen of the ball it was still going.

Clarke scored and drove in all the runs his team scored that day, and this, coupled with his marvelous work behind the bat, won the game. "Nig's" base ball star commenced to rise from this occasion, and has been ascending steadily ever since.

Jay Clarke wasn't the first man to play in Cleveland under the era-appropriate nickname; "Nig" Cuppy was a star pitcher, second only to his teammate with a much nicer moniker, Cy Young, on the old Spiders staffs. (Other Deadballers named "Nig" were Frank Smith, Charles F. Fuller, and John Grover Perrine. But the nastiest moniker from the early period has to be the one they gave to the Cleveland Forest Citys' Charley Pabor. They called him "The Old Woman in the Red Cap.") It's also unfortunate for Clarke that he hit only .254 in his nine seasons, six in Cleveland. But the catcher had enjoyed one of the most fortunate afternoons in minor league history. On June 15, 1902, he pulled eight home runs over the short right field fence in Ennis, Texas. Clarke hit six home runs in 1,536 official at-bats in the big leagues, even with an accommodating right-field fence at League Park. "Nig" Clarke was behind the plate for Addie's perfect game. Addie's passing reference to Canada is a reminder that Clarke was Canadian-born, like fellow Naps "Bunk" Congalton and Jack "Glad" Graney.

(MARCH 3, 1907, TNB)

From Massilon [Ohio], the home of Harry Smith, comes the announcement that this great backstop is to don the mask and protector for Barney Dreyfus [sic] again this season.

Two years ago Smith, while throwing to second to catch a base runner, snapped a bone in his arm and since has been practically useless as a catcher. He went south with Pittsburg last spring but the arm refused to come around and he went home.

To those who understand it, a ball player's arm is a peculiar proposition. It may go back on one in a minute and no amount of care or attention will do it a particle of good.

Then when one has about given up hope of ever regaining use of the member, it will suddenly become as good as ever, without any apparent reason. Harry Smith has given his arm two years of rest and now says it is as strong as ever.

I hope for his sake as well as the game's that this is true, as when right, he is one grand catcher. Smith received his baseball education in the wilds of Pennsylvania, with men like Claude Ritchey and a host of stars.

He went to Buffalo and thence to Connie Mack's Milwaukee team, where he did some wonderful work.

He was one of the first catchers to handle the great "Rube" Waddell successfully. He caught "Rube" for 17 innings at Chicago one day when the two teams were playing a double header and his expert handling of the eccentric one was mainly responsible for George Edward winning both games.

Connie Mack took Smith to Philadelphia when the American league was launched in the Quaker city, but he was afterwards sold to the Pirates, where he has been since. Harry was at his best when the Smoky City aggregation was winning pennants and to his efficient handling of [Jack] Chesbro and [Jesse] Tannehill was much of the club's success attributed.

He is a catcher on the same order as the great Marty Bergen, having identically the same snap throw to bases which made Bergen famous. Should Harry's arm regain its cunning, Dreyfus can rest assured his catching department will be ably taken care of and with Smith in shape the chances for the Pirates to be contenders for the bunting are brighter than ever.

Addie here lobbies, with a pitcher's love for batterymates, for a receiver who had played in only two games, over the previous two years, after the 1903 World Series. Instead of Addie's man Harry Smith, Barney Dreyfuss rode overworked and probably underpaid George Gibson all the way to the 1909 World Series. "Powder" Tannehill was a 20-game winner four out of his six seasons in Pittsburgh. The lefty control pitcher with the big curveball went on to two more 20-game seasons in Boston, teaming up with Cy Young and fashioning a no-hitter to boot. The 1901 National League ERA champ could hit, too; he was often used as a pinch hitter. He made better money when he left the employ of Dreyfuss and jumped to the American League.

(March 10, 1907, TNB)

Major League players as a rule are good waiters at bat and therein lies the difference in the pitching strength of the minor league twirler and the pitcher in the big organization.

Many a heaver who had done remarkable work in the minors is lacking when he goes up and to the fact that the major leaguers are more patient must be attributed this fact.

The majority of players in a class B league will hit at balls that a man in the big brush will not even look at and a pitcher without control will never make a success among the big boys.

All of the good hitters in the American or National are men of good judgment, but Willie Keeler, of the "Highlanders," oftener makes a pitcher put the ball over the plate than any other man in the business. His judgment on a ball is almost perfect. It is a waste of time to try and fool him into hitting at a bad one.

To begin with, Keeler isn't larger than a pint measure and he uses a short bat which he grasps in the middle, standing directly over the plate, in a natural position.

As an exponent of scientific hitting "Wee Willie" has no equal and it is worth the price of admission to see him work a pitcher.

I don't want to be misunderstood when I say he makes the pitcher put the ball over the plate all the time, for when trying to hit to left field he swings at balls considerable on the outside, or if he is trying to pull the ball, he will slash at once a bit inside.

For a man as small as he is, Keeler is a wonder when it comes to playing the hit and run game and it is practically impossible to get one by him, to give the catcher a clear throw, unless you make a wild pitch.

I have seen him deliberately throw his bat at a wide ball when a runner was going down and invariably he gets his man to second either by bothering the catcher or hitting to the infield.

It's a pleasure to see Keeler pull a third baseman in on a bluff bunt and then hit by him for a clean single which, had the third sacker remained in his position, would have been an easy out.

He can bunt better than any other man in the American league and is so adept at this form of hitting that he can cover his intentions until too late to catch him.

Keeler has absolutely no weakness at the bat and is an exceptionally fine base runner and splendid fielder.

For this memorable portrait of William Henry Keeler, Addie seems to pick up from his interview with umpire Hank O'Day (above). Conspicuous is the writer's use of "scientific" to classify Keeler's batting approach. The term was synonymous with "inside" baseball. Addie got to know Willie Keeler on the Mercer barnstorming tour. Beyond an unreal hand-eye coordination, a reason for the kind of bat control Addie describes must have been the way "Hit 'Em Where They Ain't" actually gripped his bat—nearly half way up. The five-

foot-four Keeler, usually leading off the lineup in front of Orioles team captain five-foot-seven John McGraw, hit in 44 straight games in 1897. Keeler held the record for consecutive 200-hit seasons (eight) until recently, when it was broken by the latest bat-control freak of nature, Ichiro. Suzuki towers over the lot, at five-ten.

(DECEMBER 23, 1907, CP)

Probably no other set of men in the world are as much abused as umpires. They appear on the field day after day, and no matter how well they may do their work, or how conscientious they may be, there are always thousands who leave the grounds vowing that they could have done better.

One umpire, at a time when the fans were roasting him unmercifully on a decision against the home team, and in which he was right, said to me: "Well, Ad, there seems to be a lot of amateur umpires in the stands today."

At the present time the American league staff of umpires consists of Jack Sheridan, "Silk" O'Loughlin, Tim Hurst, Tommy Connolly, Bill Evans and Jack Egan. Jack Sheridan, who by many is considered the dean of America's umpires, is perhaps the best man day in and day out there is in the game.

He is probably the only major league umpire that never uses a chest protector when umpiring behind the bat. Instead he forces the catcher to take the place of the protector.

He takes his position directly behind the pad artist, and whenever the catcher moves, Sheridan moves with him. I have never seen him hit with a ball that a chest protector would have warded off.

The nearest I ever saw him come to getting hit was in a game against Washington one day last summer.

Case Patten was twirling for the Nationals and had as his receiver a youngster named ["Bruno"] Block, who goes to Minneapolis in 1908. Case is a pitcher that is long on the quick-return delivery, and any time you take your eyes off him for a moment he will slip one over on you.

Block wasn't used to catching a fellow who had this up his sleeve.

Along about the third inning Case slipped up a fast one. Block threw it back and stooped over to give the signal for the next ball. As soon as Patten got hold of the ball he quickly assumed his position on the rubber, and, without waiting for anything, shot over another.

Neither Sheridan nor Block seemed to see the ball, and the only thing that saved Jack was the fact that the ball was high and wide.

Neither the catcher nor umpire took their eyes off Patten the rest of the day.

Tommy Connolly, on account of his conscientious manner, is called the "whitest little umpire in the game."

Connolly is personally one of the nicest fellows one would care to meet. As an umpire he is as good as they make them.

I saw Connolly do something at Detroit that didn't savor of cowardice. It happened in the spring of 1902, at the time the Detroit club was playing Sunday games on the outskirts of the city [in Springwells, Michigan].

The [Burns Park] grounds were small and the seating capacity entirely inadequate for the accommodation of the thousands of spectators who flocked out to see the games.

The last game of our opening series that season was one of these Sunday affairs and the grounds were packed.

It had been a mighty close game all the way through and the climax was reached in the last inning when the Tigers, who hadn't scored a run up to this time, sent one man across the plate, and had men on first and second with two out.

We had managed to score two runs early in the contest. The crowd outside of the stands became so wildly enthused that it started crowding in on the field.

In about two minutes you couldn't see the outfielders. Any old kind of a fly ball would have gone safe and we appealed to Connolly for protection. After trying for some time to get the people back off the field without any of them moving, Tommy went over to Frank Dwyer, who managed the Tigers at that time, and informed him that in case a fly ball was hit to any of the outfielders and any of the spectators interfered with him in any way whatever he would give the game to Cleveland.

Fortunately the next hitter grounded out and Tommy was relieved of what might have been a dangerous predicament for him.

Francis O'Loughlin, better known as "Silk," is an umpire that has probably attracted more attention than any other man in the business. "Silk" broke into the American league at the beginning of the season of 1902. He made good from the jump.

"Silk" is always absolute master of the field, and impresses that fact on the players in no uncertain way. His memorable decision in the last game of the Philadelphia-Detroit series at Philly this fall, when he called [Harry] Davis out for alleged interference by a spectator with [Sam] Crawford, when the Detroit outfielder was trying to catch Harry's long fly, will go down in the annals of the game as one of the most notable of its kind.

Tim Hurst pulled one on Ira Thomas, who was recently sold to Detroit, one day last summer, that is only a fair sample of what one has to expect when trying to get the best of the chubby arbitrator in a game of repartee.

In his last chance at the bat Ira had been handed what he thought was the worst of it, on a third strike, and was naturally a little sore at being called out in this manner.

As he assumed his position behind the plate he turned to Tim and said: "Tim, you must be blind: that ball was a foot outside."

"Is that so?" questioned Hurst.

"Yes, and you know it," came the reply.

"Well," responded Tim, "let me give you a piece of advice, Ira. If you see any more of those balls coming up that you say are a foot wide of the plate, you had better hit at them, as I don't think my eyesight has improved any in the last few minutes," and that settled the argument.

Addie reworks the part about Jack Sheridan for his January 29, 1909, story for the News-Bee *(see below, in this chapter). Sheridan was the first umpire to work from a crouch instead of standing behind the catcher. According to legend, he was never struck by a baseball in his 30-year career. Sheridan was the only ump on the field for the 1896 Temple Cup and later did four of the first seven World Series, where he was not the only umpire. He began umpiring in the Players League and served in the American League for its first 14 years, until he suffered sun stroke during a game. A young Billy Evans (but, then, "The Boy Umpire" looks eternally youthful in photographs) usually tried to team up with Sheridan, umpiring the bases while the veteran called the balls and strikes that never grazed him. The game action that Addie recounts involves a quick-pitch artist. It seems that delivery was legal in games until baseball took it away from Cleveland's Satchel Paige. Case Patten's 105 wins still rank him tenth on the all-time list for the Senators/Twins franchise, which somewhat offsets his three consecutive 20-loss seasons in the first eight years of the American*

League. Patten's name was involved in the sensational Kansas City murder trial of Lulu Prince and Phillip Kennedy, in 1903. James Block (born Blochowicz) would return to the majors in 1910, as a part-time catcher with the White Sox. He finished up his five-year career in 1914 with the Federal League Chicago Whales, playing in a new Wrigley Field.

British-born Thomas Connolly's Hall of Fame career as an umpire began in the National League in 1898. Connolly was behind the plate for the American League's first game (April 24, 1901, Cleveland Blues at Chicago White Sox), and he worked the Junior Circuit, finishing as supervisor of umpires, for 52 years. He umpired most games by himself from 1901 to 1907. The game Addie recounts here was played on May 4, 1902, his third start in the major leagues. Addie no-hit the Tigers until the ninth inning of that game, when "Doc" Casey and (former Cleveland Spider and future University of Pittsburgh coach) Dick Harley singled. Addie pitched well on Sundays. He also beat Clark Griffith in a Cleveland "home game" played on a Sunday (April 17, 1903) in Columbus, Ohio. John Francis Dwyer managed Detroit for only the 1902 season. He won 177 games in his playing career, pitching mostly with Cincinnati, ending in 1899.

Francis O'Loughlin was the first umpire to toss Ty Cobb out of a game. "Silk" came into the American League the year Addie did, and made his clarion calls there for the next 17 years.

Quotable Tim Hurst is featured in Chapter 2, on baseball humor. Ira Felix Thomas, at six-foot-two, would have towered over Hurst. The catcher went to three World Series, with the Tigers and the A's, in his 10 seasons. He was one of Connie Mack's team captains.

Having covered the league's umpires, Addie next considers a gallery of its managers. The copy editor's subhead for the following article is its own fair piece of characterization: "Mack the Fox, McAleer the Quiet Boy, Griffith the Tantalizer and All the Rest."

(DECEMBER 30, 1907, CP)

The peculiar actions of the different ball players on the field have been covered a thousand and one times, and while they are subjects that interest the fans, there is very little ever said about the actions of the men who have charge of these different players.

Upon the judgment and coolness of these men depend, in a good measure, the failure or success of their teams. It may, therefore, be of some interest to know how these men conduct themselves during the progress of a game.

There is but one real "bench" manager in the American league, by that I mean a man who doesn't put on a uniform. This is Connie Mack, the great leader of the Athletics.

Mack directs all the moves from the shade of the stands. Connie is of a very quiet disposition and very rarely says anything about baseball to the opposing players. On account of this reticent manner he has been nicknamed the "Sphinx" of baseball.

Mack goes about his work in the quiet manner that is so characteristic of the man himself.

How Connie manages Rube Waddell would make an interesting story. Mack had the Rube with him when he was in Milwaukee at the head of the team, and it was due mostly to the big fellow's wonderful work that the Brewers finished second in the race the first year of the American league.

Waddell's long suit, when he is going as only he can go, is his speed and fine curve ball. He became dissatisfied, with only these things at his command, and proceeded to develop a slow ball.

After practicing this for some time, he finally reached that stage where he thought he had it down pat, and he became so enamored with the floater that the next time he went in the box he wouldn't pitch anything else.

The opposing players were so much taken by surprise that, for the first few innings, they failed to appreciate the situation, and didn't hit it very hard; but as soon as they saw that this was all he was going to pitch, they laid for it, and soon commenced to murder every ball he handed over.

Mack implored the eccentric one to lock the slow one in his grip and save it for some future time, but he implored to no avail. Rube insisted that it was all right, and cited the fact that they weren't scoring any runs as an argument that the floater was the thing.

Connie saw that desperate means must be employed to prevent the loss of the game, as, to him, it was apparent that it was only a matter of a few innings until the opposing players would be running the bases until their tongues were hanging out.

He beckoned to a policeman, that was doing duty on the grounds, and after whispered instructions the copper went on his way.

Rube took his position on the rubber the next inning, and the first ball he tossed over was one of those slow things. The batter hit it an awful wallop and away it went sailing to the outfield.

The next batter did the same and there were two men on bases and no one out. Rube was still stuck on the slow one and handed up another. The man at the bat hit it down the left field foul line a mile a minute, but fortunately it went a few inches foul.

Just as Waddell stepped on the rubber preparatory to pitching, a heavy bass voice from the bleachers was heard to say:

"Get out of there you big stiff. You've lost your arm."

Rube looked up in astonishment for the author of the remark and failing to find him, picked up the ball with a determined look, as much to say: "I'll show you whether or not I have lost my arm," and the way he whistled them through the rest of the afternoon was a caution.

It's not hard to imagine who it was that yelled at the Rube and also what it was that Connie whispered to the copper.

Hughie Jennings has demonstrated beyond a doubt that as a leader he is all to the Merry.

Jennings gives this as his formula for success on the field:

Ten per cent baseball ability, 10 per cent luck and 80 per cent ginger fizz.

While it would hardly be fair to the Tigers to say that it was 80 per cent ginger fizz that won them the American league pennant, still it must be admitted that it had a good deal to do with the landing of the [championship] bunting.

He sent Geo. Mullin in to hit for Eubanks [probably pitcher John Eubank] in a game against Cleveland last summer along about the seventh inning with the score 4 to 1 against them and at a time when they had the bases full and two out.

George met one and away it sailed towards the left field fence. It looked good for three bases and would have meant a tie score.

Harry Bay started in pursuit and while running at full speed managed to pick it off the fence with his gloved hand.

Jennings was at first base coaching and by the time Bay made the catch Mullin had reached the initial sack.

Although the catch saved us at least three runs and practically put the

Tigers out of the game Hughie clapped George on the shoulder and said: "Good try, George, old boy," and from the manner in which the words were said one would have thought he had made the hit that won the game.

Jimmy McAleer, the manager of the Browns, is another of those quiet fellows who never has much to say in regards to baseball.

When Jim is on the bench in citizen's clothes one can always tell how the game is going by watching his hat.

If his club is ahead and seems in a fair way of winning, the head-piece is set quaintly on the back of his head. If things start going a little bad Jim will shift his position and down will come the hat until it is in its proper place, but when the opposing club is scoring runs and things look bad for the Browns Jimmy has the rim of the hat pulled way down over his eyes.

Jim McGuire had charge of the Boston team for such a short space of time that the players on the other clubs didn't get a chance to find any peculiarities about the veteran.

Joe Cantillon didn't do much work on the coaching lines last season, but while he was there he used to pull off many a funny thing.

The last months of the season Cantillon stayed on the bench in citizen's clothes. When on the lines he is a good deal on the same order as Jennings.

Clark Griffith is one of those managers who is never still. No matter how far behind his team may be he is always out on the coaching lines urging his men on.

"Griff" is a great fellow to tell the opposing pitcher how soon it will be when they will be sending him to the tall timbers [slang], and the line of talk he and "Red" Donahue used to hand one another was a caution.

"Red" is there himself when it comes to handing out a line of talk. "Griff" would get on the [base?] line and say:

"Well, come on fellows, let's [get?] at this fellow. He hasn't enough speed to break a pane [of] glass!"

"Is that so?" would come [the?] reply. "Well, old boy, I [don't?] need any speed to beat this [tear in text] of dead ones you are [torn] around the country."

Manager Lajoie never h[as much?] to say on the field. The [tear in text] [fel]low is naturally of a quiet [dispo]sition.

Larry does most of his ma[nag]ing from the coaching lines. [He?] and Fielder Jones are really [the] only two playing managers [text missing] league and their work is [torn] harder than that of the [missing] leaders. Besides having to ba[lance?] the playing end of the game [they] have the additional burd[en of] playing their respective po[sitions] to carry.

Jones has the reputation [text is torn] having worn a path from [missing text] field to the plate, coming [torn] about decisions or running [torn] see what is the trouble [torn] things are going wrong.

Neither he nor Lajoie [missing text] anything to opposing pitc[hers].

They couldn't tear the uniform off Cornelius McGillicuddy—he wasn't wearing one. In his 50 years with the Athletics, Mr. Mack always wore street clothes—dark blue business suit, starched collar on white shirt—on the bench. Only his hat changed, summer's straw hat giving way to a boater come fall weather. He didn't look like a manager, especially in the era of the playing-manager, and he wasn't to be seen engaged in the usual acts and antics of managing. He remained nailed to the Philadelphia bench, keeping a rigid posture until he might position his players with a wave of his scorecard. He didn't seem to speak, depending instead on smart, well-prepared players to make in-game decisions. It was Mack, owner and manager of the Milwaukee Brewers in the Western League, who offered the 19-year-old Addie his professional contract. Mack wanted Addie to start on a team in Albany, New York, with the promise of promotion to Milwaukee; the youngster wanted to stay in Wisconsin. About the middle of the 1900 season, Mack was obliged to take the train to Punxsutawney, Pennsylvania, to sign a reluctant Waddell and break his contract with the Pirates. Addie may seem confusing to us when he writes about the Brewers' second-place finish: today, the American League in 1900 is officially recognized as a minor league. (In the 1901 season, the one we recognize as the start of American League operations, Connie Mack's Philadelphia A's finished a distant fourth.) Still, Addie's insightful critique of the Rube's pitching is a classic.

When Hugh Ambrose Jennings arrived in Detroit, in the spring before this article was written, the Tigers had run through almost a manager a year since joining the American League. He led the Tigers to three straight World Series (the ones Addie covered in his years with the Cleveland Press*). Jennings was one of the greatest shortstops of the 1890s, playing for its best franchise, Baltimore. As a manager and base coach, Jennings translated the rowdy style of the old Orioles teams into a do-anything-to-win attitude that seemed to inspire the young Ty Cobb. Smart, Jennings was one of the first managers to* *platoon players; he also had a career as a trial attorney. George Mullin pitched the Tigers to 66 victories during the three pennant years and was a 20-game winner five times. He grew up in Toledo, Ohio, but was known as "Wabash George" from his minor league days in Indiana. A dependable batter (a career .262 average), he once pinch-hit for Ty Cobb (June 22, 1912). The game in the article was especially memorable for the sportswriter: the April 20, 1907, game at League Park was Addie's third career one-hitter.*

Jimmy McAleer's seemingly effortless style in center field earned him the nickname "Loafer" in his playing days with the Spiders. He managed the first Cleveland entry in the American League. McAleer all too frequently wore his hat over his eyes — his highest finish was second place, in 1902, his first season with St. Louis. Bill Armour, who succeeded McAleer, must have been the last Cleveland manager to wear street clothes on the bench.

Jim "Deacon" McGuire was allotted only one sentence for his "short" stay at the reins, but he actually lasted two seasons in Boston (before coming to Cleveland to manage the Naps for Addie's last two seasons and a final spring training). McGuire's playing career, on the other hand, went on for 26 years, one of the longest in history. One of the nineteenth century's great catchers, he played briefly, in 1888, for the American Association Cleveland team. McGuire was among the first to record 40 pinch hits. Joe Cantillon managed the Washington Nationals from 1907 through 1909, losing over 100 games twice, in spite of signing Walter Johnson.

Readers will readily associate the name of Clark Griffith with the Washington franchise and Griffith Stadium, but at the time of this article, Griffith was the playing-manager of the New York Highlanders. "The Old Fox" won 237 games over a 20-year career; his junk-ball style of pitching was one of Addie's favorite topics. Francis Donahue pitched on Naps' staffs from 1903 to 1905. He led the National League with 38 complete games in 1897. Fielder Allison Jones managed the 1906 World Series champion White Sox. He was a standout defensive center fielder and the kind of hitter who got on base.

(FEBRUARY 15, 1908, TNB)

In Pete Lister, President [Bill] Armour secures a man who promises to be a mighty fine ball player some day.

Pete's career as a major leaguer with Cleveland was short because he went to Cleveland from Nashville near the close of the 1907 season.

While his work during that short time was not what would have been expected from a [Hal] Chase or ["Jiggs"] Donahue, still Pete played the bag in a very acceptable manner.

Lister has a great deal to learn before he will be a star at the initial sack, but he has the good fortune to be working for a manager who will soon develop the best there is in him.

The big fellow hit .274 with the Naps, and when it is taken into consideration that he was up against the best pitchers in the country, it can be seen that he is a pretty good hitter.

One thing that particularly impressed me with his work was the fact that he is continually on the move and does not hesitate to back up all plays in the infield, that his position will allow him to.

Pete is a bright, intelligent fellow and there is no reason to believe he will not improve.

President Armour is as good a judge of young players as there is in the country, and the mere fact that Bill thought well enough of him to make the purchase is evidence enough to warrant the statement, that he has more than an even chance of developing into a star of the first water.

Pete Lister logged 22 games at first base for Cleveland in 1907, his only year in the major leagues.

(February 20, 1908, TNB)

This year's American association teams will have on their pay-rolls a good many former American league players.

Probably the one who will attract the most attention is none other than that great old veteran, Monte Cross.

The fact that he will handle the playing end of the Kansas City team gives him a little more prominence than will be shown the rest of the ex–American leaguers.

Monte has been recognized for years as one of the brainiest men in the major leagues and for this reason should make the Kaws a great manager.

Playing for years under the capable management of Connie Mack has placed him in a position to observe how Mack handles men, and this will be of immeasurable benefit to him.

There won't be a shortstop in the A.A. who will have anything on him when it comes to playing the position, and he may be able to show some of the youngsters something about how the job should be handled.

President Armour was fortunate in securing such good men as [Harry] Hinchman, [Pete] Lister and [Howard] Wakefield. Enough has been said of them recently to acquaint the patrons of the game in Toledo with their qualities.

Columbus secures ["Bunk"] Congalton, and probably [Joe] Harris, from Ban Johnson's organization. In "Connie" they have a corking good man. "Bunk" has always been a .300 hitter, no matter what company he was in, and there is no reason to believe that he will fall down this year.

Harris is a promising pitcher and it's no wonder that President [Thomas] Bryce is making such strenuous efforts to secure him for the 1908 Senators.

Charley Carr will have "Honest John" Eubanks [Eubank] to help him try to win the pennant. Under Manager Armour's guidance John developed a "spit ball," and this, with the rest of the natural ability he possesses, will make him a valuable twirler for the Hoosiers.

Minneapolis secures [Roy] Patterson and [Pete] O'Brien, while rumor has it that Rhoe [i.e., George Rohe], [Mike] Welday and [Lou] Fiene are also to be with the Millers.

Patterson will pitch good ball in the association and O'Brien is a good ball player anywhere you put him.

If Mike Cantillon is lucky enough to get the other three, just keep your eye on that outfit.

Addie kept his own eye on the goings-on in the minor leagues for his Toledo readership, who were anticipating another Mud Hens season of competition with these rosters of players mostly consigned, nowadays, to the local historical society. Montford Cross is perhaps the most visible to us. He had lately retired from the Athletics, where he had been the starting shortstop for many seasons. Starting in 1908, he was player-manager for George "White Wings" Tebeau's K.C. Blues. One of the Blues' kid pitchers that year would make a name to remember: Smoky Joe Wood. Monte also played behind Addie on the Win Mercer barnstorming tour. William Congalton arrived in Cleveland after leading Western Association hitters for two straight seasons. He patrolled the outfield behind Addie from 1905 to 1907. Harry Hinchman and Howard

Wakefield had cups of coffee in 1907. For the 1909 season, plenty of recognizable names are on the Millers' payroll, including Nick Altrock, Jimmy Collins, and Gavvy Cravath. Thomas J. Bryce, president of the Columbus club, died in his seat at Niel Park, in conversation with John McGraw. He was watching his team host the Mud Hens, on July 12 in the year of Addie's article. Strangely enough, "Bunk" Congalton was to die watching Bob Feller pitch in Cleveland (August 16, 1937). Millers owner Mike Cantillon was Joe's brother.

(OCTOBER 20, 1908, TNB AND CP)

There seems to have been a good deal of speculation recently as to whether "Rube" Marquard, who pitched such wonderful ball in the American association this season will make good with the Giants next year.

The one tryout the big fellow received while a member of the Giants was anything but pleasing to his many admirers, and when he failed to deliver right off the reel many thought he had taken the jump to the big show a trifle too early in his career.

The fact that he did not get away with his one game in the major league should not be held against him. There was never a pitcher so good that he did not get his bumps once in a while and no doubt Marquard was unfortunate enough to be sent in by [John] McGraw at a time when it was destined he should get a clouting.

After seeing him in action for a few innings at Sandusky Sunday, it is evident why he was such an enigma to the star hitters of the association.

The big fellow has a perfectly free, easy and natural delivery. Plenty of speed, a fine curve ball and excellent control. This, coupled with the fact that he is a young man and one who takes excellent care of himself makes it look as though McGraw had picked up a jewel.

One of the reasons why "Rube" may not have shown to the best advantage in his only game in the majors, was because he was unfortunate to be pitched against the Reds, a team composed of nearly all right hand hitters.

As a rule, the Cincinnati team this year, hit left handers with considerable frequency and this day proved no exception to the rule.

Once the big fellow gets started in his true form as a member of the Giants and after being coached a while by Mathewson and the rest of the Giants he should be almost as effective for McGraw in 1909 as he was for the Indianapolis club the past season.

Another "Rube," Waddell, was living at Joe Cantillon's farm in Kentucky when his heroics during a flood led to pneumonia and eventually his early death. But Cleveland product Richard Marquard was all of 22 years old, and full of life, when he pitched in this game, on September 25, 1908, allowing eight base runners in his five-inning debut. The raw rookie was put on the spot—the Giants were in the final month of a heated race for the pennant—and the strategy produced a debate among his Toledo fans. In an unsigned article on a page edited by Addie (October 24, 1908), Charley Carr, Rube's Indianapolis manager, is quoted as saying that he had warned the Giants "that Marquart had had to work too hard while with us and that he needed a rest, but McGraw thought that the big fellow would be able to stand a little more." The Cincinnati batting order that Rube faced that day featured right-handed hitting star "Hans" Lobert.

(October 28, 1908, TNB and CP)

Without doubt Honus Wagner, of the Pirates, is one of the greatest players baseball has ever produced.

The big fellow has demonstrated this year after year and a good deal of Pittsburgh's success the past season was due to the "Flying Dutchman's" wonderful all-around playing.

Much has been written and said about the great infielder, especially on his seeming awkwardness and the surprise that follows a display of his skill.

To begin with Honus has probably the largest pair of baseball hands in captivity. He is wonderfully fast on his feet for a big man. As a matter of fact there isn't anybody in the business who has anything on him in the speed line.

He has a great arm and can whiz the ball over to first from any position he may be in after fielding the ball.

But what causes Wagner to be such a wonderful ground coverer is his peculiar faculty of being able to run at top speed close to the ground.

Usually a man of Wagner's size and build has to straighten up when going full tilt and even though he does reach the ball, he is seldom able to stoop over in time to grab the sphere and toss out his man.

About the only chance a man has to make a play of that kind is to have the ball come up. In other word, have it take a big bound just before the infielder gets to it, giving him a chance to make the play without bending close to the ground.

Not so with Honus. He runs just as fast close to the ground as he does when straightened up, giving him an advantage possessed by few.

It makes no difference to Wagner whether the ball hops up or not. He is always right on top of it, and kills off many a base hit in this manner.

On the bases, the "Dutchman" has long been considered as great as they make them. Here again his speed comes into play, as with it, he is able to get a big lead.

National league players and others who have watched the big fellow for a long time, say that it is simply marvelous the way he breaks for second when stealing.

His first leap seems to carry him about ten feet, and, once he is under full steam, he simply eats up the distance between the bases.

There is no use saying anything about his ability with the stick, as his average every season shows how good he is in this department of the game.

The big fellow is certainly a wonderful player, and it looks as though he is getting better every year. More power to you, Honus!

Addie played on the same field with Wagner in postseason exhibition games in 1902 and 1904, so his observations are firsthand. Perhaps it was writing this article on "The Flying Dutchman" that led Addie to do the think piece later on why big men make the best baserunners. (See his January 12, 1909, column, in Chapter 8.)

(NOVEMBER 4, 1908, TNB AND NOVEMBER 6, 1908, CP)

For some reason or other there seems to be an impression among those who should know that Lou Criger, the star catcher of the Boston Americans, will be numbered among the missing on the roster of that club when the season of 1909 rolls around.

Why this impression should prevail is hard to understand, especially since it is considered that the great backstop caught fully as good ball last season as he ever did.

Criger seems to be just as popular with the fans of Boston now as he ever was and that is saying a good deal, as he was given as much credit for the winning of two American league pennants there as any player on the club.

It has generally been conceded by baseball players and critics who have seen Lou and Young work with their machine-like precision and efficiency, that the lean catcher had fully as much to do with "Cy's" ability to win games as had the big rail splitter himself.

In fact, Cy will tell you that Criger does all the work and that all he has to do is to pitch what Lou calls for. Of course, it would be absurd to think that Young does not do his share of the work, but it must be acknowledged that "Cy" is always seen at his best when Criger is on the receiving end of the battery.

Young's one bad year since becoming an American leaguer was in 1906 and the fact that Criger was in bad shape and caught but few games is significant.

"Cy" lost 19 games that season, by the narrow margin of one run and it is safe to presume [sic.] that with Criger back of the bat he would have annexed a lot of the close contests.

The big fellow has learned to rely on the great catcher's judgment at all times and the results they get speaks well for the ability of Criger.

Why everyone would want to break up such a wonderful combination is hard to conceive and to an outsider would seem folly, still there is an impression that such is the case.

It is to be hoped that this idea is erroneous as Young and Criger are feared and respected in every city in the American league circuit, and a battery that the game could illy [sic.] afford to lose.

The version printed in the Cleveland Press *omits the last two paragraphs of this article. Criger was Denton Young's personal catcher, wherever the immortal "Cyclone" landed, first in Cleveland in 1896 and next in St. Louis and on to Boston. Criger caught only seven times in 1906—and Young lost 21 games that year. According to biographer Reed Browning, Young, late in his career, "had found in fellow Ohioan Addie Joss ... his closest ball-playing friend since his separation from Lou Criger."*

(November 27, 1908, TNB)

An accident to one of the regular infielders of the Chicago White Sox made Frank Isbell, one of the grandest utility players in the country.

The big fellow broke out as a pitcher and as such joined the Chicago Nationals. "Issy's" career as a twirler met with only fair success and he was finally shifted to first base by [Charles] Comiskey, when he joined the latter's team at St. Paul.

When the American league in[print obscured]ed Chicago "Commy" took Isbell with him and played him at first. He covered the bag for the White Sox until Comiskey purchased Jiggs Donahue.

The two men battled for a regular position on the team and "Jiggers" was awarded the place. This left "Issy" as a sort of a general utility man.

His real worth was not discovered though, until about the middle of the season of 1906. Chicago was playing a series at Cleveland. Gus Dundon, who was the regular second baseman, was nearly put out of the business for good that day.

The members of the Chicago team were having a little batting practice before the game. Gus had just hit and after driving the ball stepped back to allow the next man the chance to get a crack at the pill.

He stood a little to the left and about five feet back of the batter, who happened to be Lee Tannehill. "Tanny" let drive at the first ball pitched with all his mite, but instead of hitting the ball, the bat slipped out of his hand and struck Dundon with all its force right in the mouth.

Gus sank to the ground, all but unconscious and for a time it seemed that he was dangerously hurt.

Fielder Jones was in sore straits for an infielder to play the position made vacant by Dundon. "Issy" offered his services and was accepted. The big fellow made good right on the jump and from that time on played every position but first, still, he gets the results and when mentioning all around utility men, old "Issy" ranks with the best of them.

"Bald Eagle" Isbell played, always attempting to keep his cap on his head and conceal his receding hair line, all nine positions on the field, including 17 games in the pitcher's "box." But he is best remembered as the second baseman for the 1906 White Sox. He'd pitched for Macalester College, in 1895, before turning pro with Comiskey's St. Paul club in the Western League. John Donahue relieved him of the starting job at first base in the 1904 season.

(DECEMBER 2, 1908, CP AND DECEMBER 10, 1908, TNB)

One thing outfielders dread to do, especially those who have had little or no experience in that line of work, is to play a sun-field.

Until an outfielder learns to play the position he finds it a very difficult task to correctly judge the distance and speed of balls that get into the sun.

Joe Birmingham, one of the Naps' outfielders, refuses to play any garden where he will have to contend with the sun's rays. It's no wonder after the experience he had at Atlanta a few seasons ago.

The Cleveland club was playing a few exhibition games in the Georgia city on its way north to open the regular season. Left field there is a fearful sun field, especially early and late in the season, when Old Sol does not get very high during the hours the game is on.

Joe was being tried out in that position and was doing very well, because there had not been many balls hit to him through the sun.

Along toward the latter part of the game, and at a time when the sun was getting low, one of the Atlanta players hit a terrific line drive straight at Joe.

Birmingham did not have to move for the ball and when he put up his hand, as though to make the catch, everyone thought he had the ball properly gauged.

Imagine the surprise when, just at the moment it seemed he was going to catch the sphere, Joe was seen to turn his head and put up his hands as though to ward off an imaginary blow.

The ball flew through his outstretched hands and hit him right on top of the head, bounding about 20 feet into the air. By the time Birmingham recovered the pill and got it into the infield the hitter was camped on third.

Birmingham had a lump on his head the size of a hen's egg for a few days. To make matters worse all the rest of the gang kidded the life out of him about the great "head work" he displayed.

Harry Bay even went so far as to give him two errors on the play, one for not catching the ball and the second for missing it when it came down after bounding into the air.

The News-Bee *version of this story is three paragraphs longer than the one that the* Press *ran, including the punch-line ending. "Dode" Birmingham played only 38 regular season games in left field over his nine-year career with the Naps. Like Jimmy McAleer before him and Tris Speaker after him, he was a gifted Cleveland center fielder who became manager of the club. His 33 assists were tops among American League outfielders in 1907. It would be interesting to know what exactly Birmingham told players who declined to play, after he became manager. Joe Birmingham died in a restaurant, in Tampico, Mexico, after umpiring a game.*

Left was the sun field in League Park, too, and especially tricky for the fly-catchers in late afternoons. New equipment for players in the early 1900s included sunglasses of "smoked glass" for fielders. Fred Clarke patented flip-up sunglasses in 1916. This exhibition was probably played in old Brisbane Park, perhaps in 1905 at the invitation of Atlanta Crackers manager Otto Jordan, a Pittsburgher. (Famed Ponce de Leon Park did not open until May 1907.)

(December 4, 1908, CP)

Many times during a season one may see a man nipped off first base on an attempt to steal second, when it looks as though he was simply caught napping.

Most players work on the supposition that it is better to be caught off first once in a while, and always be sure of a good lead, than it is to get a late start and be nipped at second by a good-throwing catcher.

Joe Birmingham practically won a game for the Naps against Chicago last fall on a play of this kind. He was on first with no one out. He started to steal and [Ed] Walsh whipped the ball to first.

[Frank] Isbell took the throw and wheeled to peg to second as [shortstop Freddy] Parent ran over to make the putout.

Birmingham was directly on a line between "Issy" and the bag and the big fellow had no other alternative than to throw where he thought Parent would be.

Instead of the ball resting in Parent's mitt, it hit Birmingham on the top of the head and bounded into left field, allowing Joe to reach third, from where he scored the only run of the game a few moments later on a passed ball.

Birmingham was not much of a runner in an era known for basestealing. His 23 bags in 1907 were his career high. Addie is recalling, in a newspaper reporter's objective tone, a crucial play from the third inning of his October 2, 1908, perfect game. Ossee Schrecongost's passed ball allowed Birmingham to score the game's only run. I place the piece here, rather than in Chapter 3, about great plays, to stress Addie's theme, in consecutive articles, of Joe Birmingham's head. (The next article refers to the threat of a beaning.)

(December 5, 1908, CP)

There is a lot of difference between being fresh on the ball field and having plenty of confidence.

Louis Evans, who finished the season with the Montreal Eastern league team, was taken south by [John] McGraw last spring. He stayed with the Giants the early part of the season. He was also with the [Chicago] Colts.

In a game the New York team was playing at Philadelphia, in which the score was close, McGraw found an opportunity to send Evans in to bat for someone; at a time when the Giants had a man on second and needed a run to win.

The youngster stepped to the plate and as he took his position, "Red" Dooin, the Phillies' star backstop, after looking Evans over from head to foot, let drop this remark:

"You had better be careful, young fellow, this pitcher is wilder than a hawk and is liable to cop you on the head any minute."

A moment later the twirler let go of a fast one that fairly whistled past Evans' face.

The next ball pitched was closer to the youngster's head than the first one, and Evans, who was wise to Dooin's game, thought it was time to take a hand. Leaning over to Dooin he said:

"Tell that guy out there that if he ever expects to drive me away from the plate he had better pack that slow one in his grip."

Before Dooin could recover from his surprise at the remark he heard Evans say: "If he hands me up another one like that I will knock the button off his cap with a line drive. Tell him to duck, I don't want to kill him."

Then to make it good Evans drove a vicious liner through the box, scoring the man from second. He was not molested again.

This article is a kind of follow up on Addie's March 10, 1907, News-Bee *piece on his own hazing. They called Clevelander Louis Richard Evans "Steve." The 1908 season was the outfielder-first baseman's only season in New York. After five years with the Cardinals, Evans emerged as a star in the Federal League. He finished his playing career for the Toledo Iron Men. Cincinnati-born Charles Sebastian Dooin was a standout defensive catcher and playing-manager for the Phillies.*

(DECEMBER 9, 1908, CP)

One constant worry to a ball player is the fear he has of losing the strength of his arm. A ball player's arm is a peculiar thing. There is never any way of telling when it is liable to go back on him. Many a player who used to be able to throw as hard as anyone, has gone to bed at night in first-class shape and awakened in the morning minus the services of the throwing member.

Take the case of Terry Turner of the Naps. "Tuck," up to the time he hurt his arm, had as fine a whip as anyone playing the infield in the American league.

He went out on the field to practice before the game one day and soon came in to the bench, complaining that his arm hurt him. All the rest of the players took it as a "kid" when "Tuck" told this, as no one ever dreamed Turner would have a sore arm.

His arm was not right again the rest of the season, although he did everything he could to restore the injured member to its usefulness.

Jesse Tannehill is another player whose arm went back on him, though "Tanny" worked a few games last fall and said it felt as good as ever.

I know of a case where a certain pitcher was out of the game for nearly two months one season with a bad arm. He tried every method ever suggested to bring it back without getting any results.

He was in the habit of pitching to the batters in practice every day before the game and, one afternoon, after warming up a bit, he noticed an improvement in his finger.

This was on a Saturday. The following Monday he asked for a chance to work, saying he thought his arm was all right again. His confidence in his whip was not misplaced, as he won a 1 to 0 game, holding his opponents to five hits and having everything at his command.

"Cotton Top" Turner set the Cleveland franchise record for career games played, but he was often out of the lineup because of injury or illness. After four seasons as the Naps' starting shortstop, the arm injury that Addie writes about moved Turner to the outfield for 1908. He was a standout infielder, twice leading the American League in fielding percentage at shortstop, and another two times at third base. His defensive accomplishments were achieved in spite of the damage to his hands from his patented head-first slides. Left-handed Jesse Niles Tannehill was a 20-game winner four times for Pittsburgh, beginning with the 1898 season. After winning 43 games for the Boston Americans over the 1904 and 1905 seasons, Tannehill developed a sore arm. He never regained his pitching effectiveness.

(DECEMBER 24, 1908, TNB)

The deal consummated at the recent American league meeting in New York, whereby Jimmy McAleer got Lou Criger, the famous catcher of the Boston team, in exchange for ["Tubby"] Spencer of the Browns and a cash consideration, said to be $5,000, looks as though the wily McAleer had once more driven a good bargain.

Of course, there is no way of telling which club got the better of the deal until after the season of 1909 is well on its way. One or the other of the men may have a bad season, and not play up to form, which will make it easy for the other side to say: "I guess we did not know what we were doing when we made that trade."

Taking things just as they stand at present, most everyone is willing to acknowledge that McAleer did not lose any of his reputation as the David Harum of the American league.

Criger is one grand catcher: a fine receiver, one of the best peggers that ever stepped behind the plate, game to the core, and, above all, one of the closest students of the game baseball has ever known.

In the days when the Boston American team was winning championships, when it had such pitchers as ["Cy"] Young, [Bill] Dineen, [Jesse] Tannehill and [Norwood] Gibson, it was simply suicide to try to steal bases on Criger.

He seemed to have the faculty of calling the turn on the base runner whenever that individual would attempt to steal, and, with the pitcher holding up the runner, and [shortstop Freddy] Parent and [second baseman "Hobe"] Ferris to take the throw, it was next to impossible to pilfer.

It can readily be seen at what a disadvantage this placed the opposition. There was nothing left for the other team to do but hit straight away, and trust to this style of game for victory.

Lou certainly was a tower of strength to the Boston club, especially when it came to coaching the young pitchers, and, while the veteran Young may go on just as well without his running mate of so many years, still the one season that he was without his services, "Cy" had his only bad year since becoming an American Leaguer.

Spencer, who goes to Boston, is a corking good man behind the bat, being a big, willing fellow, who is a good receiver and the possessor of a fine arm.

The big fellow is always a dangerous hitter, and any time he gets a hold of one it always means a chase for one of the fielders.

The one chance that McAleer took in making the trade was the fact that Criger's health, which has been none the best for the past few seasons, may go back on him.

The weather in St. Louis is always pretty warm, and this may have a bad effect on Lou, as he has become accustomed to the cool breezes of Boston.

The last thing McAleer said as he was leaving New York was: "Look out for us next season!" And, with Criger in good shape, it looks as though the Browns would certainly cut quite a figure in the race.

David Harum's novel A Story of American Life, *a best seller of 1899, is memorable for its use of the term "horse trading." Addie's interest in colloquialisms was keen; perhaps his readers would hope McAleer was not engaged in a "harum scarum," or reckless, horse swap? Keeping on a literary note, Zane Grey's brother was teammates with Lou Criger in the minors. On the subject of Criger's health issues, biographer Steve Krah notes that the catcher "became so associated with injury that he later became a spokesman for ... Dr. Miles' Anti-Pain Pills." Criger, the ur–Jim Hegan, was an old 37 at the time of the trade. He would appear in only 74 games for the Browns that season and hit .170 nearing the end. Twenty-five-year-old Edward Spencer would play 28 games for Boston, and only sporadically in the majors after that. Lou Criger had enjoyed a long career, after replacing the great Charles "Chief" Zimmer on the Spiders. England-born Albert Ferris knocked in all three Boston runs in the deciding game of the first World Series, but his .265 on-base percentage is the lowest career mark in history. Norwood Ringold Gibson won 30 games in his first two seasons with Boston, 1903 and 1904, but was only 4–7 over his final two.*

(DECEMBER 26, 1908, TNB)

Clark Griffith, the new manager of the Reds, was considered one of the best pitchers in the business in his time. Besides being a successful twirler, Griffith was one of the wisest men that ever stepped in a box.

"Griff" was not blessed with the natural qualifications of the successful twirler; that is, speed and a strong physique, and had to resort to strategy to get results.

The "old fox" was a great student of the game, and this, combined with his ability to mix them up and good control, always made him a dangerous foe.

Always on the lookout for a chance to slip one over on the opposition, or anything that might make his none too easy task lighter, "Griff" immediately took advantage of the rule which was passed some years ago, allowing the pitcher but the small rubber to stand on when getting ready to deliver the ball.

The rule says the twirler must stand with both feet on the rubber, or with one foot on the rubber, or with one foot on it and the other ahead, or towards the batter, when in the act of delivering the ball. Most box artists interpreted the rule to read: that they must stand so that the ball of the foot is on the rubber; but not so with "Griff."

He used to stand with his heel against the front end of the pitcher's plate, and then, just as he was ready to pitch, would slide up a foot or so, and, in this manner, be able to steal that much of the distance to the plate on the batter.

Where a pitcher is throwing on an average of 150 balls in a game, it can be seen that this was something of an advantage. If the opposition was not watching him every minute "Griff" was liable to be anywhere from one foot to three or four feet closer to the plate.

"Griff" was foxy enough to cover this up, too, when the inning was over. Naturally, when stealing a few feet this way he would dig a hole in the ground around the rubber, which could be readily seen by the opposing twirler. So after the third man had been retired "Griff" used to stand in the box and in a rather abstracted way scratch around the ground he had dug up with his spikes, making it smooth and even, and in this way cover up his work.

The "Old Boy" got away with this for a good many years and even though the umpires would make him stop it for an inning or two he would be right back doing the same thing again, if not watched closely.

Clark's fingers were short and this made it hard for him to get a good firm grip on the ball, especially when pitching a curve.

In order to roughen the ball so that he could get a firm hold of the sphere he used to hit the ball against the spikes on the heel of his shoes.

This would nick the ball and roughen it to the extent of allowing him to get a good grip on the pill. Any time an umpire would call him for doing this "Griff" would just say: "I am trying to get the dirt out of my spikes," and keep right on until he had the ball in such shape that he could handle it.

The rule establishing the pitcher's rubber was introduced in 1893. Notice that Addie figures an average afternoon for a starter in his era was about 150 pitches. What is it, anyway, with these crafty lefties, from Clark Griffith's movable rubber to Whitey Ford's scuff ball (Ford had Elston Howard do the scuffing, while Griffith apparently did his own)[8] *and Jamie Moyer's slow-slower-slowest ball? And they all win over 200 games. The secret of the pitching universe must be somewhere in them. Addie was known to be a flamethrower but one who pitched to contact, so he was naturally fascinated by crafty pitchers and how they got outs. He often wrote about Griffith and Nick Altrock.*

(JANUARY 6, 1909, TNB)

It seems to be the opinion among the baseball fraternity all over the country that Fielder Jones, now on the coast looking after land interests he has there, will be back in the spring to handle [Charles] Comiskey's club for the season of 1909.

The "old Roman" himself does not seem to take Jones' threatened retirement very seriously, but there is a chance, and a mighty big one, that Fielder will be missing when the White Sox are ready to board the train for their training grounds.

Jones has been threatening for the past few seasons to retire. At the close of the 1907 season he said he was done with baseball. It's better than an even bet he would have kept his word had it not been for the financial stringency.

Fielder's western interests suffered, and it was only natural that Jones would turn back to baseball when he saw it would be impossible for him to realize anywhere near the profit from his land interests that he could make out of baseball.

Last fall Fielder again said he was through with baseball, and has gone west once more. It's well known among the members of the profession in the American league that Jones has been wanting to get out of the game for some time.

Most everyone has always taken this in a joking way, but Jones insists he is in earnest. Should things shape themselves so that Fielder can put through his intended projects, chances are better than even that Comiskey will have to decide on a new man to lead the White Sox in 1909.

Many persons take it for granted that a baseball player's love for the game will cause him to give up most anything he may have in view in order to get back in the game. There is no denying the fact that the game has a wonderful fascination for everyone directly connected with it, but, at the same time, it is only right to presume that a man who is as clever as Fielder is, will not let his love for the national pastime stand in his way when it comes to seeing a chance to better himself.

Jones has had all the glory there is in baseball, and no unprejudiced mind will censure him for trying to better himself in any way that he see fit. If his western interests prove as good as Fielder says he thinks they will, then he would be foolish to come back.

The chances are that Fielder will not be back, and that it is up to Comiskey to look for a new manager.

To go from Clark Griffith in one article to Charley Comiskey in the next is to cover an awful lot of baseball history. Fielder Jones (no, that's not a nickname) had been a star for the White Sox since their inaugural season in the American League. He was their manager and starting center fielder when they upset the highly favored Cubs in the 1906 World Series. In 1909, he became treasurer of the Northwestern League and, still during Addie's lifetime, baseball coach at Oregon State. By the next decade, Comiskey's chastity belt of a pocket book proved to be a factor in his Black Sox players' desire for more income.

(JANUARY 27, 1909, TNB)

Whether or not Fielder Jones decides to return to [rest of the page is torn] this year and once more manage the White Sox, ti[torn here] remains that he is one of the greatest outfielders the [game has?] ever known.

Fielder has always had the reputation of being a heady, [torn] player and one who was always alive to the possibilities the p[osition demanded?].

There is probably no outfielder in the American league who uses better judgment than Jones in playing the hitters. He is a past master in the art of seeming to always be where the man hits.

To a good many fans this would seem a matter of luck, but after watching Jones play center field for a few games, it soon becomes apparent that he is a mighty close student of the sport.

In order for an outfielder to be able to shift his position, so as to be always where the different batters hit, it is necessary for him to first know where these batters are most likely to clout the ball and then take into consideration who is pitching and what he is handing this particular hitter.

Of course, there are times when the batter won't hit true to his form; that is if he is a natural right field hitter, he may swing a little quicker on one and pull it into left field and when he does this a fielder who plays his man as Jones does, will be crossed.

As a rule though, Jones is usually found in the right place. Many a time when the man at bat gets hold of one and sees it sailing over the infield, thinking he has made a base hit and taking a second look to see if there is a chance to make an extra base, there is Jones all set to make the catch.

So well does Fielder play for his men, that it is commonly known around the American league circuit that he never makes a one handed grab. He invariably gets two hands on the ball.

If Jones decides to stay out west and forsake the national pastime, the game will not only lose one of its greatest managers, but one of the best outfielders that ever donned a pair of spiked shoes.

Fielder led all Junior Circuit outfielders in fielding percentage in 1903 and 1906, also in putouts in 1903. And Jones was either second or third in putouts six other years. His 225 lifetime assists rank thirty-fourth all time.

(JANUARY 8, 1909, TNB)

Stanley Robison, of the St. Louis Cardinals, certainly made a ten strike when he put through the recent deal by which he secured Roger Bresnahan to lead his club.

While it has been an established fact among the players that the man most essential to a club's success, is the catcher, it has only recently become generally accepted by the fans.

There is no doubt that Roger is fully the equal, if not a little superior, to any catcher in the business and although Robison made a number of sacrifices to make the deal, parting with several of his star players, still, he surely started right by fortifying the most important position on the field.

In securing the services of the former Giant, Robison accomplished a double purpose, getting a manager and a player at the same time.

Bresnahan should make a great manager. He is a man who knows every trick in the game, can do everything a good player should be able to do and above all, is imbued with that fighting spirit so essential to a winning aggregation.

Right off the reel, Roger is going to be handicapped in his fight for the National league pennant by the fact that he will be practically forced to build up an entirely new team.

Whether or not he will be able to do this at once is something that time alone can determine, but the fans of St. Louis can rest assured that they will always get a run for their money. The team headed by Roger will be hustling every minute it is on the field.

The new Cardinal leader is certainly entitled to his promotion as a reward for his long and faithful performances as a Giant.

His career as a manager will be eagerly watched by thousands of fans all over the country and it is a cinch that no one will be pulling any harder for him than the Toledo enthusiasts. Here's wishing you all the luck in the world, Roger.

Addie and his fellow Toledoan were good friends, and tried to go partners in a 1903 deal to buy the Mud Hens.[9] *Bresnahan, who did own the Toledo club by 1916, also wrote for the* News-Bee *(see Addie's February 12, 1909, article below). Bresnahan was the new Cards manager and backup catcher for a team destined to finish seventh in 1909. It was on December 12, 1908, when Robison traded the pre–Dock Ellis version of a psychedelic trio—"Red" Murray, Bugs Raymond, and Admiral Schlei*[10]*—to the Giants for Roger. M. Stanley Robison, president of the Cardinals from 1907–10, took over from his brother Frank D. Robison—a pattern that went back to their administration of the Cleveland Spiders a decade before.*

(JANUARY 22, 1909, TNB)

President Armour is to be congratulated in securing "Sox" ["Socks"] Seybold for the coming season. A grand pair of hitters, Seybold and [Charlie] Hickman will make for the local team [the Mud Hens].

Toledo fans have had a taste of what Hickman can do in the slugging way and to show what a tower of strength "Sox" will be, it is only necessary to say that the ex–Athletic is every bit as dangerous a man for the opposing pitcher to face as is "Cheerful Hick."

These two men are great hitters in any league. Both men were very highly respected by every pitcher in the American league while they were members of that organization.

"Sox" and "Hick" are sluggers of the old school, and any time they connect with one, all the fences in the league are too short for their drives.

It takes runs to win games, and this pair will certainly do their share in driving men across the plate. With Hickman, [Homer] Smoot and Seybold coming up in a row the prospects are pretty fair for a run, especially if there happen to be any men on the bases at the time.

Both Seybold and Hickman are "no-weakness" hitters; that is, batters who can hit anything that is handed them.

Slugging Homer Smoot's nickname was not Homer. It was "Doc." The Society for American Baseball Research selected him the best National League rookie of 1902. Ralph Orlando Seybold had finished the previous season, his last in the major leagues, on the disabled list, so he was free to scout, and sign, Joe Jackson.

(JANUARY 26, 1909, TNB)

Jesse Burkett, who saw years of service in the major leagues and who for the past few seasons has been the owner and manager of the Worcester, Mass., team in the New England league, is a player that is wise to about every trick of the game. Still, Jess had a real one pulled off on him when he first took charge of the club.

It seems Burkett has a peculiar habit of always being ready to help the opposing catcher put on his chest protector or mask, in case either one of these articles are out of place, and it was through this medium that the play was pulled off on the ex–major leaguer.

The opposing battery, which was made up of a pair of youngsters, framed up the play and arranged to use it the first time the opportunity presented itself. On Burkett's first trip to the plate, the opponent's flinger, who was adept at the quick return delivery, managed to get a strike on Jesse.

The next ball pitched Burkett hit foul, making two strikes. As the ball was returned to the pitcher the backstop, according to previous instructions, took off his mask as though there was something the matter with it, and stepping a few feet to one side, commenced to tug and pull at the strap as though trying to get it fixed.

Burkett, never dreaming what was coming off, took his bat off his shoulder, and still standing in the batter's box, watched the backstop trying to fix the mask.

The twirler, who was just waiting for this move, stepped on the rubber and without waiting for the catcher to get in his position, whipped the ball over the plate. The catcher jumped back into his position and caught the ball, which "his umps" called a strike. Burkett was caught flat footed on the play and could do nothing but walk back to the bench. But what he said needs no stretch of the imagination to conceive.

Leave it to Addie to supply a detail about a baseball immortal's fixation with catcher's equipment. He might also be enjoying his revenge by portraying the ancient veteran—who had excelled at the roughhouse game he learned from Patsy Tebeau—tricked by a young battery. Keep in mind that it was this same Burkett who had taken a part in hazing Addie, and eventually spoiling the rookie's bid for a no-hitter on a disputed scratch single, in the very first game he pitched in the Bigs.

(JANUARY 29, 1909, TNB)

Jack Sheridan, dean of major league umpires, never wears a chest protector when working behind the bat. Sheridan is probably the only umpire in the game who considers a protector superfluous.

The great umpire has a way of protecting himself from foul balls and wild pitches that get by the catcher, in a manner that is as effective as it is simple.

Sheridan simply stands directly behind the catcher and uses him as a guard against being hit. Jack looks over the catcher's shoulder to get a line on where the ball is going and seems to get the results, as it is conceded that on balls and strikes he has no superior and few equals.

The "old boy" came near getting in trouble one day a few seasons ago, on account of the manner in which he officiates behind the plate. Case Patten was doing the twirling on the particular occasion and had as a receiver young ["Bruno"] Block, who was with Minneapolis last year.

Patten is one of those quick-return artists, and during the course of the contest, saw a chance to sneak one over on some batter.

Block was new to this style of game, and instead of being on the job, was just setting himself to give the sign, when the ball came whizzing up to the plate. Sheridan, who had taken it for granted that Patten had put the youngster wise, was also completely off guard. The only thing that prevented him from getting hit with the ball was the fact that the pitch was a little high. Sheridan had his head up the rest of that game.

Patten was very strong for this quick delivery thing and any time the batter got careless the former Washington pitcher would be ready to slip one over.

One day at Washington, Patten was employing this stunt to fool the Cleveland batters and was getting away with it in great shape early in the contest.

As ["Larry"] Lajoie picked up his bat to go to the plate, he remarked that if Patten tried to slip one over on him he was going to lay for just that sort of thing. When a pitcher tries this he always hands up a straight fast one and the chances were pretty good for the big fellow to belt one.

The first ball pitched was wide of the plate and Larry, with one eye on Patten, made the bluff that he was not watching. Case thought he saw a chance to get one by the big fellow and quickly stepping on the rubber slammed a nice fast one straight across.

What Larry did to that ball was a shame. He took a running hop, step and jump and let fly with all his might. He certainly gave it an awful wallop and when the left fielder had nabbed the ball and hustled it into the infield Lajoie was resting at third.

Patten tried to slip no more over on Lajoie.

Our direct line affords us a hint into Addie's writing process, when he follows his article on Burkett's fixation with catcher's equipment with this one (in part, a repeat of his December 23, 1907, article for the Cleveland Press*), on the umpire who survived a whole career behind the plate without protective equipment. The two-umpire system was introduced in 1887, when John Gaffney, "The King of Umps," and "Honest" John Kelly officiated all 15 games, in 10 cities, between the National League Detroit Wolverines and the American Association St. Louis Browns. However, in Addie's decade in the majors, most regular season games still employed a lone umpire. Wisconsin native James John (Blochowicz) Block was a spare catcher for the Senators, White Sox, and Federal League Whales, over five seasons. His last year was the first one for Wrigley Field.*

(February 12, 1909, TNB)

Roger Bresnahan's interesting description of how John McGraw treats his players, which appeared in Wednesday's News-Bee, is well seconded by a story Jimmy Jackson once told of how McGraw used him when he started in professional ball under "Mac" when he was handling the Baltimore team.

The Baltimore club was in sore straits for an outfielder and McGraw signed Jackson, who at that time was practically a novice. Jimmy's contract called for $150 a month, and, as he used to say, he was mighty glad to get that much.

The ex–Cleveland and Columbus outfielder played great ball right off the reel and when he went to the office to get his first check, he was surprised to see that it called for an amount based on the ratio of $250 a month.

Jackson called the attention of the secretary to what he thought had been an oversight. Much to his surprise, he was told that McGraw had ordered the raise as an indication of his appreciation of the player's efforts.

Jackson also says that on one of the club's trips from the west, home, the players took advantage of an off-day to stop in Buffalo to see the Pan-American exposition.

Unknown to the players, carriages were placed at their disposal for the day and as they were starting out McGraw appeared and handed each one a ten-spot.

They all expected that the carriage hire and the $10 would be deducted from their next pay envelope, but this was never done. McGraw stood for the whole thing himself.

Bresnahan's thanks to "The Little Napoleon" for recommending him to manage Stanley Robison's Cards was printed in a conspicuous place, top of the page and opposite Addie's February 10 column. In short, it was news to readers at the time that John McGraw, feared and feted for his kicks and punches as a player and for his ejections from games as a manager, could be beloved to those men who played for him. In 1915, McGraw would engineer a similar deal, trading Christy Mathewson to the Reds so his friend could have the chance to manage. Jim Jackson was a rookie with the 1901 Baltimore club, leading the league's outfielders in fielding percentage. He was a teammate of Addie's in 1905 and 1906, Jackson's last years in the majors. The Buffalo Exposition was the scene of the assassination of President McKinley.

(FEBRUARY 18, 1909, TNB)

In looking over the itinerary of the White Sox on their California training trip this spring, Sacramento appears as one of the places, [Charles] Comiskey's team will stop over for a few days.

The mention of this California city calls to mind an experience the National and American league teams had there, when those clubs were touring the west a few seasons ago.

The late Win Mercer, besides pitching in his regular turn, was made the treasurer of the trip. The great pitcher was in the habit of [add]ing up the week's receipts every Sunday night. "Merc" used to put money in a large canvas bag and leave it in the hotel safe.

There were about 30 people in the party. Each member was furnished with a round trip ticket from Chicago to Frisco and Mercer, who [had] charge of the transportation, used to keep the tickets in a canvas [bag?]. This also was left at the hotel.

About an hour after the teams left the hotel for the grounds one [Sunday] afternoon, a messenger boy walked up to the desk and handed [illegible type] a note, which read: "There is a fresh guy out here at the desk who wants to make a bet. Send out the bag with the money in[side it]." It was signed Win Mercer.

The desk clerk opened the safe and getting out the bag, which he thought contained the money, gave it to the boy who jumped on his wheel and [rode?] away.

About an hour after the clerk was surprised to see the boy come [back]. The youngster returned the bag and with it another note, which [read:] "Can't call bets with railroad tickets. Send out the money. Then, send his, too. Mercer."

Prior to the game, as is the usual custom, the players put their valuables, such as money and jewelry, in a bag and left it in the hotel [safe?].

This day Harry Davis, "Bill" Bernhard, "Topsy" Hartzel and the [players?] were dressing in the same room and as Davis had an unusually [large?] bag, the rest of us put our valuables into it. This was done in the [lobby] of the hotel and in plain sight of anyone who might be standing [unreadable].

When the boy handed the second note to the clerk he became a trifle nervous and stepping out from behind the desk, walked over to a [unreadable] in front of the hotel, where Jack Chesbro was sitting.

Chesbro never played ball on Sunday. This accounts for his being [unreadable] hotel. The clerk informed Jack of what had happened and [unreadable] the big pitcher's advice in regard to the matter.

The man who made the "spit ball" famous volunteered to take the [money?] to Mercer and jumped into a cab and was driven to the grounds, [unreadable] got there, just as the teams were starting back to the hotel.

When Chesbro told Mercer the story we were dumbfounded. The [unreadable] notes were all a hoax and was a clever scheme to rob us. The [players?] were made acquainted with the facts in the case, but their efforts to apprehend the man who was so bold, were of no avail.

When it is known that there was nearly $7,000 in cold hard cash [inside the?] bag it can be seen just how decent a haul came near being made.

Addie waits the mourner's customary year and a day after writing his eulogy to Win Mercer to tell his version of the riddle of events leading to his friend's suicide. He wrote both articles in the month of February. Naturally Addie would have remembered his friend in the winter months each year following Mercer's January 12, 1903, death. Ever loyal, Addie never publicly blamed Win Mercer for the attempted robbery, and the suicide's motives remain one of baseball's unsolved mysteries. We do know that Addie accompanied the body on the long train journey back to East Liverpool, Ohio, for burial. The difficulty in deciphering this bad page of microfilm makes the article read to us more like a gothic tale.

(FEBRUARY 20, 1909, TNB)

Near the close of every major league campaign the different managers usually secure an abundance of young material to look over before the regular season closes.

Connie Mack, who has so successfully handled the reins of the Philadelphia American league club, for a number of years, is a shrewd chap and any time he thinks his team is out of it, as far as the pennant is concerned, he has all his youngsters report early in the fall.

This gives Mack a chance to look over his new material and also saves the expense of taking a lot of deadwood on the southern training trip the following spring.

Last fall Mack secured a youngster from the championship Shamokin club, managed by Lave Cross, named [Amos] Strunk. The new comer came highly recommended by Lave and from the manner in which he showed in the few games he played, seems destined to one day be numbered among the sport's brightest stars.

Strunk certainly made a hit with the fans around the western end of the circuit. He is a tall, slender chap, and seems to be a good judge of a fly ball. But he shines at the bat and on the bases. He has all the ear marks of a fine player. He is wonderfully fast on his feet and stands up at the plate like a veteran.

Soon after he joined the Athletics, Connie put him to the test. Mike Powers, who is rated as one of the best backstops in the younger organization, is considered a little weak with the stick and Mack often sends someone to hit in his place.

It is an established fact that no matter who Connie would select to take Powers' place at the bat in a pinch, that batter never was known to make a base hit.

In fact, the Athletics' manager commenced to think that Mike was casting a spell over all his substitute hitters, thus preventing them from making good and showing him up.

Soon after Strunk joined the Philadelphia club an opportunity came for Mack to substitute someone to hit for Powers. The youngster had made a favorable impression on the players and when Connie picked him as the pinch hitter, they laughingly remarked: "Well, if he makes good here there won't be anything to it."

Strunk made good on the first ball pitched, smashing out a clean single. This is one of the reasons, Mack and the rest of the members of the club think, the youngster is sure to be a star of the first water.

Addie recalls Strunk's only appearance as a pinch hitter in the 1908 season. But he would lead the league in pinch-hit at-bats and hits in 1923. Amos Strunk, all of 19 when he broke in with the Athletics, would appear in five World Series during a 17-year career as an American League outfielder. Connie Mack was a shrewd baseball man — he built and sold off several great teams in Philadelphia over the first half of the century — but Cleveland tended to get the better of him in Addie's time. Mack sold Elmer Flick to the Blues. He was cajoled by courts into letting Nap Lajoie and "Strawberry" Bill Bernhard escape contracts with the A's. And Mack was so hot to get "Bris" Lord back in the Philadelphia outfield that he traded Cleveland the rights to Shoeless Joe, or at least he was convinced that Jackson could never tolerate living outside of South Carolina. Mack also let Steve O'Neill go to Cleveland, where he would become a stalwart behind the plate for a dozen years. Could it be that "The Tall Tactician" Mack felt a debt that could never be repaid, after Charlie Somers had loaned him the money to keep the A's afloat in the new American League? (Was there a reason for the later-day A's of Kansas City to act like a feeder roster for the Stengel Yankees?) It should be noted, when we consider character, that Mack offered Addie Joss' son a tryout with the A's, after the great pitcher's death. Mack was getting set to open the new Shibe Park, a monument to his early successes, for the 1909 season. Shamokin manager Lave Cross, a great glove at third base and near-great hitter who collected 2,651 hits, ended his 21-year career in 1907. Cross played briefly for the Spiders. (Shamokin, Pennsylvania's Stanley Coveleski would have been 19 years old when Addie wrote this piece, the year the teenager left the coal mines to sign his first pro contract, with Lancaster of the Tri-State League. With Cleveland teams, he would win 172 games to Addie's 160.)

(FEBRUARY 23, 1909, TNB)

Ball players never seem to be content with their lot. The average star pitcher would rather be a good hitter and win games for his team by driving in runs than be the best twirler in the business. The same holds good of the top-notch outfielder, who has a desire to try his hand at the pitching game.

"Ty" Cobb, that wonderful young person, who has been the sensation of the American league for the past two seasons, would rather be a good pitcher than lead the league in hitting."

"Ty" is constantly practicing the twirling end of the game and nothing delights him more than to pitch to the batters in practice before the game.

If by any chance "Ty" can make one of the hitters swing wild on one, or cause him to pop up a little fly, he is in the seventh heaven of delight. It's an everyday occurrence to see the fleet-footed southerner backing one of the Tigers' catchers against the grand stand and keeping him there while he practices curves, "spit-balls" and everything else that is known and used by the twirler.

Hal Chase, of the Highlanders, is another great player, who likes nothing better than to pitch to the batters. To Hal's credit, it must be said that if he were to quit playing first base and try his hand at twirling, he would have more than an even chance of making good. The first sacker's long suit is a slow ball and it's a dandy. To the batter it looks as though it never was going to get up to the plate.

Harry Howell, of the Browns, can always be seen playing one of the infield positions in practice, on days when he is not going to pitch. They all look alike to Harry and he is really a first class man at any of the positions. The very fact that he likes to do this kind of work, probably accounts for his being one of the very best fielding pitchers in the business.

Monte Cross, of Kansas City, was a man who always pitched to a catcher for about 15 minutes before he took his position, but this was probably more on account of the fact that he wanted to thoroughly loosen up his finger, than for any desire on his part to become a star heaver.

Only Addie Joss would think to call the notorious Ty Cobb "that wonderful young person." It does seem more in character for the ever-competitive Cobb to throw outs to his teammates in batting practice. Cobb would engage two black men in a knife fight at Cleveland's Euclid hotel before the end of this season. "Prince Hal" Chase is remembered today as probably the best fielding first baseman of his era, and its most corrupt player. Harry Howell was just coming off his best year, winning 18 games for the 1908 Browns. He won 131 games in 13 seasons. With the Orioles, in 1902, Howell pitched, played outfield and all the infield positions, and hit .268 in 377 at-bats. Monte Cross was a manager and the regular third baseman for his American Association Blues. He played shortstop for 15 seasons in the majors, beginning in 1892. Addie's own teammate, Hall of Famer Elmer Flick, made the difficult transition from catcher to the outfield in the minor leagues.

2

"The Sporting Editor"

Baseball Humor

Addie's writing interest in the lighter side of baseball may have been most immediately inspired by "a fanning bee" he enjoyed at League Park during the 1906 season, when he listened to umpire Tim Hurst tell stories. In his News-Bee *column for January 27, 1907, he called Hurst "one of the most humorous geniuses in baseball."*[1] *Joss loved the jossers of the turn-of-the-century clubhouses, dugouts, hotel lobbies, and public buses. And he must have joined in the fun, especially to pass time on the long days between his game starts. In his October 17, 1908, Toledo story, Addie goes so far as to fashion the national pastime into a metaphorical vaudeville show.*[2] *Our self-proclaimed "sporting editor" could have occasional fun at his own expense too, as we see in a thinly veiled spoof of his own free use of colloquialisms and slang (March 3, 1907, TNB), or in a non-baseball whatever-sticks-to-the-office-wall miscellany he wrote (February 12, 1909, TNB, not reprinted here) under the standing headline "Joss Sticks."*

Addie retold these anecdotes in the colloquial tongue of the turn-of-the-century American. Some gentle readers felt this was offensive, as a later generation of fans could be put off by broadcaster "Dizzy" Dean's language over the radio. Rather, I have come to think that the voice in these pieces—especially strong when he is telling funny stories—is warmly compelling.

(October 21, 1908, TNB and CP)

Without a doubt "Tim" Hurst is one of the funniest characters connected with the national pastime and some of the things Sir Timothy pulls off are great.

Anytime you can slip one over on the old boy you are going some, as

***A self-proclaimed "sporting editor," Addie Joss loved a good "jossing." The* News-Bee *ran this cartoon on February 14, 1908* (courtesy Toledo-Lucas County Public Library, obtained from http://images2.toledolibrary.org/).**

nine times out of ten Tim is there with a comeback for anything you may have to say to him.

Jim Delahanty of the Washington club put one over on Tim in a game at New York last summer. It happened in this manner:

"Del" was up at the plate and Hurst was behind the catcher giving the decisions on balls and strikes. [Jack] Kleinow, who was catching for the Highlanders, and Tim, had been having a little argument, caused by what Kleinow termed, Hurst's inability to see.

To make matters worse Hurst called a ball on Delahanty which Jack thought should have been a strike and Kleinow turned to Tim in disgust and said: "Well, old boy, you are certainly going blind. Why, I'll bet 'Del' thought it was a strike himself."

"Now, what do you think of that?" was Tim's reply. "Just to satisfy you I'll leave it to Delahanty and we will see who was right."

Leaning over Kleinow's shoulder, he said to the clever second baseman: "Jim, wasn't that a bad ball I just called on you?" "Del" nearly floored the umpire when he said: "No, it wasn't. The ball cut the heart of the plate." Of course Jim was only having some fun with Tim, but Hurst had to stand for a lot of kidding from Kleinow the rest of the day.

The next time Washington and Cleveland met in a series at League park the story was told to the members of the Naps, and they determined to ask Tim about it when they met him.

It happened that Boston was the next city the Cleveland team met Hurst and as Tim came over to the bench to give the batting order for the day [Bill] Bradley accosted him with this remark:

"Say Tim, you ought to have heard what Delahanty said about you." "Is that so," asked the umpire. "Well, I don't want to hear it." Brad insisted that he should hear it and told him a lot of things that Tim knew Del had never said. Finally he said to Hurst, "What will I say to Delahanty for you the next time I see him?"

"You can say to him for me," said Tim as he raised a glass of water to his lips, "that if he will only die I will contribute the finest Gates-Ajar money can buy."

The umpire of the day was obliged to deliver the lineups to each bench, before the pre-game meeting at home plate became a ritual. Ahead of his time, E. Lawrence Phillips became the first public address announcer when he read starting lineups through a megaphone, at Washington home games in 1902. On August 4, 1908, Jim Delahanty would be ejected from a game at League Park for verbally abusing umpire "Silk" O'Loughlin. The Cleveland native would be fined and barred from the park for a year. (Jim's brother Frank was the only Delahanty to play for the Naps—15 games in the outfield in 1907—but Tom had played for the Spiders and Ed for the Infants.) John Peter Kleinow twice caught 96 games for the Highlanders from 1904 to 1910. Popular spiritualist Elizabeth Stuart Phelps' 1868 novel, The Gates Ajar, *sold over*

100,000 copies by 1900. The book, especially popular among the many women bereaved by the Civil War, promised reunion with the dead in a domesticated Heaven. Hurst is playing Hamlet, when the prince invites Claudius to join Polonius in Hell.

(December 3, 1908, CP and December 4, 1908, TNB)

Umpires are more or less subject to injuries on the field. Probably their greatest danger lies in getting hit with foul tips.

In a game at Brooklyn a few years ago Tim Hurst met with an accident of this nature, which threatened for a time to put him out of the business for good.

One of "Roaring Bill" Kennedy's fast ones, after glancing from the bat, struck Tim on the side of the head just above the temple and the umps went out as clean as a whistle.

Tim makes his home at the Bartholdi hotel in New York and he was immediately taken there.

The arbitrator was unconscious for three days and when he did come to the first thing he noticed was a stranger in his room. Tim called him over and asked, "Who are you?"

"Why, I am your nurse, Mr. Hurst," came the reply.

Tim let it go at that for a few hours and then, being a little curious, asked him what his salary was.

"Twenty dollars a week," was the answer.

After watching him for a while Tim decided that he could dispense with his services.

It seems about all the nurse, or supposed nurse did, was to take Tim's temperature every hour, jot it down on a register and then cock his feet on the radiator and read Laura Jean Libbey stories until the time arrived for some more pulse feeling.

Tim soon "tied the can" on the nurse, and as he was leaving the room Hurst yelled: "Send that doctor up to me. I guess that will be about the best thing you have done since coming here."

The doctor soon arrived and upon entering the room was greeted with: "I want to know what my bill is."

It seems the physician was one of those fellows who was just out of college, being strong on the Van Dyke beard, long, loose ulster and cigarettes.

He had his office just below the hotel, and as Tim tells it, every time he had to go over to the Flatiron building for a package of smokes, he improved the opportunity by making a professional call on him.

"Well, let me see," murmured the doctor as he took out a pad and pencil. "Thirteen visits at $5 a visit. That makes $65. I guess that amount will just about straighten us up, Mr. Hurst."

"Sixty-five dollars!" yelled Tim.

"Why, what's the matter, Mr. Hurst? Do you think that a trifle high?" asked the physician.

"High," roared Tim; "High; why, no, that's not high; that's an Eifel Tower."

Joss adds the opening paragraph to the News-Bee *story, the version printed here. William Kennedy usually went by the nickname "Brickyard." The pride of Bellaire, Ohio, racked up his fourth 20-win season in 1900. Laura Jean Libby (1862–1925) was a writer of over 80 popular romance novels, a wedding at every book's end. She wrote at the rate of a chapter a day, 20 chapters to a novel. An ulster was a heavy, belted overcoat made from Irish frieze.*

Addie presents Hurst as a fashionable dresser in the next article.

(DECEMBER 10, 1908, CP AND DECEMBER 11, 1908, TNB)

Tim Hurst, the celebrated umpire, in private life is a fine dresser. Hurst always looks neat and natty while in citizens' clothes. On the diamond the arbitrator's Uniform has been the source of many a good laugh.

Tim is very careful of his Uniform and one day last season, when he went up to his room at the hotel where he was stopping and failed to find his togs, he was considerably put out.

As Hurst had been stopping at this particular hostelry a good many years, he was intimately acquainted with the manager, and to him Tim proceeded to tell his troubles.

"Fine joint you are running here," he opened up.

"What's the trouble, Mr. Hurst?" inquired the hotel manager.

"What's the trouble?" said Tim. "Oh, nothing. Only someone pinched my Uniform out of my room, that's all."

Naturally the manager was much disturbed at this and promised to do everything he could to have Tim's precious Uniform restored to him. After vainly trying to locate the missing paraphernalia the manager was finally forced to admit that he could not find a trace of the lost clothes and told Tim that the only thing he could do was to give him the price of a new one.

"I will give you the money to get a new one as soon as you hand me a bill for it," concluded the hotel boss.

Tim said that would be all right and just as he was leaving for another city on the following day he handed the manager a bill for 35 cents.

"What's this for, Mr. Hurst?" inquired the manager.

"For my Uniform," replied the umpire.

"Well, for goodness sake, of what does your uniform consist?" he asked.

Tim calmly replied, "My cap."

It might be well to mention that all the change Tim has from street clothes to umpiring regalia is a little blue college cap.

The one he wore last season had a red letter "B" on it and Tim had many a question asked as to what the letter was meant to represent.

Some of the players told Tim they thought it stood for "Ban," meaning Ban Johnson, president of the league, but Hurst, in his dry way, informed them it meant "best"—best umpire in the league.

Someone was uncharitable enough to suggest that it was an old Baltimore cap, which [John] McGraw had given Tim as a token of respect and esteem which Mac is supposed to have for all arbitrators.

Players and umpires came to ballparks already dressed in their uniforms. Clubhouses in the wooden ballparks were but crude affairs, better closets. Apparently, the American League didn't bother to enforce a dress policy for umpires' caps! Addie's sarcasm, concerning the great umpire-baiter they called "The Little Napoleon" (to his face) and "Bugsy" (behind his back), is a fine example of Chicago-style baseball reporting of the time and its taste for humor and entertaining rhetorical flourishes.

(JANUARY 27, 1907, TNB)

"Nig" Clarke, who last season tied George Stone for the batting honors of the American league, was a member of the Toledo club during the early part of 1901.

The dusky little catcher was given a tryout, but was found lacking in experience and as the club was well supplied with pad artists, it was decided to send him to Napoleon[, Ohio,] to get a little more seasoning.

When Manager [and owner Charles] Strobel called "Nig" to his office and informed him that he was to be "farmed," the catcher's face plainly revealed his disappointment, but the expression was nothing compared to that on Strobel's countenance when "Nig" replied:

"I don't want to go on a farm. Why, I never did any farm work in my life, Mr. Strobel."

Nig Clarke caught for Addie in Toledo and Cleveland; a sore arm, and manager Napoleon Lajoie's dislike, abbreviated his career with the Naps. For three games, in August 1905, the Cleveland club loaned Clarke to the Detroit Tigers, when injuries depleted their roster of catchers. Napoleon, Ohio, is the county seat of Henry County. According to Addie's column on February 24, 1908 (in Chapter 8), the town was under consideration for a Class D minor league franchise; however, there is no record of professional baseball being played there. Perhaps it's a little joke on Napoleon Lajoie's name, or one of John McGraw's nicknames? Also, it might be a sly reference to the site of the derailment, on August 29, 1903, of the club's sleeper car.

(JANUARY 27, 1907, TNB)

Joe Cantillon, the present manager of the Washington American league team, whose career will be watched with interest by the fans of Toledo, was umpiring the opening game at St. Louis some years ago.

The Cardinals had the Pirates as opponents and were stacked against that great southpaw, James [sic.] Tannehill, now doing box work for the Boston Americans. With the score three to two, in favor of Pittsburg, in the last of the sixth inning, two men out and three balls and two strikes on Pat Donovan, the [playing] manager of the Cardinals, Tannehill pitched what was called a strike by Cantillon, ending the game. As Joe was taking off his mask preparatory to leaving the grounds, Donovan turned and said:

"What did you call that a strike for? The ball was a foot outside."

"I know it," replied Joe, "but then it's too early in the season to be getting bases on balls."

Followers of the American Association Mud Hens would be eager for Hot Stove news about Joe Cantillon's brother Mike, who owned the league's Minneapolis Millers. Tannehill's name was Jesse. And Jesse is never to be confused for White Sox third baseman Lee Tannehill, his brother! "Pittsburg," without the "h," was the city's official spelling during Addie's time.

(FEBRUARY 3, 1907, TNB)

Junie McCree, the well-known Toledo actor, who spent the last week in the city, it being an open date, tells a good story about a game played by teams composed of theatrical people at the Polo grounds last season.

It seems the captain of one team, who was also the pitcher, was of an enthusiastic disposition and all his energy was bent upon the winning of the game. One of his players was deficient in knowledge of the rudiments of the game, but was assigned to the position of shortstop.

In the last inning with the score tied, the opposing team had a man on third with two out, when the batter hit a terrific grounder to the shortstop, who by sheer luck managed to get it by a great one-handed pickup.

He was apparently dazed by the wonderful act and stood holding the ball while the runner was tearing to first. The pitcher, when he saw him holding the ball, yelled: "Throw it to first."

Imagine his surprise when the player, walking up to him, calmly asked, "Where is first?"

Broadway's Junie McCree was born one Gonzalvo Macrillo, in Toledo, Ohio (1865). Also a songwriter and lyricist, he collaborated with Albert Von Tilzer, the man who would compose "Take Me Out to the Ball Game" a year after Addie's article. Vaudevillian ballplayers could cash in on their notoriety. "Broadway" Mike Donlin actually skipped several baseball seasons to team up with his wife on stage. Donlin and Mabel Hite commanded as much as $2,000 a week. And John McGraw earned as much as $2,500 a week, in 1912, for performing his monologue "Inside Baseball."

(FEBRUARY 17, 1907, TNB)

Umpire "Bill" Evans who did such good work as an arbitrator in the American league last season, his first year in the majors, is of an orderly, quiet and refined disposition and his "call" of a rowdy player is a contrast to the methods used by some of the older umpires, notably "Silk" O'Loughlin.

In a game at Detroit last season, "Wild Bill" Donovan, who was twirling for the Tigers, took exception to Evans' decisions and after every second or third ball pitched, would throw down the ball and look at Evans as though he thought the umpire was affected with a case of blind staggers.

This continued for some time, to the chagrin of Evans, who finally stopped the game, took off his mask and walked out of the box, delivering himself to Donovan thusly: "Mr. Donovan from your actions I am led to believe you object to my decisions on balls and strikes. Now Mr. Donovan, I want you to understand that I, in my official capacity, am sole judge of all plays upon the field and if you persist in these demonstrations, it will become my painful duty to remove you from the game."

Having delivered himself in this manner Evans walked to the plate, donned his mask and proceeded with the game.

As soon as the inning ended "Red" Donahue the Detroit joke smith who heard Evans' brief speech, walked to the plate and making a profound bow said: "Mr. Evans, as the Daniel Webster of the great national game, I salute you. I am afraid you have missed your calling. This is no place for you. They need a successor to the late 'Mat' Quay in the United States Senate and that's where you belong."

How many things can Billy Evans have in common with Addie Joss? Evans is another disappeared Hall of Famer from Ohio. And he was a newspaper reporter too—for the Youngstown Vindicator*—before he was discovered by Jimmy McAleer. Evans' syndicated column, Billy Says, appeared throughout the 1920s. Ultimately, he would serve as the Cleveland general manager in the 1930s. It was "Silk" O'Laughlin who had called John Anderson out, on a bang-bang play at first base, to preserve Addie's perfect game. Bill Donovan, in 1901, was wild (152 walks) yet overpowering (226 punchouts). Francis Donahue had seasons of more walks than strikeouts and was 164 wins-175 losses lifetime. However, "Red" was a 20-game winner three times, and he notched 19 victories with the 1904 Naps. Beaver County's own Mat Quay, a political boss so corrupt that the U.S. Senate once refused to seat him, did Pennsylvania citizens a service by dying in office in 1904.*

(FEBRUARY 17, 1907, TNB)

Jimmy West, the young pitcher whom President [Bill] Armour secured from Cleveland about a week ago, was a member of the Cleveland team on its last eastern trip in 1905.

Jim joined in Chicago and pitched part of a game there, but it was in going around the eastern circuit that he was put to the test. It was West's first visit in the east and he was naturally interested in all he saw.

"Red" Donahue, the greatest hot air merchant in baseball, was a Nap at the time and the way he hyped "Hi" was a shame [slang]. We were on route to the grounds in Washington, one day and passed a church, in front of which was a statue of Martin Luther. The statue stood some distance from the curb and the inscription upon the base could not be read from the bus.

"Who's that statue supposed to represent?" west asked innocently.

"Why, don't you know who that is, 'Hennery,' 'Red' inquired, his voice thick with surprise. Before the youngster could reply he continued, "Why that's the best sacrifice hitter in the American League."

Accustomed as we were to the stuff Donahue was constantly springing, something more than a smile greeted this bon mot and Jim Jackson has ever since declared that he heard a horse laugh from the bus team.

The butt of the joke, James Hiram West, was a September call-up in 1905. The compulsive prankster Donahue (not to be mistaken on your scorecard for Ohioan first baseman-catcher "Jiggs" Donahue, whose nickname came from clog dancing) was out of baseball after 1906, dead by 1913.

"Red" had a thing for practical jokes about statues, as next we see.

(MARCH 10, 1907, TNB)

I have been asked why I so often refer to "Red" Donahue in my tales of the diamond. The reason is an open secret to ball players to whom the rapid-fire wit of the Philadelphia boniface is as familiar as their baseball lexicon.

While Donahue's wit has never been objectionable, he never spared any one, and strange to say, his victims, after a brief spasm, always take his jokes and quips good naturedly.

After he strung "Hi" West, the Toledo pitcher, with the Martin Luther gag in Washington a year ago, when West made the eastern trip with the Naps, Donahue was constantly looking for a chance to slip another over on the unsuspecting youngster.

The opportunity came in New York, and "Red" was there with the bull [slang]. The team was en route to the Highlanders' grounds and had to pass a monument erected to the memory of Gov. William H. Seward.

As he saw the statue West asked, innocently, "Whose statue is that?"

"Why, my boy," responded the auburn-haired pitcher, with a face which for soberness would have made a Seventh Day Adventist look as cheerful as Happy Jack Gardner, "don't you know that statue? I'm surprised. I supposed every ball player knew of that memorial."

"Why, what is it?" "Hi" asked, in an injured tone.

"That statue, Hennery, was erected to the memory of the greatest hitter baseball ever knew. He played with the Giants, from 1888 to 1894, and led the National league with the stick. His grand average was .415.

"His greatest feat, however, and the one which caused all New York to chip in an erect a monument to him, was when he cleaned up the bases in the last game of the championship series with Chicago, with a home run, winning the game for the Giants in the ninth inning after two men were out. Why, that fellow had Lajoie, Wagner and even the great Casey faded before he began hitting."

I especially admire Addie's phrase "wit of the Philadelphia boniface." And there's something of the rural Wisconsin school teacher's training in his extended metaphor. Its contrast is between the widely popular minstrel showman, who billed himself "Happy Jack" Gardner, and the church, which dourly observed the Sabbath from sunset Friday to sunset Saturday. Even that would leave Sunday open for baseball, but Cleveland teams were forbidden by secular law to play home games on Sundays.[3] *As recently as June 11, 1897, Spiders pitcher Jack Powell was hauled into court and tried for playing Sunday baseball. The Naps' first legal Sunday games were played in 1911, just after Addie's death. But he had pitched on Sundays in Toledo, thanks to the vision of Mud Hens owner Charles Strobel and mayor "Golden Rule" Jones. And in Addie's first two seasons in the majors, the Naps played Sunday "home" games in Canton (3), Columbus (3), Dayton (1), and Ft. Wayne (2).*

(February 17, 1907, TNB)

"Tom" Loftus, while manager of the Washington team, used to keep the players on the bench in a constant roar, with his quaint, witty sayings.

Some of the remarks were gems. "Tom" had "Bill" Keister playing in the outfield at one time and though a good man, he could never be induced to meet a pitched ball, but instead would swing for the fence.

In fact it was a case of hit it out of the lot or strike out with him about every time he went to bat.

In a game at Washington one day [in 1902] our pitcher was fast as the wind and the last thing Loftus told Keister before he went to bat, was not to try and kill the ball.

The first one pitched Keister swung at with all his might, and on the second he swung hard enough to drive into the next county, had he connected.

Just as the pitcher was preparing to let go of the next one, Loftus called out from the bench, "That's right, Keister, just meet them."

Tom Loftus had managed the Cleveland Spiders, both the American Association and the old National League versions. Bill Keister is the seldom-remembered slugger who was the first to lead the American League in triples but was frequently traded in his seven-year career.

(March 3, 1907, TNB)

Toledo 2/18–07
Mr. Joss Sporting Editor
of News & Times bee.

i don't want you to feel harmed
at what i say in a few words
to you & I have been Reading
some of the Sporting you
have written and i find there
is not a word of sense to it
i will further more say that if
you would play Ball in the
Summer insted [sic.] of the winter you
would fare much better
as for a Sporting Editor you are
very Bum —

Yours Truly
a
FAN

you must excuse the writing for this time

For this column, Addie reproduces the holographic text of this letter, "FROM A 'FAN," along with the following note:

"The above communication was received at The Times-Bee office last month. At first I thought it was a 'kid' but the longer I think it over, the more do I believe the writer means what he says, or tries to say. Believing the public is entitled to all the laughs possible, the letter is reproduced. Whether the laugh comes from 'Fan's' peculiar adaptation of phonetic spelling license, his sage advice or his estimate of my ability does not concern me. [signed,] ADDIE JOSS."

Appreciating Addie's love of all things humorous, and suspecting the criticisms he received for writing colloquial English in his articles, I figured a spoof. Sure enough: The key is to be found in the joke letter's date — two days before Addie' first articles appeared in the newspaper!

(MARCH 3, 1909, TNB)

Herman Schaefer, known to Toledo fans as the man who played second and short for Milwaukee and St. Paul respectively in the A.A. before joining the Detroit team, is a born fielder and some of the stunts he pulls off the field are side splitting.

"Dutch," as he is commonly known, became acquainted with the German comedians, Kolb and Dill, while the fun makers were filling an engagement at the Forest City. He prevailed upon them to lend him false whiskers and a wig.

"Schaef" put on the outfit before going to the grounds and when the players arrived at the park everyone in the stands wondered who the new player was Armour had corralled. Schaefer had the crowd guessing until the umpire made him remove the disguise.

It started to rain about the second inning of a game played by Detroit and Cleveland last season and as we were ahead at the time, the "Tigers" wanted [Billy] Evans to call the game. He would not do so and the players got sore. To get even they started to burlesque the game. Schaefer was the chief offender and kept the crowd in a roar with his antics.

The climax was reached when he managed to borrow a cravanette and umbrella from someone in the stands and with the coat on his back and the umbrella over his head took his position at bat. It was so laughable that Evans didn't have the heart to make him discard the wet weather articles.

The game was played in League Park, on July 3, 1906. In another game, also against the Naps (September 4, 1908), Herman "Germany" Schaefer will steal first base, the second time in five weeks he pulls the stunt. (To think, Jimmy Piersall caught hell for circling the bases backwards to celebrate his one-hundreth home run.) Schaefer enriched the wintertime vaudeville circuit with his own zany act.

(MARCH 3, 1907, TNB)

Joe Cantillon sprung a rich one on ["Germany"] Schaefer while the German was playing short for the Chicago Nationals. Joe was umpiring and on a close play at second called a runner safe.

This aroused the "Dutchman's" ire and he told Joe what he thought of him as an umpire. Cantillon paid no attention to him until Schaefer during another outburst, threw his glove on the ground. Then Joe walked over to him and in an even voice said: "Say, let me tell you one thing. You had better pick up that glove and put it on, for if you don't there is a young fellow on the bench by the name of [Joe] Tinker itching for a chance to get out here and if you want a job on this club you had better see that he never gets here. That's all."

Joe Tinker permanently replaced Germany Schaefer for the balance of the 1902 season. Next year, Schaefer was banished to the minors, and Tinker helped the Cubs to four World Series in five years. Schaefer, of course, reinvented himself with the Tigers, and he and Tinker were the second basemen in both the 1907 and 1908 Series. He played his final game in a Cleveland Indians uniform.

(MARCH 3, 1907, TNB)

The eccentric "Rube" Waddell is a glutton for work and no matter how many games he has pitched, is always ready to go it again.

"Connie" Mack certainly has the bug on the big fellow and is the one man capable of getting the work out of him. When Connie had "Rube" at Milwaukee, his pitching was the base ball sensation of the year. If my memory serves me correctly, he won 17 out of 20 games that season. At that, he was only with the club from late in July until the season's close.

"Rube" was pitching the first game of a double header in Chicago that season and the game was a battle royal, going 17 innings, Milwaukee finally winning three to two.

As "Rube" came in to the bench after the last man had been retired Connie said, "Well Ed, you did pretty well in that game. I guess I'll let you pitch the next one."

"Rube" made no reply so Connie continued, "Do you think you can do it?" "Well, replied the great side wheeler, "give me a few minutes rest, and I will warm up to see how I feel." He did and won 1 to 0.

Addie develops this anecdote into his December 30, 1907, *Press* article.

The double-header was played in Chicago, on Sunday, August 19, 1900. Waddell also tripled and scored the winning run in the first game.

(March 3, 1907, TNB)

While Waddell was with Mack at Milwaukee, he suddenly developed a slow ball and as soon as he thought he had mastered the thing, began to use it in the championship games.

The first time he tried it the batters hit it to all corners of the lot, but everything seemed to go right at someone and in his way the big fellow got away for a few innings.

Connie implored him to cut it out and pack that slow thing in his grip, but "Rube" refused. He was getting away with it and was going to keep on as long as they didn't score.

Mack realizing the probable result became desperate and leaving the bench went over to a policeman on the bleachers and held a whispered conversation with him.

Returning, he awaited the results and not in vain. Waddell, as soon as he stepped onto the rubber commenced using the slow ball, and the first man up hit for a clean single.

Just as the big fellow was winding up to pitch the next one, a fog horn voice shouted: "Get out of there you big stiff, you're all in! You've lost your arm!"

This was too much for the eccentric one and with a withering look in the direction of the voice, he started shooting them across about the size of peas.

After this there was nothing to it and Milwaukee won hands down. Another case of the way the wise Mack handles the "Rube."

One measure of Connie Mack's genius as a manager over the years is his capacity to make a team that featured Rube Waddell's childlike irresponsibility and Eddie Collins' calculating resolve.

(MARCH 3, 1907 TNB)

When it comes to doing things on the field or in the dressing room that seem absurd to the hardened professional, the college player takes all the blue ribbons.

I was in Boston a year ago when the Columbia University team was to play Harvard, at Cambridge. Having pitched the day before I accompanied the Columbia boys to Soldier Field to watch them do battle with their opposites.

We arrived early and to pass the time went into the dressing room, where some of the players had already donned their uniforms.

"Bill" Lauder, formerly of the Phillies, was coaching the Columbia varsity and noticing one of the boys wearing two ankle supporters, asked, "What's the matter with your ankles Jack?" "Why nothing," replied the player in surprise. "Well then, what are you wearing those supporters for?" demanded Lauder. "Why because the captain gave them to me," the player responded as he laced up his shoes, preparatory to going out to the grounds.

Lauder looked at me as much to say, "I guess you can beat that."

Eddie Collins played for Columbia right about the time of Addie's visit. If he was in that locker room, you can bet he was not the dumb undergraduate. Addie kept track of baseball happenings in Cambridge. In an omnibus Toledo column on February 12, 1909, he noted: "The Harvard baseball squad has introduced a new one by having a pitching gun to shoot the little pill at the star hitters of the team." Naps from this decade who came from Harvard include Walter Clarkson, and the only major leaguer to die in World War I, Eddie Grant. In January 1910, Harvard invited Joss to coach pitchers.

The larger question is a puzzler. Was Addie a "college boy" in any serious sense? Biographical sketches routinely credit him for attending the University of Wisconsin-Madison, which is inaccurate. He did have the "college boy" reputation among his baseball peers but, like some nicknames of the period, it may simply reflect prejudice and distrust. (Fred Tenney's nickname was "The Soiled Collegian.") Baseball was divided on the issue. For decades, Rogers

Hornsby refused to manage a team with college men on its roster, but Connie Mack scouted the campuses for the smart player; John McGraw and Hughie Jennings attended classes, and coached a little baseball, at St. Bonaventure.

Eddie Plank played for Gettysburg College, but never enrolled in classes. Ed Walsh spent two days at Fordham. Christy Mathewson fashioned a media image in part from his association with Bucknell College. Certainly, Addie's story doesn't resemble George Sisler's, who was a student athlete for Branch Rickey at Michigan, or John Ward's at Penn State. (Today, in the post–Rod Dedeaux era, we take the college draft to be a media event. Stephen Strasburg is a product of postmodern America's longing to still love the national pastime.)

Up in Joss territory, Watertown, Wisconsin historian and collector David Stalker is on a mission to track down the facts about Addie's college experience. David's work could someday tell us whether Addie actually took classes, or simply enrolled so he could play baseball for two schools. If Addie was a student athlete, then the courses he took might tell us something about how he developed his writing style. The local newspapers, when Addie played for college teams, whine that Sacred Heart College recruited its ballplayers statewide, and paid them to play. The little college has been closed for 90 years, but David has pursued Addie's academic records all the way to the University of Notre Dame only to find no trace of Adrian Joss.

(MARCH 10, 1907, TNB)

Director Will Landman of the Toledo club told a story on Joe Cantillon the other day that is worth repeating. It appears that Owner "Bob" Hedges of the St. Louis Americans, and Joe, in a recent conference at Caleago[, Illinois], were discussing the probabilities of Jake Stahl refusing to play with Washington this season.

Said Hedges: "Joe, you will be on the market for a first baseman should Stahl determine not to play, won't you?" "Yes," replied Joe, "I guess I will." "Well," continued the owner, "I have a man for you." "Who is it?" asked Joe. "[Lou] Nordyke," replied Bob. "What will you give me for him?" "Well," Cantillon drawled, after a few moments' deliberation, "I will give you Cassiday." "Cassiday," repeated Hedges, in surprise, "Why, he died last spring." "Well," said Joe with a grin, "you didn't expect me to give you a live one for him, did you?"

Lou Nordyke played in a dozen games at first base with the 1906 Browns, his only time in the majors. "Cassiday" is probably Joe Cassidy, who died in the off-season, after starting at shortstop for Washington, in 1904 and 1905. Hedges' contract dispute with George Stovall will result in the former Nap's jump to the Federal League.

(MARCH 10, 1907, TNB)

Jack Doyle, who has taken the reins at Milwaukee, was a member of the Washington team in 1902, when Tom Loftus had charge. Jack was not hitting very good that season, and while at bat in a game at Cleveland drove a grounder straight at [Charlie] Hickman that looked like a sure out.

Just as "Hick" stooped to gather in the ball Jack turned towards the Washington bench and tossed back his bat. As he did so Hickman let the ball get by him, but kept on going to first just as if he had it.

Flick, who saw what had happened, tore in, picked up the ball and threw Doyle out at first, while the roar that went up from the Washington bench sounded like a southern lynching mob.

Doyle, crestfallen, took his position in the field at the conclusion of the inning, and instead of going to the bench remained at first to coach.

Some other player started out to coach, but stopped when Jack waived him back, saying, "Go back; I'm going to stay out here the rest of the game. I don't want to get near Loftus again this day."

A star from the Emerald Age of baseball, "Dirty Jack" Doyle was a talented hitter. He maintained a .299 batting average over 17 seasons, compiling 968 RBIs—just shy of .300/1,000, but my guess is he wasn't even counting. Like Charlie Hickman, Doyle was moved around on defense and frequently traded.

(MARCH 10, 1907, TNB)

When the All-Americans and Pittsburg were playing their post-season series in the fall of 1902, Joe Cantillon, who was to manage the two All-Star teams on their tour to the coast, was sitting on the bench with the Pittsburg players in the third game of the series.

[Sam] Leever and [Bill] Bernhard were the opposing twirlers and both had the batters tied in knots. Along about the tenth inning Joe came over to our bench and sat down with us. "Berny," as he as he came in at the close of the inning, said loud enough for Joe to hear: "Come on, let's get at this fellow; he hasn't a thing." "Well, Bill," said Joe, "I just came from their bench, and that's what they are saying about you."

Before the innovation of a "world's series," in 1903, teams played postseason series for state and regional bragging rights for fans. This was also the owners' way to sell a few more seats before their teams broke up for the winter. (The players also organized barn-storming tours on their own to earn paychecks after the season.) Cleveland played celebrated series against Pittsburgh and Cincinnati, and at least once attempted to organize games with McGraw's Giants.[4]

(March 10, 1907, TNB)

When Pat Tebeau had charge of the Cleveland team he was not much of a hitter. "Red" Donahue, at that time pitching for the Philadelphia Nationals, had Pat on his staff more than any other twirler in the league.

During a game at Philly one day, when the teams were hard at work, Pat took a wild swing at one of "Red's" offerings, and managed to drop a Texas leaguer just out of reach of the first baseman.

It was the scratchiest sort of a hit, and as Tebeau ran to first Donahue said: "Well, you Irish lobster, that was your first and it will be your last hit you are going to make off me."

Tebeau looked at "Red" and handed him this one: "Get out, you red headed stiff; if I hadn't slipped, I'd have hit it over the fence."

Patsy Tebeau wasn't a great hitter, but he did average over .300 for three straight seasons. He was good enough to regularly bat second in those great Spiders lineups, behind Jesse Burkett and ahead of "Cupid" Childs. Ed McKean was the clean-up man. According to some, Ollie Pickering, fresh up from the Texas minor leagues, provoked a disgusted fan to inadvertently coin the term "Texas-leaguer" when Ollie kept dumping base hits between the inrushing outfielders and the outrushing infielders. Pickering, an effective lead-off man for Cleveland in 1901, holds the distinction of being the first man to bat in American League history. It was largely a matter of luck: He led off the inning, and all the earlier opening day games on the schedule had been rained out. Addie was teammates with Pickering on the Bronchos.

(March 10, 1907, TNB)

"HESS FINDS HIS SPEED"

With a great dent in its ribs, a dead mule was found in the ball park this morning, and the chief of police and his forces started out to round up the slayer.

For some time the affair threatened to remain a mystery, until one of the Naps, in training here, announced calmly that the said mule ran into one of Otto Hess' inshoots Friday and was killed on the spot.

Under the direction of Bill Bernhard, the Cleveland battery men are working like firemen. They are routed out of bed at 7 every morning, and are hard at work by 9:30, on the diamond. At 11:30 they return to the hotel for dinner, and in the afternoon climb the mountains as a wind tester. The men are rounding to rapidly.

We can't know for certain if this unattributed short came from Addie's pen, but I include it especially to provide a correction to some team histories: Cleveland held its 1907 training camp right there, in Hot Springs, Arkansas (and not in Macon, Georgia, until 1908). The writer's simile didn't resonate in the Deadball Era, before relief pitchers were "firemen." Otto Hess was more known for his spitter than the inshoot, a pitch that breaks toward the batter. The Swiss-born lefty recorded 20 wins, and three saves, for Cleveland in 1906. Washington batters tested the rookie's fielding ability with an amazing 14 bunts against Hess, in a game at League Park, on August 5, 1902.

(December 16, 1907, CP)

Elmer Flick pulled off a stunt that amused the South-side fans in Chicago one day during the season of 1902.

The score board on [Charles] Comiskey's grounds is in right field. It is built against the fence, and in order that it may be in plain sight of everyone, is built up pretty high. The boy that hangs up the scores has a ladder that he uses to get up on the platform.

One member of the Sox hit a long fly in right, and Elmer, seeing that it was going to hit the score board stopped and waited to get it as it bounded back.

The ball must have struck something and rolled off the platform, away over on the other side from where it first hit.

"Genie" [Flick] was looking for the ball to carom back from about where it struck, and didn't see it when it landed on the ground.

In the meantime the hitter was tearing around the bases as fast as his legs would carry him. Elmer finally figured that the ball had stuck up on top of the platform.

So, taking a last look at the flying base runner, he did the only thing that he thought was left for him to do, and started up the ladder to find the ball.

[Harry] Bay quickly divined what was the trouble and sprinting over to the board from center field picked up the ball and tossed it into the infield, stopping the runner at third.

The "kidding" that "Genie" had to stand from the rooters the rest of the afternoon was something fierce.

The advisability of running out all balls hit to an infielder, no matter how easy the chance may seem, has often been demonstrated. The failure to do this caused Jack Doyle to be the laughing stock of a Cleveland audience, one time, when he was a member of the Washington club.

Jack hadn't made a hit that day and along about the eighth inning, when it looked as though he wouldn't have many more chances, he drove a fairly hard grounder at [Charlie] Hickman. Charlie was covering first for us, and as the ball came to him, he stooped as though to gather it in.

Instead of the ball finding a resting place in "Hick's" waiting hands, it took a contrary hop and rolled through his legs, continuing on its way to Elmer Flick.

Doyle, after hitting the ball and seeing that it was bounding directly at Hickman, turned towards the bench and disgustedly threw the bat among the rest of the sticks.

As he would have made the third out, Jack leisurely started towards first, as though going out to don his glove for the next inning.

In the meantime Flick, who at a glance appreciated the situation, came tearing in on the ball and picking it up tossed it to "Hick," and Doyle was out a mile.

After we had been retired, Doyle, who was never known to do any coaching, stayed on first that inning. Ed Delahanty left the bench and started out towards Doyle as though he intended to do the coaching stunt. Jack waived him back, but "Del" kept on coming.

When he got within a few feet of Doyle, he said: "What's the matter, Jack? Since when have you become a coacher?"

"None of your business," replied Doyle, "but you can gamble all you have that I am going to stay here the rest of this game."

One of the funniest things I ever saw on the ball field occurred over in Detroit a few years ago. Frank Kitson, who twirled for Kansas City last season, was the player to give the fans a laugh that day.

Kit and [Bill] Bernhard were the opposing twirlers and were having a merry battle. Frank is some hitter and it won't do for the pitcher to hold him cheaply.

Berny was going along in great shape and was using his slow ball with deadly effect.

With two strikes and two balls on Kitson he slipped at [?] a slow one and completely out guessed the Tiger flinger.

Frank took a vicious swing at the ball and missed it a foot. He swung so hard he lost his balance and fell down after turning clear around.

[Catcher Harry] Bemis dropped the ball and someone on the Detroit bench yelled, "Run." When Kitson fell he dropped directly on the third base line, and upon hearing the cry to run, he arose and started dusting [slang] up the first chalk line he saw, which happened to be the third base line.

He only ran a few feet when he saw his mistake and stopping started for the bench.

Everyone in the grounds from the bat boy to the spectators laughed, and even [Ed] Barrow, who at that time was managing the Tigers, couldn't repress a smile.

The White Sox occupied South Side Park (also known as the 39th Street Grounds) through June 1910, when Comiskey Park opened, with its spacious pasture of an outfield designed (according to an oft-told, perhaps apocryphal story) by Ed Walsh. Addie's attention to the hand-operated scoreboard brings to mind his invention of the mechanical Joss Indicator for League Park. Elmer Flick's continuing adventures in the outfield is a favorite topic for Addie. His is the only reference to Flick's nickname I've come across, so it's pretty clear that Chicago fans used the name to rib him about his Genie-in-a-bottle act. His name was being spoken throughout the league, however; this was the year that Cleveland declined to trade Flick for Ty Cobb. "Dirty Jack" Doyle was the first baseman on the championship Orioles teams that featured John McGraw at third base and Hughie Jennings at short. The game Addie remembers would have been played in the second half of the 1902 season, Doyle's only time with Washington. The great Ed Delahanty led the league in hitting that season. He would be dead within a year.

He and Doyle were great friends; they left McGraw's Giants literally on the same train to Washington. Doyle's glove would have been waiting for him in the grass behind first base, as was the custom in those days. Frank Kitson was the winning pitcher in John McGraw's first game as a manager, in 1899. He won 22 games, his career best, that season. He also won game two of the 1900 Chronicle-Telegraph *Cup. At the beginning of his career, Charlie Hickman was the starting pitcher, for the Boston Beaneaters, in game five of the last Temple Cup. Neyer and James list the slowball as Bill Bernhard's "key pitch," and mention no other pitch. Ed Barrow managed the Tigers in 1903 and part of 1904, before Addie's friend Bill Armour took the reins. Armour was the Naps' manager at the time of Kitson's wrong-way run.*

The run of News-Bee *Sunday editions has apparently not survived the years, but you can enjoy the article referenced in the following piece (unattributed in the Toledo version, but under the by line of "The Little Old Man" in the Cleveland printing) by going to the Cleveland* Press *article, of February 10, 1908.*

(February 8, 1908, TNB and CP)

"Addie Won the Bet"

Addie Joss' interesting article last Sunday on "baseball jests" was partly inspired by an incident at Cleveland last summer, when Ad "blew" a game in the ninth inning after holding New York to one hit up to that time.

After the game, as the sad and weary pitcher was taking a street car for his hotel, a stranger grasped his hand.

"Bet you don't know me," he said.

"Yes," said the crestfallen pitcher, trying to be sociable, "I know you all right."

The fan retained his tenacious grip on Addie's tired hand.

"Who am I?" he asked with an air of self-importance.

Joss struggled to get free. He was sore in mind and body and the pest who clutched his hand was clearly a nobody.

"Oh, I know you all right," said the Slat good naturedly.

"Bet you 10 to 5 you don't," persisted the nuisance.

"I'll give you better odds than that," remarked Joss in desperation, as he freed his hand and sprang into the car. "I'll bet you 100 to 1 I don't care who you are."

Addie was known to be normally a cheerful sort, great in the club house and hotel lobby. Along with fellow sports journalist Christie Mathewson,[5] however, he grew increasingly critical of the inappropriate behavior of some fans.

(February 15, 1908, TNB)

Many peculiar things arise in the course of one short year in baseball.

This is illustrated in the case of Pete O'Brien and Fritz Buelow.

About the time the American league clubs were preparing to leave for the south last spring, the Cleveland club, which was on the lookout for an experienced utility player, saw in O'Brien the man it was looking for. As Jimmy McAleer of St. Louis was in need of a catcher, a trade of O'Brien for Buelow was made.

Pete stayed with the Cleveland club until about the middle of the season, when he was traded to Washington for [George] Nill.

Fred Buelow remained with the Browns for the first two months of the season, and then, on account of an injured hand, which prevented him doing justice to himself, was transferred to Minneapolis.

Now Mike Cantillon comes out with the announcement that O'Brien, who was sent to Minneapolis, will be captain of that team this season.

As Buelow will also be with the Millers, the two men who figured in an American league trade a year ago will be members of the same team this year.

While Fred will do duty as a backstop, he will be under Pete's orders. Strange!

Fred Buelow was born in Germany, Pete O'Brien was born not in Ireland but in Binghamton, New York, and "Rabbit" Nill managed only 36 career steals.

Another unattributed article, the following fugitive piece (reprinted in the News-Bee*) comes from the Cleveland* News.[6] *Ed Bang was sports editor there for 53 years, starting in 1907, the year Addie was hired across the state* *as the* News-Bee *sports editor. As a player in Cleveland, Addie would have known, and read, Ed Bang.*

(MARCH 8, 1908, TNB)

"JOSS' DREAM"

Addie Joss had a dream the other night that he will never forget. He dreamed he was dead and had gone to a place where the chances for a snowball existing very long are mighty slim. Somehow they found out Addie's ability to pitch, and signed him to play with them.

Instead of having a baseball, the devils were playing with red-hot coals, and for bases he could see four sizzling registers, and Addie, in the pitcher's box, was standing in a pot of molten lead.

Can you beat that? When he woke up he was wringing wet with perspiration, and he was glad he was still in Macon, instead of farther south.

Notice that the reporter is innocent of Freudian dream interpretation before it became a popular indoor sport in America. After working their off-season jobs, players arrived at spring training to work themselves into shape, fast. The Naps held spring training camps in Macon, Georgia, for 1908 and 1909.[7]

(OCTOBER 17, 1908, TNB)

Had the pleasure of being on a team that represented Bloomville with a bunch of Toledo lads in a baseball tournament held at New Washington yesterday. It was a three-cornered affair, the other teams being Marion and Bucyrus.

Baseball, for players who make it a profession, becomes at times rather irksome, but in games like this, it has a rip-roaring comedy backed off the stage boards.

These tournaments are a good deal like a continuous vaudeville performance. You start playing about 10:30 a.m. and keep right on going until it gets too dark to see.

We were pitted against Bucyrus as a curtain-raiser to the big show that was to follow, but as a preliminary there was a two-round bout (not scheduled), between the field marshal and an enthusiastic spectator.

The rooter's and marshal's opinions regarding the outcome of the tournament did not agree, hence the bout. As both contestants were on their feet when time was called, Billy Smith, who was the self-appointed referee, decided it a draw.

We won the first game in rather hollow fashion, hitting ["Bill"] Bailey, the Bucyrus pitcher, who is now doing slab duty for Mansfield in the O[hio]. & P[ennsylvania]. league, and who formerly twirled for Columbus, pretty hard. Score 13 to 1.

Being winners of the first contest, we immediately started to play the other club, which was a team composed of amateurs from Marion, O. The youngsters must have been some pumpkins around their home town [colloquial] as the line of talk they started to hand us would make you think that the Cubs never had a thing on them.

Well, to make a long story short, we trimmed them 7 to 1, and by so doing, took down first money. Much joy in Bloomville. The personnel of our team:

Channell, C.; Bade Myers, 1st.; Needham, 2nd.; Ragan, ss.; Lovett, 3rd., B[ill]. Smith, cf.; M. Miller,l.f.; Barger, r.f.; Joss, p.

The Times and Times-Bee sporting editor twirled two games for Bloomville, and is now the great hero of the town.

This is an example of Addie's driest humor, related in something like the voice of northern Ohio, and aimed to inform his Toledo readers about the business of local players and regional amateur teams. It beats the Dead Sea prose Alfred H. Spink would soon make famous. I place the article in the section on humor mostly on the merits of Addie's quip about games "like a continuous vaudeville performance," even though he doesn't make the tournament sound especially amusing but too much like a part-time job.

The three Ohio towns do make a triangle on the map, with New Washington, Bucyrus, and Marion along one line and Bloomville at an axis. (Future U.S. president Warren G. Harding was the publisher of the Marion Daily Star *when Addie wrote.) Harry Lewis "Bill" Bailey was born in Shawnee, Ohio. At the age of 29, in 1911, he had a fling with the Highlanders, playing at third base and in the outfield. Bailey went 1–5, in 1906, with the Mansfield Giants and Newark Cotton Tops, and appeared in 72 more games in the outfield. (He didn't play for Columbus until 1914.) In 1908, the year of Addie's article, "Bill" Bailey was a member of the Canton Watchmakers, also in the Ohio-Pennsylvania League.*

(NOVEMBER 15, 1908, CP)

This hobnobbing with the magnates and players is great sport. Living in an atmosphere of baseball such as was on tap at the recent minor league meeting at Chicago always brings out something about this or that man that usually proves interesting.

One of the best known players and managers seen around the lobby of the hotel was Clark Griffith. The "old fox" has of late been generally considered the choice of the Cincinnati club as the man to head the destiny of that organization for the coming year.

When asked about his prospects, "Griff" intimated that as yet there had been nothing definitely doing between him and [owner "Garry"] Herrmann, but when [Washington's manager] Joe Cautillon jokingly remarked that he had a few pitchers he was willing to get rid of, "Griff" collared him, and when they were last seen both were in earnest conversation.

Another prominent figure about the hotel lobby was Jack McCarthy, who formerly played the outfield [o]n several clubs in both of the major organizations, but who more recently was with Kansas City in the American association, and who last season managed the Springfield, Ill., club of the I.I.I. league, which team won the championship of that organization.

Jack, at the time he was a member of the Cleveland club, was the possessor of a great slow ball, which was the envy of every pitcher on the team.

During the course of a little fanfest Jack casually remarked that he had a new slow one. Some one asked what he called it and also what sort of a slow one it was.

"I have named it the dry spitter," answered McCarthy.

"Well, where did you dig that up?" was the next question.

As Jack slowly lighted a large perfecto, he dryly remarked: "Why, in a local option town, of course."

August A. Herrmann did indeed hire Griffith to manage the 1909 Reds. Griffith also started (and lost) one game for the team, his last career decision. (Cincinnati needed pitching and over the winter acquired Opening Day starter Art Fromme and Ed Karger from St. Louis, in return for catcher "Admiral" Schlei.) Left fielder Jack McCarthy was Addie's teammate in the 1902 and 1903 seasons. Addie is revisiting a favorite topic—the junk ball—and even thinks to include his left fielder's warm-up tosses in the discussion.

Jack McCarthy played in Cleveland in its first three American League campaigns, so he was a Blue, a Broncho, and a Nap. (Could it have been McCarthy who taught Bill Bernhard the slow pitch?) The so-called Three-I League (Illinois-Indiana-Iowa) began play in 1886. "The local option" provided for cities and counties to vote by referendum on whether to go "dry" and ban liquor. Interesting to see the early use of the term "fan fest."

(November 16, 1908, TNB and November 17, CP)

Frank Isbell, of the Chicago White Sox, who is now part owner of the Wichita (Kan.) team of the Western association, tipped off, at the meeting held in Chicago last week, a reason why the rest of the members of [Charles] Comiskey's club always use a certain expression after hitting up a pop fly.

"Issy" did not report to the White Sox last spring, but stayed at home and whipped his Western league youngsters into shape. To do this he arranged games with some of the independent teams around Wichita.

In one of these games on foreign territory, Isbell and his men, on arriving at the grounds, noticed a colored fellow who, at the time the players entered the field, was the sole occupant of one of the bleachers.

As subsequent events developed, this member of the colored gentry was considered quite a sport about town, on account of the fact that he was always willing to wager a small piece of change on the results of the games the local team played.

This day was no exception, and "his nobs" had laid down a few small wagers on the outcome of that day's game. The independent team showed unexpected strength, and for about seven innings held Isbell's team safe. It really looked as though the independents had a corking good chance to win, and, of course, the colored man was about in the seventh heaven of delight at the prospect of picking up some easy money.

But the Wichita team managed to get a couple of men on bases, with no one out, in the eighth inning, and things looked blue. The next two men went out, leaving the runners anchored on the bases.

This caused considerable satisfaction to prevail among the supporters of the home team. The player who was next to bat was a left-hand hitter, and naturally, the opposing left fielder played close.

The Wichita slugger managed to get hold of a fast one, and drove it a mile over the left fielder's head, scoring the two runs and pulling up at third before the ball was relayed to the infield.

Naturally the home rooters were as quiet as church mice, so that when the colored man proceeded to deliver himself, which he did, he was heard all over the field.

"There you go. You good-for-nothing outfielder. I knowed you'd do something wrong. Why don't you play out when dem hard hitters come up. Youse all the time playing in for them little tippy ups," the colored rooter exclaimed.

The last remark fairly threw all the players into convulsions, and now any time one of the White Sox hits a pop fly you can always hear someone on the bench or on the coaching lines yell: "There you go hitting them little tippy ups."

Frank Isbell left his home in Wichita and returned to the White Sox as a utility player for the upcoming 1909 season, his last in the majors. Isbell was a unique player: He was a first baseman who was known for stealing bases, not slugging; he hit left and threw right; and he played every position on the field, including pitcher and catcher. He would also serve the Wichita Witches as their president from 1917 to 1926.

(NOVEMBER 18, 1908, TNB)

Heinie Peitz, who for years was one of the brainiest backstops in the major leagues, has always been noted for his dry humor and many a funny story is told of the manner in which Peitz used to "kid" the batters.

Heinie has been doing the same splendid work for the Louisville team for the past two seasons and that he has not forgotten how to hand out the "kidding" stuff is amply warranted by a story Charlie Carr, manager of the Indianapolis pennant winners, told at the recent baseball meeting at Chicago.

This particular bit of "kidding" was at the expense of the umpire who was working this day. It seems that Heinie was under the impression that his umps was not giving the Louisville pitcher any the best of it on balls and strikes, but up to the time Carr came to bat he had not complained.

Charlie took the first ball pitched and as it was one that might have been called either way, Heinie was inclined to be a little peeved when the arbitrator declared it a ball.

"It looked pretty good to me," said Peitz as soon as the umpire had made his decision.

"Well, it did not look very good to me," retorted the arbitrator, "Or I would have called it a strike. The ball was inside. Now, that settles it.

"O, very well," replied the German baron, as he tossed the ball to the pitcher.

Both Carr and the umpire thought that the incident was closed, but as Heinie stooped to give the pitcher the signal for the next ball they heard him softly murmur: "I wonder if it makes any difference how they call them in this league when the manager is at bat."

Henry Peitz wasn't a baron or even German (he was born in St. Louis), but he was a good-hitting catcher over 16 seasons, most of them with the Reds. He also led all catchers in fielding percentage in 1897. His Big League career was over, except for a cameo in 1913, after the 1906 campaign. Naps' teammates Charlie Carr and Bill Bradley operated a sporting goods store, at 724 Prospect Avenue, Cleveland, for years a meeting place for baseball players. In 1908, first baseman-manager Carr hit .301 when the Indianapolis Indians won the American Association pennant.

(December 15, 1908, TNB)

It's very seldom one has the opportunity of seeing a man steal third base after the side has been retired, but that is what happened at Armory park during the [Charles] Strobel regime, in the old Inter-state league days.

The play in question was pulled off in the fall of 1901. Toledo had been fighting it out with Dayton, then managed by Bill Armour, and Grand Rapids, for the lead all season, and, while there was then no chance to win the rag, had third place cinched.

Al Pardee was doing the heavy work this day, and, along about the fifth inning, he reached first base on a single to center. The big fellow was never noted for being a heavy hitter, and, like all twirlers, felt considerably elated after reaching the initial corner.

The day was bitterly cold, and Pardee had been complaining all day that he could not get properly warmed up. With two men out and two balls and two strikes on the hitter, Al decided that he would steal second, and accordingly, when the pitcher drew back to hand up the next one, he started for the keystone position.

Al got to a flying start, and was in a fair way to steal the base, but the batter swung at the ball, and, missing, was declared out on strikes. The catcher, in a spirit of fun, threw the ball to second, and whoever covered the bag let it get through to center field.

Pardee saw the ball go by, and immediately started for third. "Dusty" Miller, who was coaching, saw a chance to have some fun, and yelled for Al to come on.

When the big pitcher got within about ten feet of the base, "Dusty" yelled for him to slide, and, much to the amusement of everyone, Pardee hit the dirt in the most approved fashion. He got up, and, brushing the dirt off his clothes, looked around with a satisfied smile, as much as to say: "I guess I ain't some base runner."

"Dusty" by this time had started for right field on the run, and, when Al finally realized that the side was out, Miller was out of reach.

At the conclusion of the inning, Pardee was just a little bit sore, and when the players gathered about the bench he asked "Dusty" if the thought that was a smart thing to do.

"Well," replied the former big league star, "I heard you say that you could not get warmed up, so I thought a little slide might help you some."

Alfred Pardee spent his entire 11-year career performing in the minor leagues, before retiring in 1908. Both Pardee and Daken Miller played with Addie on the 1901 Mud Hens. "Dusty" Miller appeared in 51 games with the Cubs in 1902, the outfielder-first baseman's only time in the Big Leagues.

(December 17, 1908, TNB)

One of the principal figures around the hotel lobbies at the American and National league meetings held at New York was Ed Ashenback, who formerly managed the St. Paul club in the American association.

Ashenback has the reputation of being one of the wittiest men connected with the national pastime and any time he starts to tell a story, everyone within hearing distance usually takes notice.

Ashenback, in company with Charley Carr and Clark Griffith, was seated in the corridor of the Waldorf-Astoria, when the name of Howard Earl, now scout of the Pittsburg club, was mentioned.

The former A. A. manager proceeded to unravel this one as soon as he heard Earl's name:

"Howard and I were playing on the same club a few seasons ago. Anybody who knows Earl, is aware that he is a stickler for good language and no one has ever heard him use a 'cuss' word, no matter how exasperating the occasion might be.

"We were financially interested in the team and the only hitch we ever had was over my habit of swearing a 'blue streak' whenever things did not go to suit me.

"On the day I have reference to, the umpire gave us a couple of bad decisions and, of course, I made a holler, which finally resulted in my being tossed out of the game. Not having anything else to do I went into the ticket office to count up the day's receipts and was busy when the arbitrator came in to change his clothes after the contest.

"Earl followed him in and as Howard closed the door, I asked the umpire what he tossed me out of the game for.

"'None of your business,' was his reply.

"This made me sore and before I really knew what I was doing I had him by the throat and was cleaning up, when I heard Earl say: 'Edward, this is the first time in your long career that I have ever approved of your actions. And now, Mr. Umpire,' he continued, 'if you will excuse me I shall relieve my feelings somewhat by going out of doors to blaspheme.'

"This was too much for me," continued Ashenback, "and while I was in a paroxysm of laughter the umpire made his getaway."

Ed Ashenback played and managed in—at the very least—seven minor leagues. Managing the team from right field, in 1902 Ashenback took his Charlotte Hornets of the North Carolina League to a winning streak that lasted 25 games (then believed to be a record). Howard J. "Slim Jim" Earl patrolled the outfields, in 1890 and 1891, for Chicago and Milwaukee.

(DECEMBER 21, 1908, TNB)

At the National league meeting in New York "Garry" Herrmann, president of the Cincinnati club, told a story on Roger Bresnahan. Max and Julius Fleishmann, two of the stockholders in the Reds, figured largely in the story.

"One day last summer," said Mr. Herrmann, "the New York players were driving from the grounds at Cincinnati to their hotel in a bus and Bresnahan rode on the back step. The players had got only a couple of blocks from the grounds when Max and Julius Fleishmann came whizzing along in their automobile.

"'Hey, give me a ride,' yelled Bresnahan.

"'Sure,' replied Max, pulling up his machine.

"Bresnahan hopped off the step of the coach and into the auto. In about three minutes the machine was at the hotel where the Giants stop, for Max and Julius can beat every speed law ever invented. Roger was delighted with the trip.

"'Hey, boys,' he said to the Fleishmann brothers, 'that was a bully ride [colloquial]. I'll have my plunge and my citizen's clothes on by the time that old bus arrives with the rest of the gang.'

"'Give me your cards, will you, and I'll send you a couple of passes for tomorrow's game.' Max and Julius gave Bresnahan their cards and as they started to move away slowly with the machine Max called out:

"'You needn't mind the passes. We own quite a bunch of stock in the Cincinnati club.'

"And not until then," concluded Mr. Herrmann, "did Bresnahan realize that he had been the guest in the auto of two of the directors of the Reds, one of whom was the former mayor of Cincinnati."

This is a story I attribute to Addie (a little like a win for relief pitching), although it's sometimes hard to determine what he wrote and what he simply edited. I include it because it certainly sounds like a piece "The Josser" would write. How the fans of Addie's Toledo must have cherished the story of their rightly beloved Bresnahan being "taken for a ride." "The Duke of Tralee" was still a force in 1908: He'd been in charge behind the plate for 139 games for McGraw's Giants, and he led all National League batters in walks. This is the year that Henry Ford introduced his Model T. It is the first mention of the automobile in Addie's articles, although the News-Bee *is filled with ads by a Toledo car-maker. Another conspicuous historical mention in the article is the modifier "bully," popularized by "Teddy" Roosevelt in this decade.*

(DECEMBER 2, 1908, TNB)

Ball players are only human, after all, and when they are called upon to face a big game or an important series it is only natural that they might be a trifle nervous.

The one peculiar feature of this is, that, even though it is conceded that every player always feels this way before an important game, the individual never wants any of his team-mates or fellow players to know he is in this nervous state.

Just before the first game of the world's series between Detroit and Chicago, in 1907, the writer and Claude Rossman, the Tigers' first baseman, had lunch together at the Lexington hotel, where the Detroit team was stopping while in the Windy City.

As the waiter came up to take the order the following conversation took place.

"What are you going to eat, Ross?"

"Well" (this to the waiter), "you may bring me some roast beef, stewed corn, mashed potatoes — they tell me this fellow [Orval] Overall is awful fast when he is right — Oh! the rest of the order. Why, coffee and ice cream. I guess that will be all."

It's certainly a swell day for the game, Claude."

"Gee, I hope [Bill] Donovan is right today. He will make them go some to beat him. If Bill ever gets a run ahead there won't be — say, it is a great day, ain't it?"

"What's the matter. Don't you like what you ordered?" (Ross wasn't eating.)

"Say, if the 'Georgia Peach' [Ty Cobb] ever gets on, maybe [Cubs' catcher Johnny] Kling won't look so good. I guess it would make me sore to see Sam [Crawford] get hold of one.

"This beef must have been tougher than sole leather killed a month ago. It's tougher than sole leather."

"Where are you going to spend the winter, big fellow?"

"Well, I tell you, if we ever get off in the lead, we stand a mighty good chance of— Oh, I guess I will go right back on the farm as soon as it is over."

"Feel a little nervous, don't you, old boy?"

"Nervous; well, I should say not. I ain't even thinking of the game, but — say, I wish [Ed] Killian's arm was right. These fellows never did hit a left-hander very hard."

"What's the matter; you don't seem to be hungry. Did you eat a late breakfast?"

"Late breakfast! Why, I was down here this morning before the dining room opened. Say, what are you laughing at? I am going upstairs to put on my uniform."

And this was fully two hours before the game started.

The Naps came close in 1908, eventually losing the pennant to the Tigers, so Addie never went to the World Series as a player. He attended the 1907 World Series as a special correspondent, but he already knew Claude Rossman from his days playing first base for Cleveland. In retrospect, Addie's well-intentioned laugh at his friend reads like a portent of the mental illness that would in time ravage Rossman. His career was ruined when he developed what we might call the Steve Sax Syndrome, and he had trouble throwing the ball. The star of two World Series died, in a Poughkeepsie mental hospital, in 1928. Check out the Deadball athlete's idea of a sustaining pre-game meal. The day recalled was October 8, 1907, the opening game of the series against the Cubs. "Wild Bill" Donovan would pitch brilliantly in a 12-inning suspended game. Rossman will hit .400 (twice Cobb's batting average) for the Series. Ed Killian, who followed Rossman from the Naps to the Tigers, won 25 games during the regular season, but for some reason threw only four innings in the World Series.

(January 1, 1909, TNB)

Catcher Charley Street, the young man who did such fine work for the Washington club last season, never sees Dave Altizer, of the Naps, but what he starts kidding Dave about a trick that he (Street) pulled off on the ex-National when both players were drawing pay from clubs in the Tri-state league.

Street was catching for the Williamsport team and Altizer was doing stunts on the infield for Lancaster. The two cities were the bitterest of rivals and any time they met on the diamond the games were sure to be for blood.

The game this day was close and along about the seventh inning Altizer reached first on a single. He promptly started for second on the first ball pitched and by a slide, managed to beat Street's good throw.

The next man at bat flied out to one of the outfielders. Altizer was anxious to score and when the next batter hit a line drive into left field, Dave fairly tore for the plate.

Joe Delahanty, who was covering left field, started in on the ball. Altizer, looking over his shoulder, saw Joe tearing in on the drive and realized that there was a chance for the ball to be caught, but kept on going, as he saw it would take a phenomenal effort on Delahanty's part to make the play.

Joe saw that he could not make the catch and stopped short to get the ball on a short hop. As Altizer rounded third, Street, who saw Delahanty get the ball on a bound, threw down his mask and glove and fairly yelled, "Good boy, Joe. A great catch!"

Altizer took it for granted that Delahanty had made the catch, [just?] the impression Street wanted him to receive, and, stopping short [page is torn] started back for third.

The Lancaster players, who saw what was coming off, ran out on the line, telling Dave to keep on going to the plate. This completely confused Altizer, and he did not know what to do.

In the meantime Delahanty had thrown the ball to Harry Wolverton, who was playing third, and before Altizer got his bearings, Wolverton whipped the sphere to Street, who touched Dave out as he stood midway between home and third.

No matter what the league, we always seem to encounter one of the five Cleveland-born Delahanty brothers in action. David Tilden "Filipino" Altizer was the only player to have been deliberately beaned by Cy Young (1906). The journeyman utility specialist played in the major leagues for six seasons, including 29 games for the 1908 Naps. Charles Street was the possessor of two nicknames, "Gabby" and "Old Sarge." He was Washington's regular catcher for two years. In 1908, "Gabby" caught baseballs dropped from the top of the Washington Monument, a stunt that enjoyed surprising popularity with other teams, including the Indians. Harry Wolverton—they called him "Fighting Harry"—led National League third basemen in fielding percentage in 1901 and again in 1903. The Mount Vernon, Ohio, native later managed the Highlanders.

(January 7, 1909, TNB)

One peculiar thing about baseball is that no matter how bad a beating a club may be receiving at the hands of the opposing pitcher, there are always a few players on that team who never admit that the twirler "has anything."

It's really laughable at times to hear the expressions used by certain players as they come back to the bench after doing a club-swinging stunt, caused by being unable to locate the pitcher's curves.

If you should happen to be near the bench after one of the boys had taken three healthy wallops at the elusive sphere, your ears might be greeted by something like this: "Well, of all the lucky guys I ever saw, this fellow certainly has the call. I'll bet he can't get another by the plate on me the rest of the day."

Or what you will hear may run something like this: "This guy ain't got a thing. If I don't get two hits today will somebody please throw me in jail for the rest of my life."

These and many more remarks of the same nature are heard around the bench every day. It's not because the players don't want anyone to think that the opposing pitcher is simply lucky because they are not hitting him, but simply because they are so accustomed to saying these things that it becomes a second nature to them.

They, better than anyone else, know how much the opposing twirler has at his command, and are always first to recognize his merit, but at the same time they don't care to laud him by letting the rest of the team know he "has it on them."

During a series of games between the All-Americans and Pittsburg in the fall of 1902, those two great twirlers [Bill] Bernhard and [Sam] Leever, were opposed to each other in the first game of that series, played at Cleveland.

Joe Cantillon, who now handles the reins at Washington, sat on the bench with the Pirates. Neither team could score, so good was the work of the pitchers. As Bernhard came to the bench at the end of the ninth inning he said: "Come on, boys, let's get at this fellow. He hasn't a thing."

Cantillon, who had started towards our bench at the close of the inning, heard Bernhard make this remark, and before the rest of the players had become seated he turned to Bernhard and said, loud enough for all the players to hear: "That's funny. I just left the other team and that is just what they are saying about you, Bill."

Addie has told this story before, as a two-paragraph short in his March 10, 1907, column for the News-Bee. *He may be acting the good story-teller, drawing out a good yarn for his audience. Or perhaps he is stuck for copy at deadline, now that he's responsible for a daily column. "Deacon" Leever was also called "The Goshen Schoolmaster." He wrote the chapter on how to throw the curveball for James B. Foster's instruction manual* How to Pitch *(1908). Leever was a 20-game winner four times, twice led the league in winning percentage, and took home to Goshen an ERA crown. He was born in Goshen, Ohio; he was a grammar school teacher in Goshen, during Pirates' off-seasons; and he died in Goshen (population 730).*

(JANUARY 9, 1909, TNB)

One thing a pitcher, no matter how good he may be, is always in danger of his being taken out of the box. As a rule, when the twirler is derricked, it is because the members of the opposition are beginning to take undue familiarity with his offerings.

But this is not always the reason. Of late the managers have decided that it is often good policy to take out pitchers and substitute others, sometimes as often as two or three times a day. This is sometimes done in order to oppose certain twirlers against certain batters. The pitchers have begun to see the wisdom of the move and do not feel as badly about it as they did in former years.

It is very seldom that one has the opportunity of seeing a manager take out a twirler, when the opposing club has gone for seven innings without being able to score.

President Armour, of the Toledo club, pulled off this stunt once, when at the head of the Cleveland club. The Naps were playing in Detroit and, as the Tigers had a good many left-hand hitters on their team, Bill figured it would be a good move to pitch a left-hander against them.

The only southpaw in shape that early in the season was a recruit, picked up from the coast, named [John William "Jack"] Hickey. Jack went along fine for six innings and, although a trifle wild, had the Tigers eating out of his hand.

Cleveland had scored two runs early in the game, but after that found the Detroit twirler mighty hard to hit. Hickey developed a streak of wildness in the seventh inning and before anyone could bat an eye he had filled the bases, giving the first man a walk and hitting the next two.

This was too much for Armour and he promptly chased Hickey to the bench. Before the other pitcher could get warmed up Charley Carr, who was with the Detroit team at that time, slammed out a three-base hit, which cleaned the sacks and give the Tigers the game.

"Dusty" Rhoades [Bob Rhoads] was jerked one day, a few seasons ago, simply because the last man to face him that day drove out a long fly. It happened in this manner:

Washington was the Naps' opponents and with the score a tie it succeeded in getting men on second and third with but one man out.

[Charley] Jones was on second and when Hickman hit a long fly directly over Bill Hinchman's head, Charley, instead of going half way up the line, ran back to second and stayed there until "Hinch" made the catch.

The Cleveland outfielder was going directly away from the plate and it took him some time to stop and get turned around to throw the ball towards the infield.

The man on third easily scored. To everyone's surprise, when Jones reached third, he kept right on going to the plate and, though [Terry] Turner's relay way right to the spot, Charley was across long before the ball rested in [Harry] Bemis' mitt.

"Dusty" was dragged and as he left the field he remarked, "Well, it's pretty good when a long fly drives you from the box."

Addie is speaking to us from the distant origins of situational pitching and the creation of the relief pitcher. For a further treat, this is history with a punch line. John Hickey debuted on April 16, 1904. He would last six more innings in another start that season, his last game in the majors. Hickey's problem was wildness: He walked 11 batters in his 12 career innings.

(January 13, 1909, TNB)

It's pretty tough to be on the losing end of a ball game, especially when things have been going wrong for a few days, but when there is someone on the opposing team who is taking advantage of this fact, and is handing out a keen line of "kidding talk," it's harder than ever to go along, as though everything was peaches and cream.

It doesn't make a bit of difference who the player may be, and no matter how level-headed he is, there are very few who won't swell up just a little when placed in a predicament of this nature.

To have someone nagging at you when things are going wrong is just a little more than the ordinary mortal can stand. It is only human to get a little sore once in a while.

Along about the middle of the season of 1902, at the time Jimmy Collins and his Boston American league team were right on the heels of the Athletics for the lead in the younger organization, the Cleveland club went to Boston to play a series of four games.

The Naps always played great ball in the city of culture, and this trip was no exception. Cleveland won the first three games, and Collins and his team were wild to take the last one.

The Forest City aggregation, however, had a walkover in the last game, according something like 14 runs early in the contest.

The Naps were to leave for another city that evening, and the game had been called early to allow them to catch their train.

About the seventh inning, [John] Gochnaur, who played shortstop for Cleveland that year, smashed out a long drive that netted him three bases.

Collins, who had been pretty sore all day, was fairly ready to tear his hair by this time. "Dutch" saw a chance to have some fun at Jimmy's expense, so, leaning over towards the infield, he softly murmured: "Say, Jim, I'll take a big lead, so that when the next ball is pitched you can signal [Lou] Criger to throw down here and catch me napping. That will give you a chance to retire the side."

What Collins replied is unfit for publication.

This column marks a turn in Addie's recording of humor in the game to a consideration of the darker side, the cruel joke. Not to be too cruel about it, but it's good to witness Johnny Gochnaur's triple. He was perhaps the worst player ever to wear a Cleveland uniform, and its a wonder why he was the everyday shortstop for two seasons (1902 and 1903). Gochnaur "hit" .187, with a .240 slugging percentage, career. In 1903, he committed 95 errors at short. The great third baseman Jimmy Collins fielded, slugged, and managed his Boston Americans to the very first World Series title, in 1903, and they clinched the American League pennant in a September 17 win over Gochnaur's team. Addie's unspoken last laugh on his inept shortstop: apparently, Gochnaur not only couldn't hit or catch a baseball—but he was a rotten sport as well.

The next article isn't funny; Addie means it to be a serious commentary on those umpires who were "huge jokes." I've placed it here in order to retain the continuity Addie created for his humorous story in the next day's News-Bee *column.*

(JANUARY 16, 1909, TNB)

Some of the arbitrators who umpire exhibition games between minor and major league clubs are huge jokes. No one but those who have been forced to play in front of an official of this kind has any conception of how bad they are.

In games of this kind the umpire always seems to work on the supposition that the major leaguers are going to try to show up the "home boys," and he seems to take it upon himself to see that the local team gets all the best of it on every decision.

It surely is annoying to be out there trying to give the people who spend their money to see these games a good contest, when all the time the umpire is handing you decisions that are something fierce.

In these exhibition games, major league players work hard, as they want to get in shape for their season, and, as it is only natural to want to win, the adverse decisions go against the grain.

It doesn't take long for the big fellows to get wise when there is an umpire giving them the worst of it, and, instead of making it a good ball game, the contest is usually turned into a farce.

Major league clubs often are fortunate enough to run across good umpires on training trips. As a rule, the men who officiate in games for the Southern league teams are good, competent officials.

But when a major league team goes out to play an exhibition game on an off Sunday, or week day, during the regular season, it usually gets up against a man who makes many of those so-called "pinch decisions" favorable to the home team.

(JANUARY 17, 1909, TNB)

There is a champion "bug" umpire down at Erie, Pa., that certainly is entitled to all the candy. This fellow officiated at a game the Cleveland club played there a few seasons ago. The way he ran the contest was rich, but what the gang did to him was a caution.

The Naps went to Erie with the intention of playing as good a game for the fans of that city as they could possibly put up.

The teams had not played five minutes when the Naps saw what they were in for, and after a few raw decisions by the arbitrator, they decided that, if this "umps" was going to make a farce out of it, they might just as well have a little fun themselves.

This fellow was calling balls a foot over the batter's head a strike, whenever the Naps were at bat and calling drives five feet fair, foul, whenever one of the Cleveland players hit the ball.

A few of the boys started to get after his "nobs" and what they told him would have no space in a parlor conversation. Harry Bay, who had been very quiet, after having a bad third strike called on him, began to tell him what a great umpire he was (not).

As Bay was growling, Jake Thielman sauntered up to the plate and, pushing Harry out of the way, started a line of "con" that his "umps" swallowed hook, line and sinker.

"Don't pay any attention to these fellows," said Jake, "You know you are running this game. You are doing it in first class shape too, old boy." Thielman by this time was beginning to stand in mighty strong with the umpire.

Before Jake had started for the plate he had supplied himself with a generous quantity of "sneeze powder," which he placed on the back of his left hand.

"Yes," went on Jake as he put his left arm on the arbitrator's shoulder. "Don't let these guys try to show you up. You know these big leaguers are strong for that sort of thing if they can get away with it."

"Men of your caliber are wanted in the big brush," continued Thielman, blowing a generous amount of the "sneezing powder" in the umpire's face.

With this parting remark, Jake started over to the first base coaching line. It wasn't more than a minute before the umpire was sneezing to beat the band, while the players were doing side-splitting laughing stunts on the bench.

The arbitrator then got wise and was so sore that he ran over to the grandstand, sneezing all the time and looking for a policeman to take Thielman out of the grounds. Not finding one he came back to the plate and umpired the rest of the game from there.

The funny part of the whole thing was, that this fellow is supposed to have written Ban Johnson a letter in which he gave the American league's chief executive strict orders to fine Thielman $100, and Bay and ["Larry"] Lajoie too. Lajoie's fine was supposed to be because the Cleveland manager allowed his players to behave in such a disorderly manner.

Addie continues to refine his ideas on the nature of baseball jokes. In this instance, he contemplates a bad umpire (who is no joking matter) becoming the butt of a cruel prank. In an era before Organized Baseball put in place the systematic training and promotion of its umpires, it was often the case that men umpiring at low levels were simply recommended to the American League (which was Ban Johnson). Billy Evans' Hall of Fame career began, for example, when he was sitting in the bleachers at an outlaw league game in Youngstown, Ohio, and agreed to fill in for a sick umpire. John Thielman won 15 games for the Cardinals in 1905, his rookie season, two years after his brother, Henry, pitched his last game in the majors. "Jake" made 31 appearances for the Naps in 1907 and 1908.

Erie, Pennsylvania enjoys a long history of minor league baseball teams with nicknames like the Sailors and the Fishermen. In 1893, the future umpire Hank O'Day helped pitch the Erie Blackbirds to the championship of the Eastern League. Also of note: Cleveland Spiders pitcher Mike Morrison was born there (in 1887, he surrendered 590 hits to go with 205 walks); Mike Donlin, whose thirst was as big as Lake Erie, called the city home; Sam Jethroe, in 2001, died there.

(JANUARY 20, 1909, TNB)

There is no question that the lot of the umpire is anything but a bed of roses. The manner in which managers nowadays jockey with his "umps" in regard to giving him the information, as to who is going to pitch for their teams often makes the arbitrator look bad.

Here is the reason: For an illustration, Detroit is playing in Chicago. "Silk" O'Laughlin goes over to the Detroit bench and asks Jennings who is going to pitch for the Tigers.

Hughie comes back with something like this: "Who is going to work for them?"

"I don't know," replies "Silk."

"[George] Suggs and ['Boss'] Schmidt for us," says Jennings.

Now the Detroit manager probably has no intention of pitching Suggs, but announces the youngster as the boxmatch [slang] for the day's game just to get Fielder Jones to uncover his hand and show who is to work for the White Sox.

O'Laughlin goes over to the Chicago bench and asks for the battery and is told [Ed] Walsh and [Billy] Sullivan will do the work that day.

The umpire announces the batteries to the spectators and when Jennings sees Walsh walk out on the diamond, he tells Bill Donovan to peel off his jacket and get ready for a very strenuous afternoon's work.

Of course, when Donovan takes his place in the center of the diamond most every person in the grounds knows it is "Wild Bill" and "Silk" is made to look bad.

There is no question but that some rule should be passed, forcing the managers to announce the men whom they really intend to work. It's going to be a pretty hard thing to do, but no doubt the rule makers and magnates will find some means of getting the desired results.

Some action will be taken on this in the near future, very likely at the joint session of the major league magnates in Chicago in February.

"Nig" Clarke, the Naps catcher, pulled one on Jack Egan at Boston last season that caused a good laugh on the umpire and illustrates the subject of this story.

The Red Sox had been hitting pretty hard this day and late in the game Manager ["Larry"] Lajoie decided to give [Jack] Ryan a chance to work an inning or two. Ryan had just joined the Cleveland club and was practically unknown in Boston, also to Egan.

As Ryan walked out on the diamond the spectators asked the umpire who the new man was. Egan turned to Clarke and asked "Nig."

"Costello," replied the dusky catcher. "WHO?" queried Egan.

"Costello," replied "Nig." "Barney Costello is his name."

Egan turned to the press box and in a tone of voice that could be heard in nearly every part of the large field, announced, "Costello is his name."

The gang on the bench and the members of the Boston team nearly threw a fit at this announcement, and when "Nig" did tell the umpire what the new pitcher's name really was, he was afraid to make another announcement for fear he was being "kidded" again.

Here's another one I could have collected in the "Views from Toledo" chapter of this book—the broadside of a headline shouts "To Force Managers to Name Batteries"—but I couldn't resist placing it among specimens of what passed for diamond wit. The spectacle of George Suggs, who started only one game that season, facing Ed Walsh, who won 40 games in 1908, adds to the humor. Of course, no one by the name of Barney Costello ever threw for a Cleveland team. However, Russell Schneider reports a story, in The Cleveland Indians Encyclopedia, *concerning the real identity of a Cleveland pinch hitter who, in a game in 1912, told the home plate umpire keeping the lineup card that his name was "COSTELLO." This piece could also be read as an example of Addie's overruling sense of fair play. In 1905, he threw his glove at "Silk" O'Laughlin, from close range, in a game in New York.*

Who would have thought that the customary exchange of lineups by teams before the game would have cut down on game strategy? Try to imagine all the fans in the grandstands sitting so close to the field that they can hear the umpire shout out the day's lineups. And picture a team's starters learning that they would pitch moments before the games.

"Gulfport" Ryan broke into the majors in early July 1908, and pitched briefly the following season for the Boston Pilgrims. "Silk" O'Loughlin was so popular that he appeared in a 1906 soft drink ad.

(JANUARY 21, 1909, TNB)

That so many ladies have become interested in baseball and regularly attend the games, speaks well for the manner in which the great pastime is being conducted. Naturally, when a member of the gentler sex becomes enamored with the game, she wants to know all about the different plays and usually gets the desired knowledge by asking questions.

Often her ideas of the different plays are vague and some of the questions asked are certainly posers.

"Dusty" Rhoads, the Nap twirler, makes his home at Knox City, West Virginia, during the winter months. He is the only major league player that [pleads?] guilty to that city as his home and it is only natural that the [locals?] take an interest in him and his diamond doings.

A few days after Rhoads went home, at the close of the 1908 season, he met one of Knox City's fairest maids who was an ardent baseball enthusiast. The conversation turned to the national game and as the young lady was of an inquisitive turn of mind, she began to ply "Dusty" with all sorts of questions.

She seemed particularly interested in the box score of each day's game. This was an enigma to her and one of her first questions was:

"What does AB. R. H. PO. A. and E. stand for?"

The Nap twirler explained just what the initials meant. The girl volunteered the information that she was under the impression that when a player had two or three marked in the E. (error) column, he had played a very good game.

"Dusty" told her she was not far from wrong, as he never saw any player carried off the field on the shoulders of the crowd for making errors.

"Sometimes I have noticed," went on the fair enthusiast, "that the box score says some one stole a base. Now, Mr. Rhoads, will you kindly tell me what a stolen base is?"

"Dusty" explained what a stolen base was, and after showing just how this might be done, was nearly dumbfounded at what she explained her version of a theft of this kind.

"Oh my! I always thought a stolen base different than that. Down [there?] a player hits the ball and runs to first and he sees that the [pitcher?] is not looking, he will cut right across the diamond and go on to [the bench?].

"I always thought that when a player did this and reached the next [inning?] safely, it was what they call a stolen base."

This was too much for "Dusty," and, raising his hat, he excused himself and flew around the corner to enjoy the laugh of his career.

One of Ban Johnson's big ideas, when he founded the American League, was to clean up the nineteenth-century game and make it an attraction for women and kids. In the old eight-team National League, rough men played a rowdy game, one generally considered unfit for the lady fan and, too frequently, for the umpire in charge of the riot in progress. And yet, Addie met his future wife at the ballpark in Toledo. Bob Rhoads was born in Wooster, Ohio, the rural county seat that also produced Roger Peckinpaugh and Dean Chance. Addie's close buddy won 38 games for the Naps in 1905–1906. "Dusty" was the one who convinced Addie that he should wear a lucky red shirt under his uniform. For some reason (like a practical joke being played on us from the past), his name is consistently misspelled "Rhoades" in the News-Bee. *And his two T206 cards use the same spelling. However, the baseball encyclopedias agree on "Rhoads," the way he did sign his name. The artistic merits of Chadwick's box score, noted here in passing, are on display in Paul Metcalf's poem "Willie's Throw," for anyone who wishes to look.*

(FEBRUARY 3, 1909, TNB)

There's many a funny break in baseball luck and it's an easy matter for any club, especially after a close game has been lost, to figure out a way, where if this or that thing had not happened, victory would have perched on its banner.

The Philadelphia club won a game on its home grounds a few seasons ago, principally because the umpire handed the Athletics what, at the time, they thought was a bad decision.

The score at the beginning of the last half of the ninth inning was tie. With two men down Harry Davis, who was at bat, had the opposing flinger in the hole, the count standing three balls and one strike.

The next ball pitched was high and wide. The big first sacker threw down his bat and started to first, only to be called back when the umpire said: "Strike two."

Harry let out an awful "holler" and I guess the only reason he was not tossed out of the game was because the arbitrator realized he had missed one and that Davis had a roar coming.

The next ball pitched was just to the slugger's fancy and swinging hard, he lifted it over the right field fence for a homer, scoring the winning run of the game.

"Red" Donahue got out of a tight place in a game at Detroit a couple of years ago in a rather lucky manner. With the bases full and two out Donahue found himself facing ["Larry"] Lajoie.

The Detroit boxman tried to make Larry hit at a bad one and in so doing got himself in the hole. The Cleveland manager waited for a good one, but "Red" lost control for a moment and instead of getting the next ball over the plate, heaved it high and wide of the plate.

Lajoie ducked his head to let the ball pass, but left his bat on his shoulder.

The ball collided with the ash and instead of making a wild pitch, Donahue suddenly found that the ball had bounded from the bat into the infield. It was an easy matter for him to pick up the sphere and toss it to first, long before Lajoie could reach the bag.

As Larry walked out towards his position he turned toward the Detroit pitcher and said: "Pretty Lucky, Old Boy."

"Lucky," yelled "Red," "That's the longest drive you ever made off me."

A baseball platitude assures us that at-bats have a way of evening up. And every dedicated fan has noticed that a hitter will get robbed by a good fielding play, only to have a hit glance off a glove when things are going better. Well, by Addie's anecdotal count elsewhere in these pages, Lajoie is credited with a gift triple—and now he hits into a bad-luck out, on his way to 3,242 hits. Lajoie's 3,000th hit came before the League Park faithful, on September 27, 1914, in the first game of a doubleheader against New York—or did it? Some record books date the milestone hit as occurring on September 17, against Boston. And the bean counters have been adding to and subtracting from those seven bunts and a triple of his, in a doubleheader against the Browns, that did or didn't win the batting title a hundred years ago.

(February 5, 1909, TNB)

Talking about exhibition ball players, Jake Beckley, of the Kansas City team, is certainly "there" [slang] on the barn storming stunts. When the All-American and National league teams toured the west in the winter of 1902 Jake covered first for the National league team and the veteran was the life of the party.

Jake is certainly full of life and ginger at all times and he has the happy faculty of putting these two necessary attributes in his playing, which makes him a favorite with the fans, no matter where he may play.

Jake made a big hit with the fans of San Francisco, with his constant chatter on the field and his playing and ginger were in a good measure responsible for the success of the trip, while in the western metropolis.

It certainly was a hit to see the manner in which the "old boy" would fight with the umpires in these games, whenever he thought his club was not getting just what it was entitled to, in the way of close decisions.

If Jake happened to get in a close play at first base with one out he would quickly toss the ball back to the pitcher and yell, "Two out. Stay out."

If the umpire thought otherwise and called the man safe the roar that Jake would emit could be heard in Chicago.

The "old boy" got away with many a close decision, simply because he would beat the umpire to it. One of Jake's plays was always to cut a base whenever he thought the arbitrator was not looking and any time he got away with a play of this kind, the fans used to yell their approval.

Beckley pulled off a play at Oakland one Sunday morning that was a beauty.

Monte Cross was on second base with one out, when the batter hit a foul fly over near first base. The players' benches are built out near the base lines and Beckley was forced to run around this one in order to make the catch.

As the place where the players sit had a covering over it, the umpire could not see Jake as he made the catch, but the minute the ball rested in the first baseman's mitt, he yelled: "I've got it," and a moment later we saw Jake stick his head over the top of the covering on the bench, holding the ball aloft.

Cross took a good lead on second and Jake drew back as though to throw to the base. This made Monte start back for second. Then Jake disappeared. When he failed to come out from behind the bench Monte started for third, only to get about half way to the bag, when Jake's head again appeared from behind the bench. In a moment more he had tossed the ball to Charley Irwin at third, in plenty of time to get Cross, as he slid into the bag.

Beckley had seen Cross all the time through a crack in the back of the bench and certainly "killed" the life out of Monte on the rest of the trip.

Jacob Beckley hailed from Hannibal, Missouri, the town that produced that other life of the nineteenth-century party, Mark Twain. Beckley was colorful: He would shout "Chickazoola!" at the pitcher he was facing, and he had a penchant for pulling the hidden-ball trick. It took a long time for the Hall of Fame to call on Jake. He was finally elected in the same decade that would remember Rube Marquard and Addie Joss. Beckley was durable: He held the record for most games at first base until Eddie Murray. He could hit too: When he finally retired, his 2,930 career hits were second to first baseman "Cap" Anson's total. When Addie wrote this piece, the 41-year-old Beckley was managing and starting at first base on a Kansas City Blues team with Monte Cross.

Charles Irwin is another player who got his start in the nineteenth century. Irwin knocked in 100 runs for the Cubs in 1894, and led the league's third basemen in fielding percentage two years later. The closing sentence is a bit disturbing, in light of Win Mercer's suicide on that western trip. That Addie didn't notice the pun tells us something about his pleasant personality. Addie's good-humored account has its serious side. Beckley's bag of tricks harkens back to what baseball games must have been like when they were played under the one-umpire system.

(FEBRUARY 6, 1909, TNB)

It is the general impression that when a ball club goes south by train the players are off on a fine trip that will give them the opportunity of escaping the blustery days of the north for about six weeks.

In reality the southern trips are the hardest days of the campaign for the player. It's one constant grind from the moment the uniforms are put on, the first day out, until the team steps aboard the train for the place where it is to open the season.

After spending four or five months without doing any strenuous physical labor, the players naturally become soft. No wonder they are sore in mind and body soon after starting to get in shape.

Working hard for about three hours twice a day is anything but a snap and every man who has made one or more of these trips, is always glad when the season opens.

The players soon learn to save themselves as much as they can while on these jaunts and are especially careful not to give their arms too much work. It is an easy matter to ruin this delicate piece of mechanism by over-work.

It's funny to watch the infielders start to work after being so[creased]h just long enough to get good and sore. They vie with one another in seeing just how slow they can throw the ball around the bases. If the first baseman happens to be one of those fellows with an iron arm it is not long before he has to make all the throws that go to the plate.

Charley Hickman has a mighty good strong arm and seldom complains about it being sore. When a club he was with was training at New Orleans a few springs ago the infielders made it a point to see that they never threw the ball any further than they were absolutely forced to do.

If the ball was hit to short or third it was always tossed to second and then relayed to first. This made the throw short for the third baseman, shortstop and second sacker, but caused "Hick" to make three throws to their one.

Finally Charley got just a little more of this than he wanted and after a few of these plays, one morning, threw down his glove and started in towards the bench.

"What's the matter," yelled one of his tormentors, "are you quitting on us?"

"I should think I am," replied Happy. "There are too many double plays in this game for me."

Addie took advantage of this year's spring training, as a kind of family vacation, and brought his wife and two kids to Georgia. He begins his narrative in anxiety over training camp–after all, the author had enjoyed a desk job and home cooking this off-season — only to arrive at humor.

(FEBRUARY 9, 1909, TNB)

"Barn storming" is a great sport and every ball player who has had any experience in this line always manages to get more fun out of a few games of this kind than he does during the entire championship season.

When the All-American and National league teams were working their way out to the coast a few years ago the clubs were scheduled to play a game at Cedar Rapids, Ia.

This city is represented by a team in the Three I league. The season had closed a few weeks previously and as the ground keeper had not touched the diamond for some time, it was naturally a little rough.

To make matters worse the management had allowed a circus the use of the grounds just a couple of days before we got there and when the show company left the grounds it drove its heavy wagons directly over the diamond.

This left deep ruts in the soil and it was nigh impossible for the infielders to tell with any degree of certainty where a ground ball would bound.

Early in the game some one hit a ground ball to Claude Ritchey, the Boston National league second baseman, who was covering the keystone position for the National league club.

"Rich" can play a bad bound as good as anyone in the business, but this drive, just as it was about to reach Claude, hit one of these ruts and taking a false bound instead of finding a resting place in the little fellow's waiting hands hit him just above the eye.

Ritchey was blinded for a moment, but soon resumed his position. As Claude came to the bench at the end of the inning with a beautiful "shiner," someone jokingly remarked: "Well, 'Rich,' a fellow needs three eyes to get them on this ground."

"I should say he does," replied the clever second baseman, "no wonder they call this the Three I league."

Claude Cassius Ritchey was Honus Wagner's roommate and keystone partner. Ritchey first played beside Wagner on the Steubenville-Akron club in the Iron and Oil League. The 1909 season would be Ritchey's last in the majors, when he hung on as a reserve with the Boston Doves. But when he was a fixture at second for Pittsburgh, he was always among the league leaders in putouts and assists. Some rate him as the all-time Pirate at his position, even above Bill Mazeroski. It's safe to venture that he must have been the best vegetarian second baseman of the Deadball Era. "Three-I" was easier to print in newspapers than "Illinois-Indiana-Iowa League."

(FEBRUARY 25, 1909, TNB)

Frank Isbell, and his wonderful hitting in the world's series between the White Sox and the Cubs a few seasons ago, will long live in the memory of every fan. "Issy," probably as much as any member of the Sox, was responsible for their great victory over [Frank] Chance's crew.

In the last game played on the Cubs' grounds, Isbell fairly murdered the ball and when the smoke of battle had cleared, the official scorer was forced to give the old boy credit for four as nice two-base hits as ever were seen on any field.

The peculiar part of Isbell's hitting was the fact that a certain member of the White Sox, in a joking manner, called the turn on "Issy's" wonderful performance before the start of the game.

The players dressed at the Victoria hotel before going out to the grounds. Isbell got down early and not finding any of his teammates in the lobby went up stairs and laid down in his room.

It was not long before he fell asleep and when the other players came up-stairs and found him sleeping, they commenced to laugh, and someone said: "Well, there is a fellow that doesn't seem to worry any about today's game."

Finally Roy Patterson, who pitched for Minneapolis last season, walked in the room and taking a look at the sleeping player, remarked: "That old boy looks as though he was good for about four hits this afternoon."

"Issy" was soon awakened and it was not until after the boys had reached the hotel and were discussing their victory that he was made acquainted with Patterson's remark, which he had so wonderfully fulfilled.

On October 13, 1906, in Game Five of the World Series, second baseman Isbell hit four doubles. They were his only extra-base hits when "The Hitless Wonders" beat the favored Cubs, four games to two. Roy "The Boy Wonder" Patterson was a 20-game winner in his rookie season with the 1901 White Sox. He did not make an appearance in the six-game World Series five years later.

Two Octobers after that World Series, Addie won his perfect game when Joe Birmingham eventually scored following Frank Isbell's error on a pick-off play. The next section of the book opens with Addie's account, written on the day following that game. He identifies himself as the bunter who failed to score Birmingham from third.

3

"The Boys Played Grandly"

Greatest Games and Plays

Opening this collection of stories, about unforgettable games and plays, is Addie's disarmingly modest account of one of baseball's greatest pitching duels. At League Park, on the afternoon of Friday, October 2, 1908, Addie threw a perfect game to beat 40-game-winner Ed Walsh. Walsh struck out 15 Naps batters. Both teams played the contest under the pressure of a famous late-season pennant drive.

Addie speaks first.

[October 3, 1908, TNB]

About the seventh inning I began to realize that not one of the [White] Sox had reached first base. No one on the bench dared breathe a word to that effect. Had he done so, he would have been chased to the clubhouse. Even I rapped on wood when I thought of it.

I did not try for such a record. All I was doing was trying to beat Chicago, for the game meant much to us, and [Ed] Walsh was pitching the game of his life. I never saw him have so much. In the third inning with [Joe] Birmingham on third I tried to bunt and actually could not get my bat out in time.

In giving credit for my feat that now appears wonderful, don't forget that the boys played grandly behind me, while Larry [Lajoie] killed three drives that would have been hits for ordinary second basemen.

"By Ed Walsh"

"I am sorry we lost, of course, but seeing that we did have to lose, I am glad that Addie took down a record that goes to so few. It is something to be proud of—keeping a team like Chicago from reaching first base—and I guess way down in my heart I was sort of glad when "Silk" [O'Loughlin] called [John] Anderson out in the ninth. It would have made no difference anyway.

"Yes, I pitched a fairy good game myself, but Joss pitched better. May be I did strike out fifteen men, but they got four hits off me and we got none off Joss. I passed a man and Joss passed none. That shows how much better ball he pitched."

John Anderson is a forgotten man. Who would remember that it was Anderson who made the last out in the perfect game? On the other hand, perhaps it's best that the baseball expression "to pull a John Anderson," meaning an attempted steal of an already occupied base, has passed from usage. Addie's perfecto was only the second in Big League history. Along with the game accounts by Addie and Walsh,[1] *the* News-Bee *ran a feature article, with a Cleveland dateline, which credits the very first perfect game to J.L. Richmond, "now a professor in the Toledo High school, who did it twice." Southpaw Lee Richmond, a graduate of Brown University, pitched .500 ball (and even took his turn umpiring) for Frank Bancroft's Worcester Ruby Legs, a quarter century before Addie's masterpiece.*[2] *The Cleveland story also notes that Addie ran to the dressing room ahead of the crowd, which would have carried him on its shoulders: "'I am taking no chances,' he said afterward. 'Suppose they had let me drop. The season's not over yet.'"*

(FEBRUARY 10, 1907, TNB)

Terry Turner's marvelous feats are the joy of American league fans, but probably his greatest fielding play occurred that day in New York when the Naps and the Highlanders were playing a double-header and fighting for second place [in 1906].

Cleveland won the first game chiefly through Terry's phenomenal stops and throws, some of which seemed impossible. But the crowning feat came in the eighth inning of the second game. It was in this contest that [Bill] Bradley had his arm broken and ["Jap"] Barbeau was sent to third.

Terry was playing well towards third, trying to help "Jap" all he could. With the score 3 to 2 in Cleveland's favor at the beginning of the eighth inning, the Highlanders managed to get [Danny] Hoffman on second with two out.

[Walter] Clarkson, who had replaced [Bill] Hogg, came to bat and hit the first ball [Bob] Rhoads pitched, through the box. When it got by "Dusty" we gave up for lost and expected Hoffman to score the tying run. But we reckoned without Turner.

A streak of white shot across the space between short and second, as with a wonderful burst of speed he managed to spear the ball with his gloved hand. Then occurred the marvelous part of the play. While running at full speed and directly towards right field, Turner straightened up and threw the ball to [Claude] Rossman. It traveled like a rifle ball and beat the fast-going Clarkson by a step.

How Turner ever accomplished that play has always been a mystery. Although it was the play that beat New York, the spectators rose as a man and applauded Terry until he was hidden from view on the bench. It was as fine a play and as great an ovation accorded a visiting player as has ever been my fortune to witness.

Terry Turner was celebrated in Cleveland for what we might liken to his Omar Vizquel-like fielding style, dubbed "the Turner stab" by the press. William Barbeau was for a time the shortest third baseman in the league, hence the nickname "Jap," I trust. Danny Hoffman's 46 stolen bases led the league in 1905 when he was with the pennant-winning Athletics. Walter Clarkson pitched for both New York and Cleveland in the 1907 season. "Buffalo Bill" Hogg won 14 games for the Highlanders in 1906, his best year. It was his pitch that broke Bradley's wrist in 1906 (and gave Barbeau playing time).

(February 3, 1907, TNB)

Umpire "Silk" O'Loughlin, who is generally conceded one of the best arbitrators in Ban Johnson's organization, was called on to give a decision in Cleveland a few years ago, which for peculiarity, probably has no equal.

The opposing team was Philadelphia. With the mighty ["Rube"] Waddell pitching, they had us 3 to 2 at the beginning of the eighth. With one man out we had men on second and third, when [Jack] McCarthy connected and drove the ball down the first base line.

[Harry] Davis, the visitors' first sacker, made a nice play on the ball, getting it in such a position that he only had to put his foot on the bag, forcing McCarthy. At the same time he threw to the plate to catch ["Larry"] Lajoie, who was scoring from third.

McCarthy, streaking for first, ran straight into Davis' throw, the ball striking him full on the forehead and bounding over to the grand stand.

Lajoie and [Charlie] Hickman scored, but imagine our surprise when "Silk" sent Hickman back to third, basing his decision on the fact that when McCarthy was hit by the ball he was out and consequently the ball was dead, or not in play, as soon as it struck him.

The bleachers took exception to the ruling in an emphatic demonstration, and it was fortunate for "Silk" that we finally won the game. McCarthy was knocked unconscious by the blow, but in about five minutes revived sufficiently to play the game out and save it for us.

With two men on the bags in the ninth "Schrek" [Ossee Schrecongost] hit a terrific liner into left center, and "Mac" made as pretty a running catch as one could ask to see, saving us two runs and the game.

It later developed he was in a semi-trance during that inning, frequently declaring he had no recollection of the play following the blow that laid him out.

Francis O'Loughlin's trademark "Strike Tuh!" rang out across ball fields over a 17-year career, during which he called a record seven no-hit games. "Silk" and Tim Hurst were known to be the snappiest dressers among umpires. O'Loughlin was a victim of the flu pandemic.

(FEBRUARY 3, 1907, TNB)

The greatest feat of long distance hitting it has ever been my good fortune to witness occurred at St. Louis during the season of 1902. The gang had their bats working and were getting runs rather easily off Jack Harper, who was pitching for the Browns. Along about the fifth inning came the climax.

[Bill] Bradley, the first man up, hit to the left field bleachers. ["Larry"] Lajoie followed with one in the 25-cent center field seats, and then [Charlie] Hickman, who was next up, met the first ball pitched and drove it to the club house in center, crossing the plate before [Emmet] Heidrick had relayed the ball home.

[Jack] McCarthy, the next batter, before going to the plate, turned to

Manager [Bill] Armour and said, "Bill, send someone else in to bat; I haven't the nerve to go up after that."

Addie's fondness for the lighter side threatens to make his eyewitness account of a rare event into a joshing. The back-to-back-to-back home runs by Cleveland batters, on three pitches from Harper, occurred during the first game of a June 30, 1906, doubleheader. It was the first time the feat had been accomplished since 1894. A total of only 258 homers were hit in the American League that season, 33 by Cleveland. But plenty of batters that year hit Jack Harper, twice a 20-game winner in a short career; his 4.13 ERA was well above the 3.57 league average. "Snags" Heidrick hit precisely .300 over an eight-year career with both St. Louis teams. Jack McCarthy probably thought he had seen it all. The outfielder had begun his career in 1893, the year the pitchers were moved back to 60'6" and flat-sided bats ruled illegal.

(FEBRUARY 17, 1907, TNB)

Every player has his own idea of the greatest finish he ever witnessed on a ball field and each has some argument which makes his story sound like the real money. There have been many thrilling windups since organized ball became a reality and I have seen a few which are worth recording.

One great finish occurred at Detroit last season when, in the ninth inning, the Tigers had Cleveland beaten 8 to 7, but [John] Eubanks [sic.] missed an opportunity to retire the side on a double play. Then the fun started and before the hitting ceased we gathered seven runs and the game.

The next windup to startle the baseball world occurred in Washington, and again it was the hard-hitting Clevelanders who turned the trick. ["Cy"] Falkenberg had us whipped to a standstill, 4 to 1, at the beginning of the ninth, when [Bill] Bradley led off with a two-base hit, followed by [Harry] Bemis, who tripled. [Claude] Rossman, who was sent to bat for the pitcher, nearly tore off Falkenberg's head with a line drive that went for a single. Flick then laid down a nice bunt and beat the throw to first, while [Harry] Bay was retired by a fly ball to center. [Terry] Turner took up the hitting again and sent Rossman home with the tying run with a slam to left, and when ["Larry"] Lajoie hit safely to center we had the old thing in our bags.

Again, in Cleveland, we repeated the trick upon Washington with Falkenberg in the box. We were apparently overwhelmed, 8 to 1, when we went to bat for our half of the eighth inning. "Falk" had been good as money from home all day and it was dollars to 20 cents Mex. that he would get away with the game.

But, in the eighth it commenced to rain base hits, bases on balls and runs, and finally, with the score 8 to 4, ["Jake"] Stahl lifted Falkenberg, substituting [Ed] Hughes.

The bases were full when Hughes went in and Jim Jackson hit the first ball pitched down the right field foul line. When it was returned the "General" was on third and three runs had been scored. Turner followed Jackson with a hit to right, tying the score, and promptly stole second, from which base he scored when Lajoie secured his second two-base hit of the inning, placing us one run to the good, and so the score remained.

About the fastest thing in the hurry-up finish line I ever witnessed was last fall in Detroit. Earl Moore, who had been laid up all season with a broken ankle, was pitching for Cleveland and was going along in fine style. To all appearance we had the game won and had commenced to credit ourselves with it.

At last, this condition was reached: The score was 4 to 0, two Tigers were out and two strikes and no balls were on the man at bat. A few base hits and two Detroiters crossed the plate and runners roosted upon second and third bases.

Sam Crawford was up and we all pulled for Moore to walk him, for "Wahoo Sam" is dangerous all the time. Earl had the same sort of a hunch and passed up the big fellow to take a chance with [Fred] Payne, who promptly broke up the game with a three-base hit down the right field foul line.

I have seen many a player sprint around the bases, but never did I see anyone who appeared to travel as fast as Crawford did from first base to the plate.

Such games are heart-breakers and do more to down the fighting spirit of a team than half a dozen ordinary defeats.

There is no accounting for the way the members of a team will start to hit a pitcher who has held them in the hollow of his hand for eight innings.

It is absolutely unexplainable and the finishes come so fast that one hasn't time to take a breath before victory is turned into defeat.

It is said that Frederick Falkenburg had even longer arms than Addie Joss. His career took off when he developed an emery-ball pitch, in 1913 (at age 32), and he was a dominant pitcher in the Federal League. "Cy" was a member of Cleveland pitching staffs with Cy Young. "Honest John" Eubank was Addie's match in size and height, but he managed only an 8–13 career record, all with Detroit. Garland Stahl's Senators won only 55 times in 1906. He was a field genius in 1912, when his champion Red Sox (featuring Tris Speaker) won 105 games, but lasted just half of the following season (after a serious foot operation), his last both as a player and a manager. Stahl's 1906 season with Washington was also his worst at the plate, but the slugging first baseman came back big in 1910 and led the league with 10 home runs. Ed Hughes had no record in two games in 1906, his last time in the majors. Addie is reporting the revenge of Fred Payne. Months before (April 28), the Tigers catcher had dropped a sure double-play ball, and it was the Naps who scored—eight runs—in the ninth inning to win the game.

(MARCH 3, 1907, TNB)

One of the most remarkable catches I ever witnessed on the diamond, was made by Harry Bay at Philadelphia a few seasons ago. It was in the last game of a series of four and both teams were going the limit to win.

The score was close and along toward the latter part of the game, the Athletics had ["Topsy"] Hartzel on second with [Harry] Davis at bat.

Davis is always dangerous and able to hit one a mile any time. This time he met one of ["Red"] Donahue's slow curves and drove it towards the center field corner and from the bench appeared to be ticketed for over the fence.

Bay took out for it, running as only he can run. He was watching the ball and therefore didn't notice how close he was to the fence, until too late.

Just as he crashed into the boards he leaped into the air and the ball striking his outstretched hand, stuck there.

To us it looked as though the ball had pinned him against the fence, but quickly recovering, he threw to Larry [Lajoie], who touched the bag completing a double play, as "Topsy" left the bag as soon as the ball was hit, thinking it a sure three-base hit.

"Jasper" Davis was not a big man but he was one of the premier sluggers over the first decade of the American League. The Athletics first baseman won four consecutive home run crowns, led the league in RBIs twice, and three times in

doubles. "Deerfoot" Bay was the regular center fielder during Donahue's three seasons with Cleveland, starting in 1903. The Nap was once clocked, running from home to first base, at 3.5 seconds. A high school track star, he set the Illinois record for the 220 low hurdles. Back home, in the Peoria area, Harry was a popular trumpet player for many years.

(MARCH 3, 1907, TNB)

The fact that the Boston Americans have signed Jimmy Barrett for the coming season recalls a catch the fleet-footed Jim made in Cleveland during the season of 1903.

It always seemed that Barrett played his best ball against the Cleveland team especially when Detroit was playing in the Forest city. Jim played a deep field and when Hickman came to bat this day, went out farther than usual.

"Cheerful Charles" [Hickman] caught one of [Frank] Kitson's fast ones on the nose and the ball started on a dead line for the fence, about midway between left and center.

Barrett was off at the crack of the bat but did not seem to have a chance in the world to get it. In the meantime "Cheerful" was tearing for first. Jim rapidly overhauled the pill and with a last, desperate effort, reached out his bare hand and grabbed it.

To make it good, he tossed the ball high in the air and caught it again as he kept on running for the fence.

Hickman reached second and when the ball was relayed in and one of the players told him he was out, he refused to believe the statement, thinking he was being kidded. It was not until [umpire Jack] Sheridan told him he was out that he would believe Barrett ever made the catch.

League Park's left-center field wall was 362 feet from home plate, and it stretched to 409 feet in dead center. Jimmy Barrett was the starter in center field for Tigers teams before Ty Cobb changed not only the lineup but the game itself. Barrett led the league in walks this season. Frank Kitson won 128 ball games for five teams over his 10-year career. He never knew that he led the league in saves in 1900. Jack Sheridan was the target of one of Addie's rare on-the-field temper tantrums, the pacific pitcher's second flair-up in the 1905 campaign. (He'd been ejected earlier that season, and suspended by Ban Johnson for five days, for throwing his glove at "Silk" O'Loughlin.) Addie would deal much better with the pressures of the pennant race of 1908, as exemplified by his perfect game performance.

(March 3, 1907, TNB)

[Charlie] Hickman was the victim of another catch that was highway robbery and "Chick" Stahl, now manager of the Boston Americans, played the star role. This drive was made on "Cy" Young and when a batter like Hick meets one of "Cy's" fast ones, it usually travels some.

Charley hooked the ball in the eighth inning with a couple of men on the sacks, with two out, and it looked like dollars to lead nickels that the fire was out [colloquial].

The ball was headed for right center when Stahl started in pursuit and when he put out his bare hand and it stuck in his fist, the groan that went up could be heard in Painsville.

Euphonious Painsville, Ohio, is pretty much a straight shot, if you're driving, about two counties north and east of League Park. (Chagrin Falls is sister town in northeast Ohio.) Charles Stahl (not to be confused with "Jake" Stahl) was another terrific center fielder, the Red Sox's best before Tris Speaker. Stahl's shoestring catch on a line drive by Ollie Pickering preserved Cy Young's May 5, 1904, perfect game. On March 28, 1907, having recently resigned his post as Boston Americans manager but awaiting replacement, Stahl committed suicide while the team was in West Baden, Indiana.

(March 3, 1907, TNB)

Elmer Flick pulled off one in Detroit last season that wasn't so bad, as President [Bill] Armour will testify, the catch defeating [his?] Tigers. [Harry] Eells and [Ed] Killian were the opposing heavers with the score 2 to 1 in Cleveland's favor in the ninth. Detroit tied the score and had [John] Warner on third with two out and Killian at bat.

Ed drove one on a line in to center, Flick was covering the middle field that day on account of [Harry] Bay's having, a few days previous, tried to make a base hit with his thumb. The drive was sharp and appeared good for a single.

It often happens when a ball is hit sharp, that it sinks, or curves down making it harder to get and this drive took such a course. There was no use for Elmer to try to catch Warner at the plate by waiting for the bound so he took the only way left and that was to drive for the ball which he did.

He came tearing in at break-neck speed and when at the right distance made the slide. It was one chance in a thousand, but he came up with the ball, having caught it with both hands, not over two inches from the ground.

Talk about your swell catches! That one made our hair stand. The judgment Flick used in making the wonderful play was only second to the catch itself.

After managing the Tigers for two seasons, Bill Armour had returned to Toledo, where he was president and manager of the Mud Hens. It was Armour who discovered Ty Cobb and signed him for $500. "Twilight" Ed Killian was a good hitting pitcher, averaging .320 in 1907. Killian debuted with Cleveland. His nickname is an indication of how effectively he pitched in the late afternoon light. His career record for fewest home runs per innings pitched will probably never be broken. John Warner twice led National League catchers in fielding percentage. Thanks, in part, to Flick's circus catch and throw, Harry "Slippery" Eels won four of his nine decisions for the Naps in 1906, his only season in the Bigs.

(MARCH 3, 1907, TNB)

But the greatest catch I ever saw by an outfielder, Clarence Beaumont, who figured in the trade Pittsburg made for [Ed] Abbatic[c]hio, pulled off in the Cleveland-Pittsburg series in the "Smoky City," in the fall of 1904.

This game had gone as far as the twelfth inning with the teams battling for supremacy. We had men on first and second, with two out and [Bill] Bradley at the bat.

[Charlie] Case, who will be with [owner George] Tebeau at Kansas City this season, handed Bill one about waist high and the way Brad belted it was a caution.

The wallop was headed for the center field fence corner. "Beau" started as soon as it was hit. Taking but one look he sprinted as hard as he could to head off the ball. On the bench it seemed that the ball would never come down.

But soon we saw Beaumont look again and with hands outstretched, running directly away from the home plate, he grabbed the little joker as it came down over his shoulders.

It sure was a grand catch and one I never expect to see duplicated.

The way those Pittsburg fans stood on their feet and yelled was a pleasure to witness. They applauded "Butch" all the way from the field to the bench and the award was not too much for the play. The game went to the fourteenth inning remaining 3 to 3.

Addie recalls action from yet another exhibition series. Obviously, the players did not let down in these extra-season games. The contests were played like the early equivalent of interleague play, only the games didn't count in the regular season. Clarence Beaumont led the league in hits for the third consecutive season in 1904. The previous fall, he became the first man to bat in a World Series. His nickname, "Ginger," did not reflect his brand of play, which was easy, but rather his auburn hair. Bill Bradley was a stellar power threat for half a dozen years. Brad did things that amazed fans, like slamming three triples in a game, homering in four consecutive games, and hitting safely in 29 straight. After 1906, when a pitch broke his arm the year after he was hampered by a stomach complaint, he lost all his power at the plate. Over his last two seasons in Cleveland, he hit well under .200, with only 12 extra-base hits.

Middle infielder Ed Abbaticchio wasn't nicknamed "Batty" for his bat—he hit only .254 over nine major league seasons. Abbaticchio replaced Claude Ritchey at the Pirate keystone for 1908, when he led the league in fielding percentage and proved that Honus Wagner made everybody around him better. (Barney Dreyfuss had traded Beaumont and Richey to the Boston Nationals for Abbaticchio.) He was the first Italian-American baseball player, and he also competed in pro football (he invented the spiral punt). Ed ran the hotel in Latrobe, Pennsylvania's Abbatacchio Building (now demolished), on the corner of Depot and Jefferson streets. Charlie Case won 21 games in two years with Pittsburgh then finished his professional career in the minors. George "White Wings" Tebeau did not display great speed as a player: His nickname came from a novel by William Black. He homered in his first major league at-bat, against Cleveland, in 1887. George ended his career as an outfielder on his younger brother Patsy's Spiders.[3] But his great success was in business. He is said to have become a millionaire in the Midwest.

(December 2, 1907, CP)

The real test of a man's ability and greatness is not holding opposing clubs hitless, but rather having the other team hit him with regularity all during the contest and still be unable to score runs. Any time that a pitcher is mowing down the opposing batsmen, inning after inning, without allowing them any safe drives, you can gamble that everything is breaking just right for that man. But when he has to face a proposition where the other team, by virtue of their being able to hit, have men on the bases in every inning, and he is still enough master of the situation to prevent them from scoring, then that man is pitching in a manner that to the experienced spectators, is the true art.

Nick Altrock pitched a game against us at Chicago one Sunday during the early part of the race in 1905, which I think was one of the finest exhibitions of twirling I have ever seen. Each club scored a run early in the game, and from then on until the sixteenth and last inning, there was no more scoring.

Up until the ninth we had Nick for three singles, but from then on until the end he was in trouble every inning.

There never was an inning from the ninth that we didn't have a man as far as second, where a base hit would have won the game. In several of the innings we had men on third, sometimes with two out, and a couple of times with but one man down.

Nick was always equal to the emergency, and aided by a stone-wall defense was able to prevent us from scoring.

In the fourteenth inning, with the first man out of the way, [Elmer] Flick strode to the plate. Elmer hooked one of Nick's benders and when the ball was returned to the infield he was resting on third.

With ["Larry"] Lajoie up next it seemed a certainty that we would score, but Nick took another hitch in his trousers and planting his wad more firmly between his teeth, proceeded to make Larry hit a ground ball to Geo. Davis [at short] on which Flick was run down between third and home.

The break finally came in the sixteenth. Flick was again the first man at bat and he singled to center. Lajoie bunted between Altrock and [first baseman "Jiggs"] Donahue. Jiggs came tearing in on the bunt, but Nick fielded the ball and turning to throw Larry out at first found no one covering the bag. [Second baseman "Gus"] Dundon, whose place it was to cover, was caught flat-footed on the play. [Bill] Bradley moved them over, and it was up to [Terry] Turner, who delivered in fine shape with a line drive far over the left fielder's head, good for three bases, scoring Flick and Lajoie.

[George] Stovall, who had been hitting the ball on the nose all day, but unluckily, fouled out to Donahue. [Harry] Bemis singled to left, driving in Turner and giving us a lead of three runs.

The Sox came back for a dying effort and scored a run with but one man out. [Ed] McFarland hit a fast drive, a little to the right of Turner, who made a swell stop and tossing the ball to second forced Davis, who had been on first. Larry [from the second base position] hurried the ball to Stovall [at first base], completing a fast double play and shutting out the last hope of the White Sox.

Although I happened to be on the winning end of the game, still it seemed to me that Nick was pitching by far the better game, as, while I was on easy street all through, on account of the fact that the team behind me was playing nothing short of a marvelous fielding game, Altrock was continually pitching himself out of holes gotten into either by himself or through some error on the part of the men behind him.

I don't believe that I ever saw a better exhibition of up-hill pitching than that performed by Nick on that long Sunday afternoon.

Addie relied on his fastball to author two no-hit masterpieces and another seven one-hitters, but he was known primarily as a control pitcher. In the May 5, 1905, extra-inning game recounted above, Addie allowed no White Sox runner to reach second base all day. That game was Altrock's longest appearance of a year in which he logged a career-high 315 ⅔ innings. Altrock's pitching career took off when he came to Charles Comiskey's White Sox. His menu of junk pitches induced batters to beat the ball into the South Side infield.

Columbus, Ohio's Dundon was a good glove (led the league's second basemen in fielding percentage in his rookie year of 1904) whose weak bat (.202 BA/.265 OBP/.236 SLG) made for a three-year career in the majors. Ed McFarland's career as a catcher extended over 14 major league seasons, only one (1898) as a starter. His fielding percentage behind the plate led the league in 1900. The Cleveland-born McFarland broke in with the Spiders of 1893. "Handsome Harry" Bemis' career—1902–1911, all with Cleveland—matched his battery mate Addie's. In 1905, he shared playing time with catchers "Fritz" Buelow and "Nig" Clarke. A year later, he was run over by Ty Cobb in a controversial play at the plate eerily similar to the Pete Rose-Ray Fosse incident; it may have led to the catcher's decreasing quality of play and the eventual end to his promising career. In retirement, Bemis operated a furniture store in Cleveland.

(December 10, 1907, CP)

One of the beauties of baseball is the fact that no two games are alike. No matter how much of a fan one may be, or how often he attends he is always sure of seeing something different.

Unusual happenings on the field form one of the attractive features of the game, and we, in the position of players, have a better opportunity of seeing, and therefore appreciating, these peculiar happenings, than have the spectators.

Jack McCarthy, who last season did outfield duty for Jimmy Burke's Kansas City [American Association] team, was the victim of a peculiar play when he was a member of the Cleveland team during the season of 1903.

We were playing the Athletics in Cleveland and with the big "Rube" [Waddell] on the slab, we were having an awful time getting runs. [Bill] Bernhard was twirling for us and was in rare form, thus making the game a pitcher's battle and one in which a run was liable to win for either club.

At the beginning of the eighth inning they had us 1 to 0. Larry [Lajoie], the first Nap at the bat, singled, and [Charlie] Hickman followed with a double, putting Larry on third and "Hick" on second, with no one out.

It looked mighty good for a run at least. McCarthy, the next man up, hit a wicked bounder down the first base line. Harry Davis hurried over to the bag, and, by a great effort, managed to grab the ball just as he stepped on the bag.

Without a moment's hesitation he wheeled and threw the ball home, intending to head off Larry at home plate. Whether or not the attempt would have been successful no one will ever know.

Jack had been running as fast as he could down the line and when Davis snapped the ball home he was directly in line with the heave. Instead of the ball finding a resting place in [Ossee] Schrek[engost]'s big mitt, it hit McCarthy full on the forehead and bounded over to the grand stand.

Jack went down and out as though kicked by an army mule and, while the Philadelphia players were running after the ball, both Larry and Hickman scored.

["Silk"] O'Loughlin, who was umpiring, decided that only Lajoie's run could count, and sent Hickman back to third.

We finally managed to score the winning run in the next inning and "Silk" wasn't bothered by the infuriated fans.

McCarthy was restored to consciousness before the inning was finished, and gamely went out to his position in left field.

In the Athletics' half of the ninth, they had men on second and third with two out. Schreck hit a vicious liner directly over the shortstop's head. McCarthy came tearing in on the ball and made one of those wonderful shoe-string catches for which he was famous, thereby cutting off two runs and winning the game.

In the club house after the game, McCarthy didn't remember a thing of what he had done after the ball hit him.

One of the most peculiar things I ever saw happened in Detroit last fall. It was the sight of a man scoring a run without one ball being hit out of the infield and not an error being made.

It happened in this manner: [Joe] Birmingham opened the eighth inning by beating out a slow hit to [shortstop Charley] O'Leary. [George] Mullin, in endeavoring to catch him off first, made a balk on which Joe went to second. With no one out, it was up to [George] Stovall to bunt, which he did, laying the ball down along the first ball [i.e., base] line about half way between first base and the plate.

Mullin and ["Boss"] Schmidt both started for the ball, while [first baseman Claude] Rossman went back to the bag to make ready to take the throw. Schmidt yelled that he would take it, and Mullin stopped [i.e., stepped] back to let the catcher field the ball.

When Schmidt finally fielded the bunt he was about 30 feet away from the plate. Birmingham rounded third and seeing that no one was covering the bag kept right on coming and was across [home plate] before the astonished Tigers realized what had happened.

It was laughable to see Rossman holding the ball in his hand, and just aching to throw it, but there was no one to heave it to.

Connie Mack arranged for Harry Davis, his team captain, to manage the

Naps for 1912, replacing the popular George Stovall. He resigned, before the end of the season, in favor of Joe Birmingham. It was to be Davis' only managerial job. George Mullin, like his friends Addie and Roger Bresnahan, resided in Toledo. It's no wonder that Mullin let his catcher have the ball. Charles Schmidt is known for his knock-down fist fights with teammate Ty Cobb, and he may have once sparred with Jack Johnson. Charles O'Leary singled in a pinch-hitting appearance for the St. Louis Browns 21 years after he'd played his last game with the St. Louis Cardinals. His vaudeville act paired him with Germany Schaefer, his double-play partner with the Tigers.

(JANUARY 6, 1908, CP)

Manager "Larry" Lajoie can hit a ball harder, when it is about a foot away from the plate, than he can when the sphere splits the heart of the rubber.

Larry once won a game for the Naps against the Boston Americans in this manner: It was in 1904 when [playing-manager Clark] Griffith's Highlanders and [playing-manager Jimmy] Collins' Pilgrims were having a neck and neck struggle for the coveted bunting [i.e., the pennant].

[Bob] Rhoads and [Norwood] Gibson were pitching. Both men were in great form and the game soon developed into a pitching duel. Each team managed to get one run and thus the score stood until the eighth inning.

In Boston's half the visitors were easily retired and the first two men at bat for us went out. [Elmer] Flick then singled.

Larry was the next man to face Gibson. [Lou] Criger, who was catching, felt sure on account of Elmer's speed he would try to steal. He accordingly signaled Gibson for a waste ball. Flick stayed on the bag. Criger again called for a waste ball and this time Elmer went. Larry saw him going and reaching out about two feet slapped the ball into the right field bleachers for a home run, sending Flick in ahead of him and giving us two runs, one more than enough to win.

After the next man had been retired, Criger came back to the bench, swearing he would never have a pitcher waste a ball again against the big fellow.

"It's just like suicide," said Lou. "Why, the further you pitch them out the harder and farther he drives them."

Otto Hess lost a game to Philadelphia in a peculiar way.

[Eddie] Plank and Hess had been having a merry battle all afternoon, and, at the end of the ninth inning the score stood 3 to 3.

Cleveland failed to score in its half of the tenth inning. The first two men were quickly disposed of by the Filipino. Harry Davis was next at bat, and Otto in trying to make him hit at a bad ball got himself into a hole, until the count stood three balls and one strike.

The next ball Otto pitched the umpire called a strike. Davis, who had thrown down his bat and started for first, let out an awful roar at being deprived of free transportation. Harry must have been quite sore, as the next ball Hess pitched he hit a mile over the right field fence.

Umpires have a good deal to do with the winning or losing of a game by tossing out an unruly player whose successor may be the means of winning for his club.

Tommy Connolly helped the Naps win a game from St. Louis in this manner last season: It was the morning game on Labor day and the two clubs were tied at the beginning of the tenth frame.

The Browns were retired without a run. With one out Flick drew a base on balls. [Edward] Spencer, who had been catching, thought that Connolly was wrong and didn't hesitate to tell him of it. Tom put him out of the game and [manager Jimmy] McAleer sent in [Jim] Stevens [sic., Stephens] to handle [Harry] Howell's "spitter" for the rest of the game.

The first ball pitched to [Bill] Bradley, who was at the bat, was called a strike. On the next one, Elmer started to steal and easily reached third on Stevens' [sic.] high throw to head him off.

Connolly, who was umpiring behind the pitcher, called it a strike, and "Brad," who had not swung around, yelled murder. Tom put Bill out of the game.

Larry sent [Harry] Bemis up to hit, and the first ball Howell pitched him, Harry drove between third and short for a clean single, scoring Flick with the winning run.

Ollie Pickering beat the Naps out of a game at Philadelphia in 1903. Rube Waddell and myself were the opposing twirlers and we were both having a good day.

Each scored a run early in the game, but from then on to the fourteenth inning there was nothing doing.

In our half of that inning it looked like a score, as with one out, [Charlie] Hickman and [Jack] McCarthy singled, placing men on first and second.

Flick had the Rube three balls and no strikes and things looked mighty fine. The big fellow steadied and got over a couple of strikes and with the count standing three and two handed up a curve ball.

Hickman and Mac started a double steal just as the Rube began to pitch. Elmer swung and missed and [Ossee] Schreck[engost] snapped the ball to third to Lave Cross, who put it on Hick before he reached the bag—and the Athletics were out of a dangerous place.

["Topsy"] Hartzel was the first man at the bat for Philadelphia and Topsy hit a fly ball to [Harry] Bay, which the Sliver easily caught.

Pickering, who hit second in the batting order, strode to the plate. The first two balls I pitched him were fast ones and he fouled both of them. Bemis signaled for another fast one, but I shook my head. I figured I could afford to waste a curve ball on him. Pick can murder a low ball, and instead of getting the pellet on the outside where I tried to pitch it, the blamed thing took a fast break and curved just a little inside of the plate and right down in his groove.

The right field fence in Philadelphia is short [280 feet], and in order to keep the hitters from making home runs whenever they feel so inclined, Connie Mack has built a wire screen about 50 feet high on top of the fence.

Pickering gave the ball an uppercut—in fact played cricket with the sphere. There was a strong wind blowing directly toward the fence and when the ball got high enough to clear the stands the wind got a full chance to carry it.

The ball kept on going until it hit the screen right over the score board. The wind was blowing so strong it had beat the screen out a ways from the bottom of the fence.

Instead of the ball coming back from the screen, as it naturally would, it rolled down and hit the top of the score board.

It hung there, as if it was making up its mind which way to fall.

To us it seemed an eternity, and when it finally decided to drop behind the score board it was time to pick up the bats, as the meeting was over.

A franchise in the Deadball Era often went by more than one nickname. Boston was known as the Americans, the Pilgrims, and also the Beaneaters, before they were the Red Sox. Cleveland, in Addie's rookie year, was called the Bluebirds, the Blues, the Bronchos, and the Bronchs; they would be the Naps before they were the Indians (starting in 1915). Cleveland newspapers liked the shorter nicknames to fit their headlines. Barton Rhoads' surname is spelled "Rhoades" in this Cleveland article, as it is in Addie's Toledo stories too. His mound opponent on that day had an interesting name, as well: Norwood Ringold Gibson, "Gibby" for short. Gibson won half of his career 34 victories in 1904, when his Boston team beat out New York for the pennant, by a game and a half. This season, Lajoie would win his fourth consecutive batting title, while also leading the league in hits, on-base percentage, slugging percentage, and RBIs.

Fireballer Otto Hess was a veteran of the recent Spanish-American War, serving in the Philippines. "Jasper" Davis led the league in home runs every year from 1904 through 1907 but collected only 75 lifetime. Flick's 64 walks in 1907 were good for fourth among American League hitters. "Tubby" Spencer, of Oil City, Pennsylvania, was a backup catcher not known for his bat. He enjoyed his best offensive year in 1907, hitting .265 for the Browns. That's Jim "Little Nemo" Stephens who was Spencer's replacement. The Salineville, Ohio, native was in his rookie season.

Pitcher Harry Howell was also one of Ban Johnson's umpires during the 1904, 1906, and 1907 seasons. Umpire Connolly was calling balls and strikes from his position behind the pitcher's mound. It so happens that Ollie Pickering—the first Cleveland player to bat in the American League, and here recalled playing with the A's—was in the outfield for the Browns in the Labor Day game. Addie went 13 ⅓ innings that day, without walking a batter. Joss had first pitched against Waddell in an October 20, 1901, semi-pro game (after his season with Toledo), when his Racine team bested Waddell's Kenosha team for the semi-pro championship of Wisconsin. Add another nickname to skinny "Deerfoot" Bay's résumé.

(November 10, 1908, TNB and CP)

No two persons who attend a baseball game with any degree of regularity will ever agree on what they consider the greatest play they have seen.

This not only holds good with the spectators, but applies to the players as well. At best great plays are only the opinions of individuals, and as we all have the right to express ours, I am going to try to tell what I consider the greatest plays of the year in these lines.

Necessarily the plays I have reference to were made by or against members of the Cleveland club.

This article will deal with the fielding stunts which loomed up as great to me. There are two kinds of fielding plays that come under the head of top-notchers.

The first, commonly known to the members of the baseball fraternity as "stabs." In other words, plays that are made simply because the only way a player has to make them is to take a chance on getting them in this manner.

The best one of this nature I saw last season was pulled off by Bill Bradley, at the time he was playing short stop for the Naps, along about the middle of the season.

It occurred in a game against Chicago one Saturday afternoon at Cleveland. With Cleveland one run to the good at the beginning of the eighth inning Chicago had men on third and first, with no one out.

John Anderson, who was at bat, drove a terrific liner to left field. When the ball started, it looked like dollars to doughnuts that it was going for a hit, and consequently, the man on first started as fast as he could to go around to third.

Bradley took a look at the flying sphere and, running towards third, jumped as high as he could and then stuck up his gloved hand. The ball struck the mitt and remained there. He landed on his feet and threw the ball to first in time to complete an easy double play.

It was a marvelous play on account of the fact that Bill made it back-handed; that is, he did not get in front of the ball but seemed to hook it after the pill was past him.

Hal Chase, of the Highlanders, has the reputation of being one of the greatest first basemen in the country and well has he earned this distinction.

The nimble Californian certainly pulls off many a great one around the initial sack. Hal is there with the judgment on any kind of a play that may arise and very seldom, if ever, does he do the wrong thing.

Chase plays just about ten feet deeper than any other first baseman in the American league and many a time he has as far to run to cover the bag on a throw, as has the base runner. He was playing a little farther back than usual one day last summer in a game against Cleveland on the Highlanders' grounds. ["Larry"] Lajoie, who was at bat, hit a fast grounder to deep short. Shortstop [Neal] Ball stepped back to get the sphere on a good bound and just as it seemed he was going to gather it in the pill took a false hop.

The shortstop grabbed the ball with one hand and without waiting to straighten up, shot it over to first. Ball is the fortunate possessor of a fine arm and he let this one go as fast as he could.

Chase in the meantime had been running almost as far as Lajoie in his effort to take the throw. Hal managed to reach the bag just after Ball had let go of the sphere.

Instead of the throw being true, where it would have been comparatively easy for Chase to handle, it was wide to the right of first.

How the big first baseman ever managed to get shifted on the bag will always remain a mystery to me, but that is what he did, and reaching out as far as he could he scooped the throw out of the dirt, just the fraction of a second before Lajoie's foot struck the bag.

The great part of the play, was the fact that he shifted feet on the bag so fast. When he reached the base, after coming on the dead run from where he had been playing, it seemed the height of impossibility for him ever to stop in time to get on the right side of the base again. He not only did this but came up with the ball as well. It sure was a grand play.

The Cleveland Press *cut the final paragraph of this story. Bill Bradley was once Jimmy Collins' pick for the best third baseman in the league. In this vignette, "Brad" is playing out of his normal position, which makes the play even more impressive. He saw action at shortstop in 30 games for the 1908 Naps. On July 19 of the following year, Neal Ball will complete the first unassisted triple play (and slug an inside-the-park home run)— while playing for the Naps.[4] The previous season, Ball's 80 errors led American League shortstops. (League Park fans, a decade hence, will witness the only triple play in World Series history, performed by Bill Wambsganss.)*

(November 17, 1908, TNB and November 18, 1908, CP)

In such a close race as the American league had this season it is always easy for the losing clubs to look back and see where the change of a few plays would have won them the bunting [i.e., pennant].

These post-mortem affairs are interesting to show just how close certain clubs came to being the winners of the flag.

The Cleveland club lost the championship by half a game and the members of the team can look over the season's work and recall many battles that were dropped by some great play the opposition or a little bad break in the luck.

In our last game at home with the White Sox we had several chances to win, but could not get the hit that would send home the winning runs. At that, we might have won but for a little bad break in luck and a couple of swell plays by [third baseman Lee] Tannehill and [first baseman Frank] Isbell.

With the score 3 to 1 against the Naps at the beginning of the sixth inning they managed to get men on second and third, with one out.

[Bill] Bradley, the next man at bat, worked [Ed "Piano Mover"] Smith for a pass, filling the bases. At this stage of the game [Fielder] Jones sent in [Ed] Walsh.

Here is where the luck broke badly for us, as [Bill] Hinchman hit a slow roller down the third base line, on which there was no chance for Tannehill to get anyone but [George] Perring, who was tearing for the plate.

"Tanny" made a great play on the ball, getting it on the dead run with his bare hand and without stopping to straighten up, whipped it in to [Billy] Sullivan, just the fraction of a second ahead of Perring.

Had "Brad" not received a pass and filled the bases there would not have been a chance for Tannehill to get Perring at the plate, as George could have slid away from Sullivan easily, but it was a force play and gave the Sox third baseman the only chance he had to get his man.

Isbell also pulled off a play in the ninth that went a long ways towards winning the game for the Chicago club. With one out Bradley hit a fast grounder right over second.

It looked like a hit, but [shortstop Freddy] Parent made a swell play on the ball. His throw to Isbell was high and directly in the path of the runner. A less courageous first baseman might have flinched a little and side-stepped, but not so with old "Issy." He jumped for the ball and after getting it came down on the base line as "Brad" reached the bag.

They came together like a couple of football players, but the first sacker held the ball and was awarded the decision. Hinchman followed with a slashing drive to right on which Bradley could easily have reached third.

Larry [Lajoie]'s long fly to center, which ended the game, would have scored bill and tied up the score. So Isbell's play was directly responsible for the Nap failure to score in that inning.

Both plays were gems and while they practically beat us out of a good chance for the championship, Tannehill and Isbell should be given credit for their wonderful work.

The Cleveland Press *did not print the last paragraph of this story, either. I wonder if Ed Walsh got any rest that offseason, after pitching 886 innings (64 wins) over the last two White Sox seasons? His 66 appearances for 1908 included this one in relief, on October 3, 1908, on the day after he had struck out 15 Naps on who knows how many pitches! The Hot Stove League this year is far from restful for Addie or anyone connected to the Naps. Their offseason is preempted by followers and critics, all posing the kind of question that supplies its own answers: How come Cleveland finished that one-half game behind in the pennant race? In short, Addie is asked to replay the season all through the winter. In this postmortem, Addie duly reflects on a loss to the great Walsh—never allowing himself an off-season basking in the memory of the perfect game he had pitched that fall on the previous day, when the Naps were still in the running. The defeat had to be one of the great disappointments in his short career.*

Bill Hinchman would set American Association season records, in 1914, for hits, doubles, and total bases, while playing for the Columbus (Ohio) Senators, before returning to the majors to lead the National League in triples, in 1916. (He authored another come-back, at age 48, in the minors.) Hinchman was the Pirates scout who discovered Lloyd Waner and "Arky" Vaughan.

(DECEMBER 31, 1908, TNB)

Triple plays unassisted are seldom seen. Often players have chances to pull off this stunt and only fail because they are so anxious to get their men that they fail to grasp the opportunity.

Terry Turner, the Naps' shortstop, had a swell chance to get away with a play of this kind in a game the Cleveland club was playing in Washington a few seasons ago.

"Dusty" Rhoads was on the mound for the Naps this day and the Nationals got to him in the first inning. The first man walked, the second singled, advancing the runner a base, and the third beat out an intended sacrifice, filling the bases, with none out. Lave Cross, who was next at bat, hit the second ball "Dusty" pitched on a line between Turner and second base, and when the ball left the bat it looked like a hundred dollars to a plugged nicket it would [be] a base hit.

All three base runners started [with] the crack of the bat and were under full headway, when Turner [made?] one of his characteristic plays. He scooted across the turf at break-neck speed, and while on the dead run grabbed the ball in his gloved hand, not over two inches from the ground.

[Fold in paper] he was going toward second to make the catch, it was a simple [matter?] for him to step on the bag, completing a double play. All that would have been necessary for him to do to get the triple unassisted, was to have touched the runner coming from first, who saw there was no chance for him to get back, and had almost stopped right in front of "Tuck."

Terry was too anxious, however, to retire the side, and before he realized what a golden opportunity he had to get his man, tossed the ball to first.

[Unreadable here] [Joe] Nealon, while playing first base for the Pittsburg team a few seasons ago, overlooked a swell bet when he failed to make the best of an opportunity offered him to pull off the unassisted triple play.

The Pirates' opponents this day had [men] on first and second, with no [one] out. A double steal was attempted, and both runners got a flying start. The man at bat pulled a vicious liner down the first base line and Nealon, making a wonderful play, managed to spear it in his left hand, just as he fell on the bag.

Wagner saw the possibilities of the play, and yelled to Nealon to hurry up, meaning by this for Joe to hustle to second, touch the base, and get credit for the unassisted triple play.

The big first baseman had his back to the play, and, when he heard Honus yell, he thought the "Flying Dutchman" meant for him to [hurry?] the ball to second, and, naturally he wheeled and threw it there.

Pirate Joe Nealon led the National League with 83 RBIs in 1906, with a slugging percentage of only .353. Teammate Honus Wagner led in runs scored, batting average and total bases.

(January 14, 1909, TNB)

Unassisted double plays made by outfielders are very uncommon. It is only occasionally that one has the opportunity of seeing some gardener pull off a stunt of this kind.

About the only man who has much of a chance to make an unassisted double is some fast fielder, who after making one of those seemingly impossible plays, on a short fly, or low line drive, keeps on tearing in towards one of the bags and beats the runner to that station.

One would hardly imagine that a man the size of "Socks" Seybold, who will probably be a member of the Toledo team next season, would pull off a play of this kind. The big fellow did it, however, in a game the Athletics played at Cleveland a season or two ago.

"Socks" always played great ball in Cleveland park and this day was no exception to the rule. The play that made "Socks" look great, happened in this manner:

With the score a tie in the seventh inning and one man out, "Nig" Clarke singled. With the count standing two balls and no strikes on the next man at bat, the hit and run play was tried.

Clarke got a good start and when the batter hit a short fly just along the right field foul line, "Nig" kept on towards second.

It did not appear to anyone that Seybold had one chance in a million to make the catch. "Socks" kept on coming though, as fast as he could and by a supreme effort, managed to grab the ball, not over two inches from the ground.

He was running in the direction of first base, and as Clarke was just rounding second, when the catch was made, it was an easy thing for "Socks" to keep on going until he completed the unassisted double, by planting his foot on first.

This is a category of the twin kill that must inevitably bring up the name of Tris Speaker. "Speak" had a knack for completing the unassisted double play at second base in part because he played a shallow center field. Right fielder Ralph Seybold was an unlikely candidate to make such a play because of his oft-maligned chubster's physique. He was a much more likely hitter than Ollie Pickering to knock a ball out of Columbia Park (see article from January 6, 1908, above). He grew up and played ball in Jeannette, Pennsylvania, a town close to where I live, and he died in a car crash on the Lincoln Highway, straighter these days but still a death trap. "Socks" Seybold is buried on a hill-side in Brush Cemetery, Adamsburg.[5] Socks would have been in Toledo in the months before the 1909 season. The great slugger had recently retired from the Athletics to work as player-coach, and then manager, of the Mud Hens.

Addie wrote this article in the wake of his January 12 piece (see Chapter 8) on fast big men in the game. It makes sense that he would draft several pieces at a sitting, in anticipation of his now daily deadline at the newspaper.

4

Of Fanatics, Kranks and Bugs

THE FANS

They went by various names in the press. In these articles, Addie lets baseball's fanatics, kranks,[1] *bugs, and fans speak.*

(January 27, 1907, TNB)

"An Unappreciated Truth Told by a Fan at League Park"

During the progress of a game at Cleveland a few years ago the park policemen who were stationed at the left field bleachers had occasion to remove a spectator who had been imbibing too freely and was in condition bordering on utter collapse. Our team was having a bad field day, Larry [Lajoie], [John] Gochnaur and [Bill] Bradley having contributed costly miscues, and consequently the spectators were not in any too good humor. As the officers were carrying out the man, someone in the bleachers yelled:

"Hurry back, there are a few more dead ones in here for you to lug away."

James Egan points out that the first ballpark Frank Robison built in Cleveland (on Perkins Avenue) featured what was called a "kicking pen" for "VIP 'kranks,'" which was "a box to keep the rabid rooters isolated from normal people." (To kick was to complain.) The lowlight in the history of Cleveland baseball fans' behavior has to be the Beer Night forfeit game of June 4, 1974.

(January 27, 1907, TNB)

While the Cleveland club was at San Antonio, Tex., for spring training in the season of 1904, "Red" Donahue, at that time a member of the Naps, was pitching for the regular team against the locals the first Sunday of our stay. Red was not extending himself to any extent and the result was that the Texans were connecting with his delivery rather freely. Some spectator in the stand undertook to kid Donahue a little not knowing Red's ability in this line and when he said, "Oh, Red, you are easy," Donahue's reply nearly took him off his feet.

"Easy, eh, well I ain't half as easy as you are. Why you gave up a half a dollar to see me pitch today."

The 50-cent admission was standard at most major league fields of the era. In his two and a half seasons on the Naps' pitching staffs, Francis Rostell Donahue was a seemingly endless source of anecdotes for Addie. This would have been Red's first spring training with the club.

(February 3, 1907, TNB)

Many a good remark is heard by occupants of the grand stand, especially from persons who are not thoroughly conversant with the details of the game.

Some years ago a Toledoan who had never seen a ball game, was induced to become at an exhibition of the great national pastime. The game proceeded and to all intents the uninitiated spectator seemed to be enjoying the performance.

About the middle of the game Eddie McFarland, who was catching here at that time, went to bat and hit a foul directly over the grand stand. At this the uneducated bug suddenly became enthusiastic and exclaimed:

"That's the greatest thing I ever saw. All the rest of the players hit the ball out straight and this batter hits it over the stands, the other way."

Owner and manager Charles J. Strobel's Armory Park stood on the present site of the federal courthouse. Ed McFarland's 16 home runs happened in 1894, three years before Armory Park was opened. (His season total was the Mud Hens record for 36 years.) Cleveland-born McFarland hit but 13 round-trippers in his 14 major league seasons.

(FEBRUARY 24, 1907, TNB)

When "Dutch" Gochnaur was playing short for Cleveland in 1903 many of the fans took unique means of letting the "Dutchman" know they didn't like the article of ball he was giving them.

"Goch," in company with [Jack] McCarthy and [Bill] Bernhard, hopped on a Wade [Amusement] Park car at the square [downtown Cleveland's Public Square] one day on their way to the grounds and took a seat way in the rear. About half way out the conductor came around for their fares and recognized them as members of the team, being a fan.

In the course of his remarks he mentioned Gochnaur, and the "Dutchman" immediately began to tell him what a rotten ball player this fellow Gochnaur was.

The conductor took the bait, hook, line and sinker, and the way he raked the "Dutchman" over the coals was a caution. This continued until they reached the grounds, to the amusement of the players.

Just as they were about to alight, Bernard said to Johnny in a stage whisper, "This fellow must be a friend of yours, Gochnaur." The two bells the motorman received must have made him think the conductor was affected with the spring halt.

"The spring halt" was an ailment that affected old horses. The joke invokes the days when streetcars were still "oat powered," or horse drawn. But most of the streetcars that Addie rode to major league ballparks had been electrified. Starting in December 1888, the East Cleveland Street Railway Company operated the first electric transportation service in the United States. By the end of that decade Frank Robison's electric streetcars took fans out to his ballparks.[2] *The Wade Park line that Addie writes about was probably not a street car but one of the old cable cars from the nineteenth century. (See the illustration in* Base Ball on the Western Reserve, *on page 194.) Jack McCarthy was a hero in the Blues' first year at League Park. On May 24, 1901, Cleveland was losing to Washington, 13–5, with two men out in the bottom of the ninth, when McCarthy singled. His second hit drove across the ninth run in the inning—for an unlikely 14–13 comeback victory.*

At this point in his career, Addie's amusement can turn to irritation with baseball fans. The only times the sports editor lectures his audience occur in such columns.

(FEBRUARY 24, 1907, TNB)

It's bad policy for an outsider to ask questions of a ball player on the way back from the grounds, especially if the team has lost a tough game. We were playing at Chicago during the time the National Republican convention of 1904 was being held in that city.

Stopping at the Lexington hotel were, among others, the West Virginian delegates. The game that day was lost in the last inning, after being apparently won, and the players were not in a cheerful mood.

Upon our arrival at the hotel the boys alighted from the bus, and as they were passing through the doors were met by a courteous southern gentleman, who inquired of "Dusty" Rhoads, "How was the game?" The Beau Brummell didn't answer at once, and the man from West Virginia repeated his question.

He was taken off his feet when Rhoads, with a sour look, answered, "Great!" and without pausing, continued to strike through the corridor.

That GOP convention, meeting from June 21 through 23, 1904, nominated incumbent president Theodore Roosevelt. Roosevelt enjoyed playing a vigorous game of baseball, but he was only a reluctant fan of the Washington team. George Bryan Brummell (born 1778) was a famous English fop.

(FEBRUARY 10, 1908, CP)

If there is one thing a ball player dreads it is to be caught in the clutches of a fan who wants to talk baseball when the ball tosser just left the field tired and sore, is the fellow known as the "all-wise bug."

He will come up to you while you are standing in the lobby of a hotel and in some manner or other start a conversation.

He will begin asking you questions about this or that player and finally will tell you that he was the one who started the now great star in the business.

The first thing you know he is telling you all about this player's family. He knows his father, mother, sister and in fact all the members of the family.

Nine times out of ten he will whisper real confidentially in your ear that the player's mother used to take in washing while the father carried the hod.

After thinking he has established himself in your good graces by this wonderful bit of information he will start on another line which usually runs something like this:

"You fellows DON'T want to win the pennant.

"There ain't nothing to it. That club of yours can win the rag in a gallop.

"I'm wise in [to?] the game. There is more money in it for the club owners to be up among the leaders every year than to cop the rag."

When you inform him that there is nothing that a club would rather do than win a pennant he will look at you with a knowing smile and wink and say: "Nix cull, I'm on" [colloquial].

The chances are ten to one that before he gets away he will inform you that Buck Orth lives next door to him in Des Moines, when you know Orth makes his home in Lynchburg, Va.

Then there is the familiar fan who will rush up to you on the street or around the hotel and, grasping you by the hand with a coal miner's grip, say, "Well, well, how are you, old man? I haven't seen you since we were out that night in Chicago."

It's better than an even bet that you haven't the slightest remembrance of having even seen him before, but for appearance sake you will suffer him to lead you to a chair and there he will proceed to tell you all about how many times he has watched the papers to see what kind of a record you were making.

It isn't long before he invites you in to have a drink, and when you tell him that you don't indulge he will put on a surprised look and say: "How long since you climbed on the wagon?" When you tell him you are off for good, he will assume a patronizing air, and proceed to give you a little good advice about the benefits to be derived from total abstinence, and will usually wind up by saying: "I'm going to quit myself and just as soon as I get back to the house — well a new leaf for me."

If you don't handle him with kid gloves the chances are he will attempt to borrow a fiver from you before he starts around the corner to find a cheap lodging house in which to sleep for the night.

The man who used to play is another kind of fan that the players have to put up with very often during the season.

If allowed to, he will tell you about the games he used to play in and how on one occasion when a member of the Bean Blossoms he struck out 21 of the Poseyvilles in a contest for the championship of Brown-co[unty].

And if you are not careful he will have you out in the alley showing you just how he performed the marvelous feat.

Or if his long suit has been hitting them "where they ain't," you had better be careful or the first thing you know you will be dodging imaginary wild pitches or watching some of this bug's home run drives.

You often run across the fellow who used to play with one of the now big league stars and some of the stuff they tell you about how they used to catch this pitcher, or play the outfield alongside of this or that man, is enough to make one wish for the simple life.

Albert Orth did reside in Lynchburg. In fact, he was part owner-playing manager for the Lynchburg Shoemakers. Orth went by a couple of nicknames—"Smilin' Al," for his demeanor, and another, "The Curveless Wonder," out of respect for his pitching style. The control pitcher was yet another master of the slow ball; batting against him, Ossee Schrecongost once caught a pitch in his bare hand. For several seasons, the Highlanders' pitching staff featured both Orth and fellow change-up artist Clark Griffith.

The Cleveland Press *ran a box, "Perhaps This Incident Inspired Addie's Article," attributed to the regular columnist called "The Little Old Man," beside the story. It turns out to be an almost verbatim reprint of Addie's story of February 8 (see Chapter 2).*

(February 16, 1908, TNB)

The "consolation fan" is a form of pest that players often encounter during the season.

This fellow, as a rule, tries to create the impression on the player that he is for that particular man first, last and all the time. After you let him go along on this line for a while, he will usually start something like this:

"Well, old boy, that was a swell game you pitched today."

You acknowledge the compliment, and he proceeds: "They certainly broke bad for you all day. Why, that kind of a game will win nine times out of ten. Say, what is the matter with that fellow Turner? He is getting so he can't take the ball out of his pocket without dropping it. If you had any kind of a team behind you, it would be a cinch for you to lead the league."

Right here you begin to weary of this kind of stuff, but keep your temper and tell him that the chances are "Tuck" [Terry Turner] fell down on one that no other shortstop in the league would have tried to get.

He comes back with something like this: "Well, I guess that's right.

Turner is certainly the goods when he is going right, and it just goes to show how lucky that other gang is to have him fall down on a chance that he would eat up ordinarily.

"At that, I would like to see you with the Highlanders. There is a team for you. If they had a fellow like you on their pitching list, they would win the pennant by the Fourth of July."

You remind him of the fact that there are some great twirlers on that team, and that you guess they have as good a chance as any team to win the rag just as they stand.

He will proceed to tell you how much he thinks of your own playing, and, after some more of this kind of "bull," which he thinks he is getting away with, he proceeds to roast the home team, which is probably in the lead.

After telling you how lucky it is, and how he can't see where it has a license to be in the race, he will wind up by saying:

"Say, this fellow [Ed] Walsh is certainly the candy. Any time he has the 'spitter' working he has it on anyone in the league. I guess Jiggs Donahue is a bad man for first!" and as you walk away you can faintly hear: "Why, the White Sox will win the whole series from this bunch of dubs."

Apparently, people "bugged" people a long time before the literary Beats used the term in the 1950s. The running headline for this numbered series is "Baseball 'Bugs.'" Terry Turner had more than one nickname. Dubs: slang for a duffers. The New York Highlanders were a second-division team in 1907 and finished last in 1908.

(FEBRUARY 18, 1908, TNB)

That species of fan who thinks he knows a little more about the inside workings of the club than do the players themselves, is the fellow who is more of a bore than any of the other brands.

It's a strange thing, but for some unaccountable reason there are a lot of people who imagine they are on the inside of all that goes on between the players, both on and off the field.

Where they get this supposed information is hard to conceive, but get it they do and nine times out of ten, they are telling you something about your fellow players you never heard of yourself.

It's amusing at times and then again it gets on your nerves and you feel like telling the informant just how little he knows of what he is talking about.

This sort of fan will nail you to the mast anywhere he may happen to find you, but a good many times you will be caught in his clutches while going out to the grounds in a street car.

You are probably sitting in one of the rear seats enjoying a smoke, while reading the last edition of one of the afternoon papers. The first thing you know someone slides into the seat next to you.

If the car be a little crowded and you make room for him he will call you by your first name and as soon as he thanks you, you have a feeling that you are in for it.

You haven't gone a block before he has one arm resting on your shoulder in a real confidential manner and is pouring in your unwilling ear something like this:

"Now look here, old man, of course I know you don't want to say anything about this, but on the level what is the matter with ["Larry"] Lajoie and ["Heinie"] Berger?"

You inform him that as far as you know there is nothing the matter and tell him they are the best of friends.

He assumes a patronizing air and says: "Well, I have it on the very best of information that Larry doesn't like the German [Berger] and I did hear they had a fight in the clubhouse the other day."

By this time you are looking around for some much needed help and as it is not in sight you have to sit there calmly and listen to him while he says: "I have it from a particular friend of Bill Bradley's that he is playing for his release. I know absolutely that [Elmer] Flick ain't trying."

It's getting pretty tough by this time and you are making the cigar you have been smoking look like an over-worked piece of tobacco, while the wise one proceeds to tell you that half of the men on the team don't take any care of themselves and are full of liquor three or four nights in the week.

When he informs you that he saw "Dusty" Rhoads coming out of the grill room of the Hollenden so drunk he could hardly walk, night before last, you feel like committing murder, especially when you were with Rhoads yourself all that evening at some show and know that "Dusty" never drank a drop in his life.

When the conductor calls "ball park" you try to get away from the "bug," but it's a ten to one shot that he will follow you to the gates and want you to get him a pass for that day's game.

Poor, beleaguered Addie just wants to smoke his cigar and enjoy his sports page. Cigars still enjoyed a greater popularity than cigarettes in this decade. Deadball Era ballplayers commuted, on public street cars, to the day's game.[3] *The Hollenden (now demolished) was located at the corner of Superior Avenue and East Sixth Street, in Cleveland's Grand Canyon district. The luxury hotel opened in 1885 and over the years hosted five U.S. presidents, probably including Theodore Roosevelt.*[4]

(OCTOBER 24, 1908, CP)

No matter how successful a baseball manager may be, or how good are the results he gets from his players, there will always be many who are ready to criticize him on the slightest provocation.

No matter how conservative the enthusiast may be in his own line of business, the minute he becomes an ardent admirer of a certain club, and roots hard for that team to win, he develops into a rabid fan.

When the club is winning and everything is going along in apple pie order, he bubbles over with enthusiasm and praise for the players and manager. But as soon as things begin to look a little bad and the club starts to lose, he begins to offer suggestions and tells what he would do if he were running the club.

There was considerable comment in Chicago during the third game of the world's series because Manager [Frank] Chance let [Jack] Pfeister finish out the inning that Detroit hit him hard and scored the winning runs. On the face of it one would naturally think that Chance was making a mistake in allowing Pfeister to remain in, when up to this time Chicago was leading by a score of 3 to 1.

But a little thought will show that the manager of the Cubs was only doing what any other leader would have done under similar circumstances.

[George] Mullin opened Detroit's half by drawing a pass, the only one Pfeister had issued. ["Matty"] McIntyre followed with a single, and when the big southpaw threw [Charley] O'Leary's bunt to [third baseman Harry] Steinfeldt too late to get Mullin, the bases were filled with one out.

With three left-handed batters—[Sam] Crawford, [Ty] Cobb and

[Claude] Rossman—coming up, would it have been policy to take out a left-handed pitcher and substitute a right-hander?

Hardly. This is no doubt the way Chance figured it, and so he let Pfeister continue. Crawford hit one at Chance that he knocked down, but could not recover in time to get anyone.

Cobb beat out a slow bounder to [shortstop Joe] Tinker, and when [Claude] Rossman singled to right, Detroit was two runs in the good. It would have been suicide to burn up another pitcher at this stage of the game, as Mullin was holding the Cubs safe, and it did not look as though they had a chance to score on him.

This is only one instance of where a manager is often-times criticized for doing just what he thought was right, and which was about the only course to pursue.

Of course, after it is all over, the manager, as well as anyone, can see where he might have done differently, and possibly with better results, but it is a cinch that he was doing just what he thought best at the time, and if everyone would take that feature of it into consideration there would be less criticism.

I've decided against placing this article in either the World Series reports chapter or the one on "Inside Baseball" because the writer seems to be directly addressing the kickers. The headline was "Fans' Knocks Often Unjust." Addie writes at the beginning of an off-season in which he must have grown weary of explaining to fans why Cleveland had lost the pennant by the closest of margins. To make matters worse, he had recently returned from witnessing the 1908 World Series and, no doubt, thinking about what could have been for the Naps. Game Three, when the Tigers teed off on Ohioan Jack Pfiester's curves for six hits in the sixth inning, was the only Detroit win against Chicago in the Series.

(January 15, 1909, TNB)

Have you ever unintentionally "butted" in on a ball club when the players were gathered in some public place? Or have you ever seen some other person, who did, with the deliberate intention of hearing everything that was said and discussed by the players?

If you ever have, let it be known that the reception that unfortunate person receives is about as warm and cordial as an iceberg.

If there is one thing ballplayers hate, it is to have someone entirely foreign to them hang around, trying to edge into the crowd and the means they take of letting this unfortunate individual know that he is not wanted are, to say the least, unique.

"Hap" Ward, of the [vaudeville] team of Ward and Vokes, is a great friend of the players and is known by nearly every prominent member of the profession.

Ward boarded a train at Boston one night last summer, intending to go to Philadelphia. On the same train was the Pittsburg team headed for the Quaker City.

"Hap" decided he would go up ahead and mingle with the players for an hour or so. When he reached their car he failed to see anyone he knew and, thinking he would wait a few minutes, stood near a table, where a few of the Pirates were enjoying a game of cards.

No one paid any attention to him at first, but when it became evident to the players that "Hap" was there to see the game, they resented his intrusion and commenced to make him aware of this in their own peculiar way.

Remarks passed between the players, intended for Ward, were soon flying through the air. "When did you get in?" "Well, why don't you sit down and take a hand?" "Anybody issue invitations for this party?" "Who's your friend?" "Getting an earful?" And any number of remarks similar to these were hurled at "Hap."

Ward was on in a minute and played the part of the rube to perfection. The card players were still in the midst of this "kidding" game when Fred Clarke and Honus Wagner happened along.

"Hello, 'Hap,'" said both Wagner and Clarke, when they saw the actor. "Here, fellows," continued the Pirates' manager, "I want you to meet Mr. Ward."

The "kid" was on [slang] the card players, which they acknowledged very gracefully.

This brings us back to the serious part of Addie's essays on the unwelcome attention of strangers.

Before radio and big-figure attendance at the parks, most fans followed baseball in their daily newspapers. Sports writing was in its Big Bang period when the Press *and the* News-Bee *hired Addie Joss. Established newspaper personalities Elmer Flick, Napoleon Lajoie, and Bill Bernhard brought to the American League experiment an immediate legitimacy.*

The dilemma was that modern performance industries, such as organized baseball and acting, at the dawn of the American Century, were dependent upon public exposure and recognition, which may have ranged from general popularity to star-making. This obvious fact meant that social boundaries would inevitably become blurred in the minds of some consumers. That is, notoriety will be taken for fame in this culture. And, somewhere in a fan's cognitive response to these industries, private sectors will become public. Addie's stranger could read "all about" his favorite player, and almost come to think he knew him. The "direct line" that fans enjoyed, and players took for granted, becomes a boundary line dangerous when crossed.

(January 18, 1909, TNB)

Public men, no matter what may be their professions, are bound to be more or less annoyed by over-enthusiastic admirers. Baseball players, undoubtedly, get it worse than anybody.

It's really amusing to watch these so-called fans and the manner in which they take [sic] to occupy the players' time and attention. This is especially true of those who come around the hotels and try to mingle with the players.

Encouragement they never receive and no matter how many or how strong are the rebuffs they receive, it never seems to f[a]ze them.

Sometimes the player or players who are forced to stand for this sort of annoyance find that the usual hints to vacate are completely ignored and in order to forcibly impress upon the "bug" that his presence is not desired, it is imperative for someone to flatly tell him to "beat it."

Josh Clarke, of the Naps, sent a fellow on his way at St. Louis last fall in a rather startlingly new and novel manner.

It happened in the corridor of the Planter's hotel, the evening of the day, that the Browns by winning, the first game of a double header, put the Naps out of it, as far as the winning of the American league pennant was concerned.

It needs no stretch of the imagination to conceive the melancholic feelings of the players that night as they gathered in small groups around the lobby to talk it over.

As the boys were thus congregated it was noticed that some fellow, an entire stranger to everyone on the club, persisted in "butting in." While the stranger never said a word he kept crowding right in and seemed to drink in every word said by the players.

As soon as the Naps noticed him they all started for another part of the hotel lobby and had no more than got nicely settled when over comes Mr. Stranger.

This was done a couple of times and commenced to get the boys sore. Josh, who at the time had on one of those cowboy sombreros, which made him look like the typical man from the west, said: "Leave it to me. I'll chase him."

Clarke always carries one of those hunting knives with him and, reaching in his pocket, he took out this murderous looking implement. Opening the large blade, he backed the stranger against a large pillar and, holding the point of the knife against his ribs, said: "Look here, whoever you are, we have had you around here as long as we want you, and now it's up to you to 'git.'"

The stranger took one look at Josh's determined face, then a hasty glance at the dirk, and the way he flew out through the front door would have done credit to a ten second man.

Joshua Clarke's nickname was "Pepper," for the obvious reason. His knife threat occurred on October 5, 1908, but was never made a gun-in-the-NBA-locker-room scandal. Clarke was born in Winfield, Kansas, which is West if you're in St. Louis, the farthest outpost of major league baseball in those days. Representing the United States at the 1900 Olympics, Francis W. Jarvis ran the 100-meter dash in 10.80 seconds. The sprint has been a standard event since the modern Olympic games of 1896.

5

"Another Remarkable Instance"

THE INSIDE GAME

Baseball's "inside game," also known in Addie's day as "scientific baseball," is usually traced back to "Foxy Ned" Hanlon's recipe for Temple Cup championships when he managed the Baltimore Orioles.[1] *This theory of play evolved, in the Deadball decades, most conspicuously through the innovations of two of Hanlon's star players, John McGraw and Hughie Jennings, now managing their own teams.*[2] *Addie took his regular turn on the mound against Jennings' Detroit teams, but he didn't have to look beyond his own infield for model practitioners of the inside game, Terry Turner and Bill Bradley. Addie witnessed Bradley's mid-career transition from slugger (in 1902, Bradley ranked second in the league in home runs, third in doubles, and sustained a 29-game hitting streak) to insider (a record 60 sacrifices in 1908 and only nine extra-base hits in 1909), after four consecutive seasons of injuries and illnesses sapped him, and his bat "Big Bennie," of power.*

The inside game was the thinking fan's delight. It was a new way of watching and, especially, talking about baseball.[3] *On the field, the scientific game both introduced and rediscovered much-debated strategies, including the sacrifice bunt and the hit and run,*[4] *pinch hitting and relief pitching specialists, platooning and lefty-righty matchups, professional baseline coaching and signs, pitchouts and working the count.*

Addie singles out, in his baseball writing, Jimmy McAleer and Bill Armour, his first professional managers, for their formative influences on his concept of the inside game. And two of the young Addie's teammates in Toledo, Bobby Gilks and "Cupid" Childs, were schooled in the scientific method.[5]

You might even speculate that the Hanlon tradition continued right into the Cold War.[6] *No fewer than three Deadball strategists, Tris Speaker, Bill McKechnie, and "Muddy" Ruel, were coaches for the Cleveland Indians' championship team of 1948. And the starting third baseman for that club, Ken Keltner, was discovered by scout Bill Bradley. Casey Stengel, whose Yankees teams featured platooning and the hit and run, learned the inside game from John McGraw himself.*[7]

(JANUARY 27, 1907, TNB)

Everyone who follows baseball at all knows what a great factor "the luck of the game" is to a team that wins games and pennants.

As prominent a baseball man as Jim McAleer, manager of the St. Louis "Browns," is authority for the statement that 60 per cent of the game is luck.

While McAleer's estimate may be a trifle far fetched, it is safe to say that at least one-third of the games won or lost by a team during the season's play are determined by some prank of dame fortune.

Many a great player has discovered his calling as a pitcher, infielder or outfielder, through a lucky beginning.

For instance: Bob Wallace, the great short stop, who has been doing such wonderful work for the Browns, was originally a pitcher, in Cleveland, in the days of Pat Tebeau, "Cupid" Childs, Ed McKean, Jesse Burkett and the rest of that wonderful team.

"HOW WALLACE FOUND HIMSELF"

Chip McGarr, who was the team's regular third baseman, was injured one day and Tebeau sent Bob to play the bag, with the result that he never was asked to pitch again and is now considered one of the greatest infielders the game has ever produced.

Another case is that of Weldon Henley, who pitched such great ball for Connie Mack's Athletics a few seasons ago.

Weldon is a native of Georgia and was a student at the Georgia School of

Opposite: ***The 1906 edition of the Cleveland Naps would produce three 20-game winners (Bob Rhoads, Otto Hess, and Joss, pictured), but only a third-place finish*** **(Cleveland State University Library, Cleveland Press Collection).**

CLEVELAND BASEBALL TEAM
1906
Naps at Home
APRIL 30 . . . . ST. LOUIS
MAY 1, 2, 3 . . . . ST. LOUIS
MAY 4, *5 . . . . CHICAGO
MAY 7, 8, 9 . . . . DETROIT
MAY 10 . . . . CHICAGO
MAY 29, (30), (30), 31 . . . . ST. LOUIS
JUNE 4, 5, 6, 7 . . . . . . BOSTON
JUNE 8, *9, 11 . . . . . WASHINGTON
JUNE 12, 13, 14, 15 . . . . . NEW YORK
JUNE *16, 18, 19, 20 . PHILADELPHIA
JUNE 28, 29, *30 . . . . . . CHICAGO
JULY 3, (4), (4) . . . . DETROIT
JULY 5 . . . . CHICAGO
JULY 26 . . . . WASHINGTON
JULY 27, *28, 30, 31 . . . . NEW YORK
AUGUST 1, 2, 3, *4 . PHILADELPHIA
AUGUST 6, 7, 8, 9 . . . . BOSTON
AUGUST 10, *11, 13, 14 . WASHINGTON
AUGUST 31 . . . . CHICAGO
SEPTEMBER *1, (3), (3) . . . . CHICAGO
SEPTEMBER 5, 6, *8 . . . . ST. LOUIS
SEPTEMBER 14, *15 . . . . . . DETROIT
SEPTEMBER 17, 18, 19 . WASHINGTON
SEPTEMBER 20, 21, *22 . . . . BOSTON
SEPTEMBER 24, 25, 26 . PHILADELPHIA
SEPTEMBER 27, 28, *29 . NEW YORK
OCTOBER 1, 2, 3 . . . . . . DETROIT
* Saturday † Sunday ( ) Holiday
Naps Abroad
APRIL 17, 18, 19, *21 . . . ST. LOUIS
APRIL †22, 23 . . . . CHICAGO
APRIL 25, 26, 27, *28 . . . . DETROIT
APRIL †29 . . . . ST. LOUIS
MAY †6 . . . . CHICAGO
MAY 11, *12, 14, 15 . . . NEW YORK
MAY 16, 17, 18, *19 . . . . . BOSTON
MAY 21, 22, 23, 24 . PHILADELPHIA
MAY 25, *26, 28 . . . . WASHINGTON
JUNE 1, *2, †3 . . . . CHICAGO
JUNE 21 . . . . DETROIT
JUNE 22, *23, †24 . . . . . ST. LOUIS
JUNE 25, 26, 27 . . . . . . DETROIT
JULY †1 . . . . CHICAGO
JULY *7, 9, 10, 11 . PHILADELPHIA
JULY 12, 13, *14, 16 . . . WASHINGTON
JULY 17, 18, 19, 20 . . . NEW YORK
JULY *21, 23, 24, 25 . . . . . BOSTON
AUGUST 15, 16, 17 . PHILADELPHIA
AUGUST *18, 20, 21, 22 . WASHINGTON
AUGUST 23, 24, *25 . . . . NEW YORK
AUGUST 27, 28, 29 . . . . . . BOSTON
SEPTEMBER †2 . . . . CHICAGO
SEPTEMBER †9 . . . . ST. LOUIS
SEPTEMBER 11, 12, 13 . . . DETROIT
SEPTEMBER †16 . . . . . . ST. LOUIS
OCTOBER 4, 5, *6 . . . . . CHICAGO
OCTOBER †7 . . . . ST. LOUIS
* Saturday † Sunday ( ) Holiday
EVERYBODY READS
THE CLEVELAND PRESS
PINK SPORTING EDITION

Technology [now Georgia Tech], where he received his baseball training as the club's first baseman.

It was during a practice game that he was pressed into service as a pitcher and with remarkable success, striking out 16 of the opposing team.

The varsity had scheduled a game with Cornell, which was making a tear of the south that spring and when the day for the big game arrived it was discovered Tech's regular pitcher could not take part in the contest and that the only man who could pitch was Henley. Cornell was shut out 4 to 0 and Henley's mark as a pitcher was made. It was not long before Weldon was doing great work in the American league.

"When Luck Played a Hand"

A remarkable instance showing how luck will break on the field, was experienced by Cleveland at Philadelphia one day in 1904.

[Earl] Moore and ["Rube"] Waddell were the opposing twirlers. At the beginning of the 12th inning we had men on second and third with one man out. [Harry] Bay who was the next batter, hit an easy grounder to [second baseman Danny] Murphy, who gathered the ball clean and made the throw home to catch the runner scoring from third.

As Bay dashed for first he dropped his bat in front of the plate. Murphy's throw, although low, appeared to have the base runner beaten easily.

Just as Schreck [Ossee Schrecongost] reached to catch the ball it struck Bay's bat and bounded off to one side so far that by the time Schreck recovered it both runners had crossed the plate and Bay was on second.

As "Rube" struck out the next two men it can be seen how important a part luck played in winning, that game.

"Things Which Change Games"

Many times such small things as pebbles, sticks or small holes will cause an infielder or outfielder to miss a play that will lose a game for his club.

In a series the Cleveland club was playing at Baltimore in 1902 an instance of this sort occurred. It was the ninth inning of one of the games and we had the Orioles beaten by one run, apparently. They had a man on second and two out when the batter hit one right at [John] Gochnaur, our shortstop.

"Gooch" played the ball all right, but just as he was about to pick it up and retire the runner at first it struck some small object, presumably a pebble, and took an awkward, high bound out of his reach.

Of course the man on second scored and they eventually beat us.

Gochnaur was the victim of another circumstance that robbed us of a game one day the following season. It was when [Charlie] Hickman was playing first base for Cleveland.

Charley had been complaining for a long time about the "bag" at first being worn out and so small that whenever he had a close play to make it was hard to find it, so Manager [Bill] Armour had the ground keeper put on a set of new bases. When the bags are new they are about three or four inches thick, hard and solid.

Along about the seventh or eighth inning we were one run to the bad and had men on second and third, with two out and "Gooch" at bat. About the second or third ball pitched he hit with an awful jolt and sent it down the right field foul line. It looked like a sure two-base hit and we had those two runs counted.

Of course the minute "Gooch" hit the ball Harry Davis, who was playing first for the visitors, started toward the foul line, but with no expectation of getting the ball.

Well what do you suppose happened? The ball hit that new bag at first and bounded straight into the hands of Davis, who stepped on the bag and put out the runner.

As the score remained the same this play finally lost us the game.

"Luck in Tight Places"

Another remarkable instance showing the important part luck plays in close games was shown in that great series at Philadelphia near the close of the season of 1905, when Chicago and the Athletics were fighting it out to see which would win the championship.

With Chicago one run in the lead during the latter part of the deciding game, the Athletics had runners on second and third and the batter hit a sharp single to Jim Callahan, who was playing left field.

As is the custom when an outfielder comes in from the field, he will drop his glove about midway between the infield and his position; and Topsy Hartsel had dropped his when he went to the bench at the end of the inning.

The hit the batter made was so sharp that it seemed like suicide for the runner at second to try to score, especially as Callahan is the possessor of a fine throwing arm. But the occasion demanded an attempt at least, so the runner was coached home, as Callahan set himself for the pick up and throw.

The ball was seen to stop in its course and Jim had to come running in and make a hurried pick up and throw.

In the meantime the runner tore for the plate and by a long slide scored in safety, just ahead of Callahan's perfect throw.

That ball had hit Hartsel's glove and probably prevented [Charles] Comiskey's team winning the pennant.

"Columbus Luck, of Course"

Coming close to home probably not a few Toledo fans remember how "Lefty" Davis won a game here for Columbus a few seasons ago, by hitting a ball that stuck in the telegraph wires along the right field fence, the hit going for a home run and scoring a man ahead of Davis, when Toledo apparently had the game won by a margin of one run.

All Toledo fans remember how Otto Krueger broke up a brilliantly contested 16-inniing game one Sunday last season, by hitting the first ball ["Bull"] Durham pitched into the center field bleachers, but probably only a few knew that the ball struck the outside rail of the bleachers first and then bounded in, making it possible for Toledo to win one of the best games it has ever been my fortune to witness.

Numberless instances could be related by all players who have been playing the game for any length of time, but they would only tend to strengthen the opinion that luck is an essential factor in a team's pennant aspirations.

In this omnibus column, typical of his early efforts for the Sunday edition, Addie continues a January 27, 1907, article on luck in baseball (above). Luck is a favorite theme throughout his sportswriting and a preoccupation in the player's mind.[8] *As we have also seen, Addie was disposed toward finding humor in the game, in this case "some prank of dame fortune."*

James B. "Chippy" McGarr was the regular third baseman on the notoriously chippy Spiders clubs that went to the Temple Cup in 1895 and 1896. He was released before the start of the 1897 regular season when Bobby Wallace was named the starter at third. Unless Addie is recalling a spring training game, he is mistaken: Wallace never replaced an injured McGarr. Rhoderick

Wallace, of course, made yet another position shift—he's in Cooperstown as a shortstop. Addie might have included Danny Murphy on his list of players who changed positions during their careers. Murphy was the starting second baseman in his first World Series with the Athletics, and their right fielder in two more. Weldon Henley, one of the college boys, went 27–27 with the 1903 and 1904 Athletics, and won only five more games in his career. Earl Moore was the Naps' hard-luck pitcher in 1904, losing four games in extra innings (twice to Waddell). Addie recalls Moore's August 8 loss to Waddell, in 12 innings. John Gochnaur seems to have made his own bad luck in the field; his unfortunate fielding average for 1903 was .863. When he teamed up with Charley Hickman, not even the presence of slick-fielding Bill Bradley and Napoleon Lajoie could save the Naps' infield. In the time before Emil Bossard, no less than two star Cleveland infielders were conspicuous for their nervous habit of clearing the infield dirt of pebbles: "Pebbly Jack" Glasscock and Bill Bradley.

Alonzo Davis pitched for the 1903 Mud Hens, but he never made the majors. Playing under the name of Louis Durham, "Bull" would win five consecutive doubleheaders pitching for Indianapolis, in 1908. Bill Haber devoted 13 years to tracking down the identity of this pitcher whose birth name is Louis Raphael Staub. "Topsy" Hartsel's glove, without "Topsy" in it, was found by the ball Harry Davis hit, in a game on September 28, 1905. It was routine for a player to leave his glove on the field, between half innings, until a 1954 rule. As his reward for a happy playing career in Philadelphia, Harry Davis was sent by Connie Mack to manage Cleveland for most of the unhappy 1912 season.

Addie is in Toledo during the Naps' season to be present for the birth of his daughter, Ruth Theresa Joss. Notice that the Mud Hens are playing on Sunday, still illegal in Cleveland. A photograph of Armory Park, on facing pages 24 and 25 in John Husman's Baseball in Toledo, *clearly shows the telegraph lines strung above right field.*

(February 10, 1907, TNB)

Now that "Nig" Clarke has signed his contract for 1907, the officials of the Cleveland club are breathing easy and the story circulated in Detroit regarding a combination formed by certain alleged dissatisfied Naps to hold up the club for more salary this year, is as dead as Mrs. Peaney.

"Nig" is conceded generally to be the coming catcher of the American league, and an occurrence in Philadelphia in 1905 will illustrate, in a measure, why he is thus regarded.

Clarke received his first thorough try-out with Cleveland at Philadelphia during the season of 1905, at the time the Athletics were winning the right to dispute with the Giants the title of "World's Champions."

Foxy Connie Mack had his team doing all sorts of inside playing, and one of their favorite tricks was to tip off the opposing catcher's signals to the man at bat. This was usually done when a man was on second, and "Nig," who had been put wise, framed it up to beat them at their own game.

The usual signal between a catcher and his pitcher is commonly known as "one and two." One finger showing means a fast ball and two fingers a curve. But Clarke changed this somewhat, making the pitcher understand that whenever the thumb was in sight it meant a curve, no matter how many fingers might be shown, while anything else meant a fast ball.

About the sixth inning, with "Topsy" Hartsel on second and [Harry] Davis at bat, Clarke signaled for a fast ball, using one finger for his sign. Davis fouled, making one strike. The second was a repeater at which Davis swung and missed.

By this time Hartsel thought he had the signs, and when "Nig" showed two fingers for the third ball "Topsy" gave Davis the office for a curve.

The pitcher started the ball for the center of the plate about waist high, and Davis, believing the ball would curve, let it go by, expecting every instant to see it break away from the plate. But when [Jack] Sheridan called "Three strikes, batter's out," he looked all sorts of things at Hartsel.

That was the last time sign tipping was tried on Clarke by the Athletics.

Count the News-Bee *sports editor among the unsigned Naps who were dissatisfied with their contracts. (See the February 24, 1907 story in Chapter 1.) "Topsy "Hartsel, who called himself Fred, was a smart ball player and terrifically effective lead-off man on Connie Mack's Athletics. The year after Addie's death, Hartsel managed in Toledo and later ran a downtown business with ballplayer Harry Hinchman. "Topsy" Hartsel is buried in Toledo, not too far from Roger Bresnahan and Addie Joss. Speaking of matters funereal, Mrs. Ollie Peaney was killed on the night of March 1, 1895, in the sleepy village of Tontogany, Ohio. The "drug store murder" remains unsolved. Connie Mack kept back-up catcher Morgan Murphy on the roster specifically to steal signs.*

He read the other team's signs through a pair of binoculars—for away games, from a rented room across the street from the ballpark—and relayed them to Philadelphia batters via the base coaches! The subject of signs—lucky ones, not baseball signs—is continued in the following column.

(February 17, 1907, TNB)

Ball players as a rule are the most superstitious men in existence and the stuff they go through to evade a supposed hoodoo is as ridiculous as it is entertaining.

Not only the players, but managers and club owners are affected by this malady. The ancient 13 is evaded on every occasion, and it is as much as one's life is worth to ask a player to take No. 13 locker in the clubhouse or to assign him to berth No. 13 on a Pullman.

A load of barrels is considered a good omen, as is the finding of a hairpin. Should a team pass either the barrels or a load of hay, the boys all raise their hats and then it is an assured fact the day's game is as good as won.

One thing a player positively refuses to do, is to change a baseball shirt after having put one on for the game. This custom is so strong that I have known players to go out on the field with their shirts on wrong side out, rather than run the risk of provoking dame fortune by changing them.

Another thing the players are particular about is the direction taken by the teamster on the way to the ball grounds. Should a club win the first game of a series, the players want to be taken over the same route the next day, and woe unto the driver who tries to take them in another direction. To meet a cross-eyed person is a sure sign, in the player's opinion, that it is all off for that day's game.

"Armour Has It Bad"

President [Bill] Armour of the Toledo club has always been very superstitious, and as the Cleveland players, at the time he was at the helm there, were aware of this, they would take advantage of every opportunity to spring a joke upon "Bill."

[Bill] Bradley, who is as fond of a joke as any one, once managed to find a small boy who was so cross-eyed that it was hard to decide whether he was coming or going, and in some way smuggled him into the grounds.

"Brad" knew Armour was on the bench and he sent the kid in with instructions to ask Armour if he wanted a good mascot.

The boy did as he was told and when "Bill" saw those eyes he nearly fell off the bench.

When a regular player has fallen off in hitting, the means he resorts to in order to regain his batting eye are varied. About the first stunt is to change bats; if this fails he will assume a different position at bat, and as a last resort will have some member of the team, in whom he thinks there is good luck, rub his hands on the bat. Or if he is real superstitious, he will have him spit on the end of the bat three times. Should he make a hit the next trip to the plate, he will come back to the bench exclaiming: "Nothing to it! I knew that was all I needed to start me hitting."

All players have their peculiarities at the plate. Some are involuntary; others are from force of habit, but the majority from superstition.

Ball players are not the only class afflicted with a superstitious vein, and it is an established fact, that traveling men will lay over a day or two on a trip, in order to travel to their destination with a ball club.

"Traveling Men Afflicted."

The knights of the grip [slang] are never afraid of a railway accident while a baseball team is on board. When it is taken into consideration how infrequent are the accidents to baseball clubs in the face of the amount of traveling done, it can be seen that there is method in the madness of the traveler who waits for the club train.

"Always have the broom the umpire uses to clean the plate, on the opposite side of the batter's box. Never have it between the batter and our bench." Manager Armour is a stickler for this and drills it into his players.

"Never have the bats in front of the bench crossed, and always have their handles pointing towards the bench," is an old superstition. Some players have a certain way of walking to the plate. One may believe it is good luck to walk around the catcher, while another will do just the opposite, but each will do what he thinks is the lucky way.

Pitchers as a rule are superstitious about striking out the first man, considering it an ill omen. Others are bad on the shut-out proposition. It is laughable to watch a pitcher, who doesn't believe in blanking the opposition, trying to have them get a run in the game, when his club has what he considers a commanding lead.

It is impossible to enumerate all the superstitions of the players, but instances mentioned serve to show how strong a hold the belief has on some of them.

Addie was a super superstitious ball player. He wanted locker number 13 in the club house, and he wore a lucky red shirt under his uniform when he was winning. The major leagues in Addie's time required travel on the railways. The Naps' team train derailed, just after midnight on the morning of August 29, 1903, outside of Toledo. Addie's luck held, and he and his teammates managed to escape serious injury. The Cleveland club purchased an insurance policy of $100,000, against injury in the case of train wrecks, in April 1904. And in March 1908, Bill Bradley and Harry Bay were cut by flying glass when someone threw bricks through their Pullman's window.[9] Legend has it that Clark Griffith was so zero-phobic that he would let in a late run in games to avoid the shutout. But the record shows that Griffith twice led his league in whitewashes.

(JANUARY 13, 1908, CP)

One of the first essentials of team work, and one that is absolutely necessary for success on the diamond, is a thorough understanding between the different members of the club. There is only one way in which team work can be successfully attained so that the opposing players will not be able to discover what is going on; that is by the use of signs.

Signs between pitcher and catcher are most common on account of the fact that they are used on every ball pitched.

There are really but two sorts of balls pitched, one being what is called a "fast one" and the other a curve. There are slow balls, too, but what is generally known as an inshoot comes under the head[ing] of fast balls.

Most all battery men have two or more set[s] of signals that they use during the progress of the game. This is to confuse the batter in case the opposing club has a man on second base that is liable to get the sign and tip it off to the batter.

Many times when the pitcher shakes his head at the catcher after receiving the signal for a certain ball he is doing so not because he doesn't want to pitch what certain [batters like?] because he is trying to [word obscured] the batter.

The man at the bat may be weak on a certain ball and know that the pitcher and catcher are aware of the fact. Being weak on this particular style of delivery he is naturally looking for that kind of a ball.

The catcher signals for a ball the batter might hit and the pitcher shakes his head. The batter then thinks the catcher has signaled for a curve he is more liable to meet and when the pitcher shows that he doesn't want to pitch that[,] the man at the plate takes it for granted that he is going to get the other kind of a ball.

The catcher goes down and signs for the same ball again and the pitcher nods as much as to say, "all right."

In reality he is going to pitch the same ball that the backstop first called for and nine times out of ten the batter will stand there and watch one go across the plate, that he would murder under ordinary circumstances.

The battery men work signs in many ways. One most in use is the "waste ball." With a base runner on first — one that is liable to make a break for second — it behooves the pitcher and catcher to keep a strict watch on his movements. He may betray on which ball he is going to make the attempt.

It is taken for granted that the man at bat will also know when the runner is going, so that he may be able to help him along in any way he can.

Sometimes the sign is given by the man at the bat and at other times the base runner is the one to give it.

In order to cover both places the pitcher watches the man at the bat, while the catcher keeps his eyes on the base runner.

If either of them think[s] the play is to [be] attempted on that particular ball, it is made known, and, the sphere is pitched out, so as to prevent the batter from hitting, and also to give the catcher a clear field to throw out the runner.

The second baseman and the shortstop also come into this play to the extent that they decide who is to take the throw, then signal the catcher. The backstop imparts the information to the pitcher and he is thus put on his guard.

Suppose there is a man on first and it has been decided that the shortstop is going to take the throw.

With a right hand batter at the plate it is the pitcher's place to see that he doesn't get a ball inside to the hitter, that is a ball pitched in so close that he can pull it into left field and possibly be able to hit through the place just vacated [by the shortstop].

With a left hand hitter at the plate the ball must be pitched on the inside.

The same is true of the second baseman when he is covering. Of course the pitcher is not letter perfect and he can't always get the ball just where he wants it, but nine times out of ten, when you see the hit and run play pulled off, it's the fault of the man in the box.

There is nothing that can happen that will so quickly take all the fight out of a club as to have a few of its men get caught off the bases. With this fact in view all clubs make it a point to try to perfect a system of signs whereby they will be able to catch these base runners.

With a man on second, it's a common occurrence to see the shortstop and second baseman circling around, as if trying to catch him napping.

Often this is what they are trying to do, but usually their object is to keep the runner as close to the bag as they can, thus giving the outfielders as much chance as possible to head him off at the plate on a base hit.

In these few ways of utilizing signs for team work, I have made no mention of how these signs are given.

With a bench manager the signs are sometimes given from the bench, but more often not, as the members of the opposing club are always studying the bench manager and in order to throw them off guard he has some member of his club giving them and at the same time making a bluff, as though he were directing all the plays.

They may also be worked from the coaching lines, but, as a rule, they are given by the players themselves, especially by those who are directly connected with the play.

Addie's discussion of signals was written in the style of the day's popular baseball periodicals, which included Lajoie's Base Ball Guide. *His clear-minded analysis is muddied by the Cleveland copy editor's inept job in this series of articles. Opponents found it easy to solve second baseman-manager Lajoie's signs to his outfielders—he'd tip off what kind of pitch was coming.*

(JANUARY 20, 1908, CP)

When the great world's series [games] between the Cubs and the White Sox were in progress in 1906, "Cy" Young was "watching" the contests from his home through the medium of the telegraph wires. When the man at the ticker announced the pitchers for one of the games, the big fellow said: "Never mind the pitchers. Who are the men behind the bat?"

No one is so well able to appreciate the fact that on the catcher's judgment and ability to do the right thing at the right time depend[s] the success of a club, as is the man who is pitching to him.

There are a great number of things the pad artist does that are not appreciated by the fans simply because they haven't the opportunity to realize what an important factor the catcher is in the game.

The backstop's work as a rule is not of the spectacular kind, because he doesn't have the chance to make that sort of plays.

About the only chance a catcher gets to make a spectacular play is when he has to go up against the stands for a foul fly, taking a chance of breaking an arm or leg in the effort.

Catchers are only human and can't be blamed if they don't care to make these spectacular plays very often.

Many a good catcher has been hurt in this way. Jack Warner, while a member of the New York Nationals, sustained a broken arm by crashing into the grand stand while going for a foul fly and was out of the game for nearly a whole season as the result of the injury.

The man behind the bat is the one man on a team who is in a position to see every play on the field. He has everything in front of him. He is the field general and can direct the plays as they come up.

Many times during a game the pitcher in fielding a bunt cannot see where the base runners are or how far they may be from the base to which they are going. At a time like this he depends entirely on his catcher, who is in a position to see both the bunt and the base runner, for his instructions as to where to throw the ball when he does get it.

Not only alone [sic.] on bunts must the catcher do this, but also on all short hit balls to either the third baseman or the guardian of the initial sack.

It can therefore readily be seen how important are the catcher's duties in this respect. The rest of the infielders soon learn to rely solely on the backstop's judgment and it's always up to him to see that the right play is tried.

All the signaling is done by the catcher. He decides what the pitcher shall serve to the batter, and while it is optional with the twirler whether or not he wants to pitch this ball, ordinarily he will rely on the catcher's judgment in this respect.

In order for the backstop to readily call for what the batter is less liable to hit, he must necessarily be a close student of the game and one that has the happy faculty of remembering the batter's weaknesses.

When we remember there are about a hundred different players facing the [battery?] during a season, it can readily be seen that the catcher's work in this respect is no joke.

He must remember that every pitcher he catches has a different style of delivery and all twirlers are correspondingly different in effectiveness against the hitters.

What one twirler will find a batter cannot hit will be easy picking for that same hitter when opposed by another pitcher. The catcher must know all these things and never for a moment lose sight of this fact.

In order not to have his team wholly on the defensive all the time, the catcher must be able to know just when the base runner is going and in addition to this must be able to make a good throw to second after "calling the turn" on the runner.

It makes no difference how well the catcher may have planned the play. If the pitcher doesn't perform his part of it in accordance with the plans of the backstop, the play becomes a failure.

The catcher calls the turn on the runner and signals the pitcher to waste the ball. Instead of doing this the twirler puts the ball where the batter can take a swing at it, and even though the batsman is unable to connect with the ball, he can interfere with the catcher's throw.

Nine times out of ten the backstop will make a poor throw, and the people in the stands will yell murder at the catcher, when it was really no fault of his.

Again, the pitcher, instead of getting the ball out where the catcher can easily handle it, will toss it low and inside. This is the hardest kind of ball for the catcher to handle, and still the public expects the man behind the bat to throw out the runner just the same.

Glance over the roster of the four world's champions and you will find thereon the four men who are considered by many unprejudiced critics the best quartet of catchers in the business: [Roger] Bresnahan and [Johnny] Kling in the national, and [Lou] Criger and [Billy] Sullivan in the younger organization.

It's hard to imagine that Cy Young could have a telegraph line, and an operator, in his home. Cait Murphy notes that, in October 1908, "Visitors to farm country report that after a long day in the fields, [Ohio] farmers are driving miles to the nearest telegraph office, to stand around and talk baseball until the operator gives the scores." Addie must mean his Peoli, Ohio, hometown, where they later opened a post office for the express purpose of the retired Hall of Famer to get his fan mail. Addie wrote about Young's catcher, Lou Criger, especially in Chapter 1 articles. William Sullivan's career batting average (.213) was eight points below Criger's, but the defensive stalwart was the first to catch 1,000 games. His son, Billy, Jr., caught in the 1940 World Series for Detroit, after playing briefly with the Indians. John Warner was an outstanding defensive catcher for 14 seasons, his last four in the American League. With the Giants, he led National League catchers in fielding percentage for 1903 and 1904. The injury Addie remembers was probably from Warner's 1900 campaign. Harry Bemis and "Nig" Clarke shared catching duties for the Naps in 1908.

(January 27, 1908, CP)

It will be but a short time now until all the major league teams in the country will be starting south on their training trips, and it will be of interest to the fans to know how the players prepare themselves down in Dixie for the more arduous work to follow.

After signing a contract, the player receives orders from his club owner when and where to report. His spring training commences then and there.

About the first thing a player does is to go up to the attic and look over his baseball paraphernalia. Shoes and gloves are given a thorough saturation with oil or Vaseline, to soften the leather and make these parts of his uniform ready for the work they are to do.

He then packs his clothes and starts to join the club. After a long and tiresome ride, which sometimes takes two and even three days, the team arrives at the training quarters.

The rest of that first day is spent in getting settled in the new quarters, and the following morning, weather permitting, all the men are taken out on the field for the first practice.

The first hour or so is spent in doing nothing but tossing around the ball to get limbered up.

The manager will then [call?] on some of his numerous twirlers, usually one of the youngsters, to go out on the rubber and hand in a few to the hitters.

After about a half hour's work at this, the men will assume their regular positions on the field. Someone will hit to them and the usual practice work, always seen just before the commencement of a championship game, is gone through with for another half hour, at the conclusion of which the men are sent back to the hotel.

About the third or fourth day, the manager will call all the men together for a little talk, the purpose of which is to outline a plan of work which is to be followed for the rest of spring training.

It can readily be seen that if there is not some change made in the daily work it soon becomes very monotonous to the men. Most everyone on a team has a different method of getting himself in condition and it depends on the man what this sort of work will be.

The veterans, as a rule, take things easy for the first week, contenting themselves with trying to get in condition to stand the harder work which is to follow.

Some will run around the park a few times each morning and afternoon. Others will go out to the outfield and have someone hit fly balls to them and chase until one would think they would drop from exhaustion.

One of the easiest and best ways for a man to get in shape is to have someone hit short ground balls to him. This is about the best way there is of getting off weight.

Anyone who has never had experience in this line of work would be surprised at the manner in which this form of exercise brings every muscle of the body into play. A couple of weeks of this style of training soon gets the men in the finest condition imaginable.

As a means of diversion the manager will pick a team from his surplus men and pit them against the regulars and a game of five or seven innings will often be played.

Here is where all the new plays that are to be used during the regular season are tried and perfected.

Sometimes a whole day is spent in this way. Runners will be stationed on the bases with instructions to try by any means they may devise to get to the plate, and the regulars will play their hardest to prevent this.

A lot of good natured rivalry enters these contests and on account of this they are, to say the least, very interesting. There is nothing that the second team so much enjoys as to defeat the first team, and in order to do this they will play their hardest.

While the Cleveland club was in Macon last spring Doc Payne introduced the medicine ball, and the players soon found that throwing the great sphere was one of the finest things known to start perspiration.

"Nig" Clarke had a football on the grounds every day and when the men became tired of the daily routine of work on the field some of them would get down in one corner of the grounds and soon an impromptu game of association football would be going merrily on.

The players have little time to themselves while off the field on one of these trips, and are usually so tired when night comes that they are perfectly willing to sit around the hotel until bedtime.

All members of the club are expected to be in the dining room by 8 o'clock in the morning, and are usually sent out to the field by 9.

Baseball players are generally irritable, and this part of their makeup is more apparent in the spring than at any other time of the year.

This is no doubt caused by the fact that: after a winter spent in resting, the muscles of the body are in no shape to withstand the rigors of a hard training and, naturally, the players are sore in mind as well as in body.

An important factor in a team's success in getting in shape is the trainer. When a club is fortunate enough to have a first-class man to handle them, the work of the men is lessened to a perceptible degree.

This man has no snap [slang]. There are usually from 20 to 30 players taken on a training trip, and, while all of them do not care to be handled by the trainer every day, still he has at least half of these to take care of twice a day.

The Cleveland club is fortunate in having one of the best trainers in the country. Doc Payne is the man and he certainly knows how to get athletes in condition.

Doc has plenty of experience in work of this kind, as he used to be sparring partner for "Kid" McCoy and Bob Fitzsimmons.

Besides being a first-class man in his line of work, the genial doctor has the happy faculty of being one of the best entertainers a person could find in a day's travel.

Addie reported to training camp in 1905 at 215 pounds, as much as 30 pounds above his playing weight, and had to sweat them off in the New Orleans sun. The Cleveland Press, *April 2, 1907, ran a photo across the top of page 10 showing Addie, on a spring training field, kicking (perhaps a change in routine?) a medicine ball in a line with Harry Bemis, "Bunk" Congalton, and Bob Rhoads. The aptly named trainer is Dr. James E. Payne, a Cleveland-born physician who gave up his practice for a career in boxing. His record, as a middleweight, is 12 wins (10 KOs), 11 losses (8 KOs), and five no decisions. The close associate and sparring partner of Charles "Kid" McCoy was the Naps' trainer for 1905. James Payne took his own life only five years later.*

(FEBRUARY 3, 1908, CP)

Ask the average man or woman which is the hardest position in the infield to play, and the answer will be: "They are all hard." And so they are, but the position more trying than all the rest is third base.

The third-sacker can't come in too close to play for bunts. If he does, the batter will, instead of laying the ball down, hit it out, and if he happens to drive the ball fairly hard in the direction of third, and not directly at the guardian of that corner, it gets by and goes for a base hit.

With a batter on first and no one out, the third baseman must move in on the grass in order to be in a position to get the bunt.

If the man at the bat lays one down, the third-sacker must come tearing in and get the ball in time to force the runner at second, if he can. If he is unable to get his man there, he must throw out the runner going to first.

With a fast left-handed batsman at the plate, the third baseman has not only his position to play, but at the same time he must be able to go over and get all short-hit balls in the direction of the shortstop. If he waits for the shortstop to come in to handle these kind of hits, it's better than a two to one shot that the batter will be safe at first.

One of the hardest situations a third baseman encounters is when a fast man is on second with no one or one man out and a good bunter at the bat.

He never knows just what sort of a trick these two men will attempt to pull off and consequently must be constantly on the alert in order not to be caught unawares.

Another play in which a third baseman has to perfect himself is the one where there are men on second and first, with no one out, and the man at the bat bunts.

In this play the third sacker is usually between the devil and the deep sea, for if the man bunts along the third base line, he must start in to get the ball. If he sees the pitcher is going to handle the ball, he must tear back to third to cover the bag, so the heaver can toss the ball there and force out the runner.

Bill Coughlin is seen at his best on hard hit balls and in this respect has no superior and few if any equal him in Ban Johnson's organization. He is fine on ground balls and plays bunts with excellent judgment.

Jimmy Collins is without doubt the most graceful third baseman that ever donned a uniform. He makes the hardest kind of a chance look easy.

Lee Tannehill, who up to last season covered third for the White Sox, is one of the finest fielding third basemen in the business.

"Tanny" had the misfortune to be spiked in a game at St. Louis early last season. [Lee] Quillan [sic] and [George] Rohe alternated at third and both of them played good ball at this position.

Quillan can recover himself after knocking down a hard hit ball as quickly as any one I ever saw.

In speaking of that peerless third baseman, Bill Bradley, my comments may be a trifle more of a glowing nature than they would be were he and I not on the same club.

Fielding bunts is his one great specialty. He never comes in on the grass to get these little love taps.

No matter how fast a man may be, or how well he can lay them down, Bill always plays back for him. This is a great advantage to his team, as by doing so he protects his territory, so that it is possible for the batter to cross him and hit one through there.

Brad can sacrifice as good as any man in the business. Taking everything into consideration it is hard to see where one can get a third baseman that will have anything on Bill. I have always contended and still think that Brad is not only the best third baseman in the American league, but one of the grandest ball players that ever wore a pair of spiked shoes.

In a game in 1905, Addie played third base for the Naps, cleanly handling two chances. Nicknamed after his Pennsylvania hometown, "Scranton Bill"

Coughlin is an eccentric choice to lead off (above the immortal Jimmy Collins) Addie's somewhat selective lineup of crack third basemen. He was a regular at the hot corner, for Washington and Detroit, over the first eight years of American League play. Addie also watched his work in the first two Tigers' World Series. Leon "Lee" Quillen's glove wasn't enough to keep him in the major leagues. He hit an even .200, in his 160 at-bats, with Chicago, in 1906 and 1907. "Whitey" Rohe was a utility player for his three years in Chicago, and finished up his major league career in 1907. Bill Bradley was always a great fielder, even when his batting skills were fading.

(October 22, 1908, TNB and CP)

How many times does one hear the expression in regard to certain pitchers: "I can't for the life of me see how he gets away with his games. Why, he hasn't a thing"?

To a good many fans, and especially those who are not close students of the game, the pitcher who is not blessed with tremendous speed and a fast breaking curve ball is always called lucky whenever he wins a game.

In reality the twirler who can win consistently and who is not fortunate enough to have been endowed with the natural ability some of his more fortunate fellow pitchers possess, is entitled to at least as much if not more credit, than is the other slabster.

In order to accomplish the same results he must have developed something which he can use that will even up his effectiveness, to the same standard of the other twirler.

This is usually accomplished by three things: control, a change of pace, and last of all, plenty of nerve. A pitcher of this class is termed, by the baseball fraternity, "a mixer."

By this is meant a pitcher who is constantly mixing them up on the batter. Not relying on tremendous speed nor a good curve ball, but one who is depending for his success on the fact that he can pitch what the batter is not looking for.

One of the greatest examples of the successful twirler of this type is none other than Clark Griffith, who for years, was a top notcher.

"Griff" never was accused of having enough speed to knock the mitt off the catcher's hand nor did he have a wonderful curve ball, still he managed to win a handsome percentage of his games every year simply because he knew how to pitch and had the nerve to hand up a slow one any time he thought he could outguess the batter with it.

There are any number of major league pitchers who depend on this style of work to win their games and they are about as hard to beat as anyone.

Instead of being called lucky they should be given credit for the wonderful work they accomplish and are to be complimented for the advantage they have taken of a few things nature has endowed them with, thus putting them on an equal footing with their fellow twirlers who have more natural ability.

Addie's equivalent of a canned speech is a column on junkball pitching. Jack Pfiester was the slowball specialist at the recently concluded World Series, but Addie returns to his on-going consideration of Clark Griffith's sleight of hand. (Perhaps Addie is largely concerned here with fulfilling his quota of post–Series columns for the Press?) Griffith's luck, if you want to call it that, held up for a career .619 winning percentage over 20 seasons.[10] He was the White Sox' best pitcher in 1901, when he led the league in winning percentage and led the team to the very first American League championship. (Clark Griffith's luck would seem to run out, however, when Jack Chesbro's wild pitch, in the final game of the season, denied his Highlanders the 1904 pennant.)

(October 23, 1908, CP)

Few lovers of baseball realize the meaning of the word nerve on the field. The general impression seems to be that the man who appears to feel he can defeat the opposition, and has no hesitancy in saying so, is the one possessed with nerve.

While it is a good thing to have confidence in one's ability to do certain things that are required to win games, there is more to the meaning of the word nerve than this alone.

If the man who fears the opposition and realizes its strength and knows he must be able to give his club the best he has to win, can go in and triumph, he must be given credit for possessing real "sand."

There is always a place in every game where some player is called on to show whether or not he is made of the right kind of stuff.

A striking example of this was shown during the world's series. Pitcher

[Mordecai] Brown of the Cubs was called on to make a play that required nerve, and lots of it, and right nobly did he respond.

With the score 2 to 0 in the Cubs' favor, Detroit had men on second and first with no one out. [Ty] Cobb laid down a perfect bunt along the third base line. Brown came in like a flash, and fielding the ball perfectly, wheeled and threw the sphere to [Harry] Steinfeldt at third, forcing [Charley] O'Leary at that station.

Had Brown hesitated the fraction of a second, or thrown the ball the least bit badly, every one would have been safe, and the bases full with no one out.

Roger Bresnahan, the Giant's great backstop, last year clearly demonstrated that he is made of the right kind of stuff. After being hit in the head by a pitched ball late in the season, an injury that nearly ruined his baseball career, he came right back and hit at a fine pace for [John] McGraw and his team the rest of the campaign and continued it this year.

After getting a wallop such as Roger received, most anyone would have been "plate-shy," but not so with Bresnahan. He simply would not be driven away from the plate. It takes some nerve to face a pitcher three or four times a day all season after being handed a jolt like that.

Geo. Stovall of the Naps is another example of what nerve will do for a man. The big first baseman has had his left wrist broken twice by trying to get badly thrown balls, which forced him to go after them directly in the path of the runner.

One would naturally think after two such experiences, Stovall would play them safe and duck any chance of a collision. But it has made George all the more determined to get those bad throws, and no one ever saw him step aside and give the runner the right of way.

What takes as much nerve, probably, as anything a player has to face, is to have the home crowd get after him. A man who can stand for the abuse handed out by the home bleachers day after day and in the end win them over is to be admired.

Grover Land showed Bill Armour that he had plenty of nerve in a game at Minneapolis one day two seasons ago. The local team was giving a fine exhibition of club swinging all day. Finally with a couple of men on bases, a situation where a hit would win the game, Armour looked around for a man to send in to hit for the pitcher.

He cast his eye up and down the bench, but before he could pick his man, Grover grabbed his bat and said: "Bill, let me go up there, I can hit this fellow."

Of course, Bill let him go. He made good, but whether he did or not, it showed he had the nerve to try.

These incidents show that it takes something besides natural ability for a player to make good in a pinch, and the fellow who can deliver, when called upon to do so, is the one you have to hand it to for having the nerve.

Three Finger Brown's play was a highlight of Game Four of the 1908 World Series. The wonder is that the game's greatest overall player bunted, with nobody out and his team about to lose its third game in the series. Brown went on to shut out the Tigers on four hits that day. Bresnahan was limited to 95 games behind the plate in the year of his beaning, and 1908 was his last season as a regular. Slick-fielding George Stovall was known for his nerve, both on and off the field. He once struck his own manager, "Larry" Lajoie, over the head with an oak chair, and it was "Firebrand" who threatened a team strike when Ban Johnson wanted the Naps to play on the day of Addie Joss' funeral. Grover Cleveland Land was hitting for his Toledo Mud Hens in a contest against the Millers. After appearing in 95 games with the Naps over five seasons in six years, Land landed the regular catching job for his two Federal League seasons with Brooklyn. Note that the term "pinch," meaning in the clutch, was not yet specifically applied to pinch hitting.

(October 27, 1908, TNB and CP)

"What is the reason left hand batters find it so hard to successfully hit left hand pitchers?" is a question one often hears asked.

After seeing a few of the star southpaws working against a club of left hand hitters it is plain why this question so often comes up.

As a rule the port side hurler invariably makes the left hand batter look like he was tied to a post.

There are two explanations for this. One is because no club has more than two southpaws, who are worked regularly, on its payroll, while most of them have only one and some have none at all.

This gives the left hand batter but little chance to hit against a side wheeler. That is, he sees one about every four days and sometimes not as often.

Not having much of a chance to hit against this style of pitching it is only natural that when an off side sticker does get a crack at a left hander he is usually lost.

When facing a right hand twirler the left hand hitter has the advantage of knowing that every time the flinger hands up a curve ball it is going to break in toward him. With a southpaw in the reverse is the case.

One thing every batter does, and an act which is perfectly natural, is to pull a little as soon as the pitcher starts to deliver the ball.

By this is meant, stepping back just a little, so that in case the ball is in close, the batter can step back and hit it, or he can step aside and let it go without being hit by the ball.

The best hitters in the business do this and no matter who the man is he will naturally pull a little.

With a left hand pitcher on the slab and one whose curve ball, instead of breaking in to a left hand batter, breaks out and away from him, this act of pulling just about ruins his chances of ever hitting this sort of ball successfully.

Anytime a southpaw can keep his curve ball low and over the outside corner of the plate, to a left hand batter, it's a pretty tough job for the man at the plate to get many drives into safe territory.

There are a few port side batters who can hit the southpaw successfully. "Matty" McIntyre, of the Tigers, hits them just as hard as he does the right hand flingers, but as a rule most left handers are practically helpless when facing a side wheeler.

Richard Smiley finds that Mathew McIntyre became one of the best left-handed hitters against southpaws after he deliberately took batting practices against lefties during the 1905 season. With Detroit in 1908, McIntyre hit .295 and scored a league-best 105 runs.

(October 29, 1908, TNB and CP)

What is more spectacular on the diamond than the view of an outfielder cutting across the field on the dead run, picking up the fast bounding sphere and without stopping to hesitate the fraction of a second, throw the ball to the plate in time to nip a base runner, trying to score from second on the hit?

The act of throwing men out at the plate on hits of this kind is always appreciated by the spectators, no matter whether the feat is accomplished by a home player or a member of the opposition.

Any time an outfielder does throw a man out at the plate he is sure to come in for more than the ordinary amount of applause from the spectators and the critics.

While there is no question in regard to the merit of the play, and, while the player is entitled to receive all the credit given him, few realize that there are more men directly connected with the play than the results show.

Everyone who understands baseball and attends a fair share of the games, must have often noticed the shortstop and second baseman continually hovering around the second station when there is a runner on base.

Very seldom, if ever, do they catch anyone napping and at first sight it would seem a waste of time and energy to keep up this sort of maneuvering.

By so doing, however, they force the runner to stay close to the bag. That is, he is constantly in fear of being caught and in order to be on the safe side must keep close enough to the base, so that he can return there easily in case of a throw.

When a base hit is made on which he should score, he still has another obstacle to face. This is in rounding third base. A third sacker who is in the game every minute, will always force the runner to go out around him in a play of this kind.

Instead of giving the runner a clear field, he will stand directly on the inside of the bag, forcing the base runner to make quite a long turn to get by him.

When it is taken into consideration the number of times a man is nipped at the plate by inches, it can readily be seen that there is something to the play besides the outfielder's throw.

This type of routine interference was facilitated in those days by the deployment of only one umpire on the bases and one behind home plate. In the 1890s, the umpire-baiting Orioles and Spiders took ever more blatant advantage of the lonely ump.

(October 30, 1908, TNB)

How many times during the season does one see plays pulled off on the field which, after completion, make some certain player look very bad?

No matter who this unfortunate player may be, he is sure to come in for his share of criticism from the fans. Often it may appear as though he was really responsible for the mistake, when, as a matter of fact, it might not have been his fault at all.

Just as an illustration: In a game between Cleveland and the Highlanders at League park last summer. New York had men on first and second, with no one out.

The Highlanders were but one run to the good at this stage, and it looked like dollars to doughnuts that the man at the bat was going to sacrifice.

I happened to be pitching the game, and, as "Nig" Clarke gave me the signal to pitch, I took a look around towards second to see what sort of a lead the man there was taking.

Just as I turned my head, or possibly a little before, Larry [Lajoie] gave "Nig" the sign that he was going over to try to catch the man napping. This was a tip for Clarke to call a waste ball, so as to keep the batter from making a play on that pitch.

On account of the fact that I had my head turned to watch the man at second, "Nig" was unable to impart this information to me, and, when I handed up the ball and the man bunted down the first base line, we were all crossed.

[First baseman George] Stovall came in to field the ball, figuring to throw it to Larry at first, but Larry had gone to second to take "Nig's" expected throw. This left first base uncovered, and, naturally, the batter reached first in safety, filling the bases, with no one out.

Most everyone took it for granted that the "Big Frenchman" had lost the play for us, when, in reality, "Nig" and I were the ones at fault.

George Perring came in for a lot of criticism early last season in a game against Detroit, for which he really was not to blame. It happened in this manner: With the score a tie in the ninth, we had men on first and second, with one out.

Perring was on second, and, when the batter hit a ground ball between third and short, George started for third. [Third baseman Bill] Coughlin went after the ball, and at first it looked as though he would get it.

Perring figured he would, and, in order to block an easy double play, he stopped, so that the Tigers' third baseman would be forced to make the difficult double by throwing to second and then having the ball relayed to first.

Had he gone on he would have given Coughlin a chance to touch him with the ball between the bases, which would have resulted in an easy double at first. The third-sacker, however, booted the ball, and by the time Perring recovered and started for third again, Coughlin managed to get the horsehide, and, in the race for the bag, beat George by a stride.

There was considerable comment on the play by the fans, and Perring was severely criticized for his apparent lack of judgment.

Just a couple of incidents like this go to show that many a time when a man does something which looks bad, he is only doing what anyone would do under the same circumstances.

George Perring, not especially known for his baserunning, was a utility infielder in a brief career with the Naps and George Stovall's Federal League club. He was the shortstop for Addie's perfect game.

(OCTOBER 31, 1908, CP AND NOVEMBER 7, 1908, TNB)

The high art of touching base runners, a feature of baseball that is generally overlooked by most fans, means a whole lot to any team that has an infielder skilled in this department of the game.

How many times is an umpire hooted by the fans for calling a man safe at second, on an attempted steal, when the catcher's throw reaches there in plenty of time to get the runner? The "ump" is generally right, because the infielder fails to touch the runner, the arbitrator being directly on top of the play, is able to render the right decision.

Some infielders have the art of touching a runner down to such a point that it is almost impossible for a man to get away without being tagged.

Then there are others who never learn to properly tag a man on the paths, and the loss of more than one game during a season can be directly traced to this lack of skill.

It's a pretty tough thing for the infielder to be directly in the way of a fast coming base runner, who he knows is going to slide into the bag feet first, and at the same time set himself to catch the ball and put it on the man as he is about to hit the dirt.

Bobby Wallace of the St. Louis Browns never seems to get hurt or spiked in a play of this kind, and yet very seldom, if ever, does anyone get away from him.

Bob plays a throw a little different than most infielders. When he sets himself for a throw he straddles the bag: that is, he stands directly over the base with his feet spread far enough apart to insure him secure footing.

In doing this he forces the base runner to slide directly in front of him, as it is the only way the runner can reach the base, and naturally, if Bob gets the throw in time, all he has to do is to tag his man.

Anyone who is afraid of getting spiked will never be overly successful at touching runners. And it's the man who forgets all about the danger of the play that usually gets away without a scratch.

The one they called "Mr. Shortstop" was indeed durable: from 1899, when he was moved to shortstop, through the 1912 season, he played an average of 133 games a year. His 17 chances in a game, on June 10, 1902, set the league record for the position. Addie must have witnessed the serious spiking which shortened Lajoie's 1905 season (blood poisoning), and led to the rule requiring players to wear sanitary white stockings under their team-color stirrups.

(NOVEMBER 3, 1908, TNB AND CP)

There is probably nothing in baseball that so quickly takes the life out of a club, than to have a man or two caught off the bases. With this fact in view every club tries to perfect itself in this department of the game.

It's a delicate matter and in order to be pulled off successfully must be worked to the queen's taste by everyone directly connected with the play.

When the play is properly made it causes the man who is unfortunate enough to be caught, to look cheap.

To the spectator, there usually appears but two men who are directly connected with the play, when in reality the pitcher has as much, if not more to do with it, than any of the other players.

This is especially true where the catcher throws to one of the bases to catch a man napping.

The infielder usually gives the catcher the sign that he is going to attempt the play, but often the backstop signals the baseman to this effect.

The pitcher is next tipped off on what is coming, and knowing what is expected he must pitch the ball where it will be easy for the catcher to handle and at the same time, such a distance away from the batter that it is impossible for him to hit the ball.

This gives the catcher a clear field for his throw and also prevents the man at the bat from hitting the ball and spoiling the attempted play.

It can readily be seen that if the pitcher does not keep the ball out or away from the hitter what a swell chance the man at the bat has to not only break up the attempted play, but at the same time to hit through the spot vacated by the infielder.

The infielder must start for the base as soon as the pitcher starts to deliver the ball and consequently this spot is left open.

If the ball is not pitched out it would be a snap for the hitter to push the sphere through the open spot.

[Mordecai] Brown, [Johnny] Kling and [Joe] Tinker pulled off the play on Sam Crawford in the fourth game of the [1908] world's series at Detroit, when they picked the Tigers' slugger off second.

It was a swell play all around and while most of the glory of the play went to Kling and Tinker, Brown must not be overlooked, as he made the play a success by the manner in which he handed the ball to Kling.

A play of this kind often makes a lot of difference in the result of a game and any time a club can put one of these kind over in a pinch the chances are better than even that it will win.

"Wahoo" Sam Crawford was the complete player. He hit for double figures in triples for 17 seasons in a row and stole 41 bases in 1912. He was good in the outfield, too—he sometimes played center field in place of Ty Cobb, whose own fielding is immortalized by Richard Bak's terrific title, Cobb Would Have Caught It.

(NOVEMBER 4, 1908, CP)

From a spectator standpoint, sliding head first into a base has the call [colloquial]; but from any other way one may look at it, the fellow who jumps into a base with his spikes towards the man covering, has it all over the other man.

There are several reasons for this. Probably the one which causes most everyone to slide feet first nowadays is the fact that it not only lessens the chances of the one sliding to be hurt, but, at the same time, causes the man who is covering the base to be ever ready to get out of the way of the spikes.

But let the infielder once be assured that the base runner is coming in head first, and he will stand directly in his way, knowing that even should the man bump into him there will hardly be any chance of his getting hurt.

Harry Bemis of the Cleveland club nearly put a Southern leaguer out of the business a few years ago, simply because he was forced to block him as he tried to slide into the home plate.

It happened in Birmingham, in an exhibition game the Naps were playing with the Southern league club of that place.

Some young fellow, who had just joined the Coal Barons, singled. He immediately stole second and third. Bemis paid little attention to him, but when he started to try to steal home Harry thought it was time something was done.

He was one of those fresh young fellows who was always there with the "kidding stuff." The way he was going around the bases it was even money he would steal the ball if not watched closely.

He finally made the break for the plate. The ball was thrown low and on the inside so Bemis was forced to get down on his knees to block the ball.

Harry picked up the sphere, and instead of getting up, just remained there waiting for his man. He slid head first and when his cranium came in contact, with Harry's knee it stopped him about as quickly as it would had he been hit on the head with a bat.

Bemis was not even so much as jarred, but that young fellow learned a lesson about sliding that day that he will never forget.

The famous practitioner of the head-first slide in the American League was Addie's teammate Terry Turner; in the National League, it was Giants first baseman Fred Merkle. Merkle was born in Watertown, Wisconsin, eight years after Addie's birth nearby. Addie probably first saw the younger player when Merkle was a pitcher in Toledo, where he played high school and semi-pro ball with teams like the 1905 Shamrocks. The two were teammates on the Cuban tour of 1909. The game in Birmingham would not have been played in famous Rickwood Field, the oldest minor league park still in use. Rickwood, whose design was influenced by Shibe Park and Forbes Field, was constructed in 1910.

(NOVEMBER 5, 1908, TNB AND CP)

"You fellows certainly deserve a lot of credit for the way you keep up your nerve in front of such large crowds," is a remark often heard by many ball players.

To the spectator it may seem that it takes a lot of sand to be able to play at top speed in front of crowds that number thousands. While this is true, the actual work of playing the game is nothing compared to the strain on the players' nerves before the contest.

In races such as the American and National league had last season, no one who has never had a similar experience can begin to realize what an awful strain the players are under.

In order for a player to be able to give his club the best there is in him, it is necessary for him to be keyed up to about 99 per cent of his full energy all the time.

This is especially true when he is on the field. Between games it would seem that he then has an opportunity of relaxing a little, but such is not the case.

The moment one game is over the player begins to figure on the next day's contest and the more he thinks of it the more he is sure to worry.

It's not particularly agreeable to go to bed at night, when one is sorely in need of a rest, and be unable to close an eye.

To lie there and toss until the small hours of the morning, seeing nothing but baseball in all its varied forms, is not conducive to much rest, and even though a fellow does finally fall into a fitful slumber, it is better than even money he will dream something about the great pastime.

One wakes up in the morning feeling fully as tired as when one went to bed. Then there is the long wait until it is time to go out to the grounds for the game.

This is especially irksome owing to the lack of anything to do but to wait for the time to pass. There is nothing quite so hard as this.

To make it worse, there are always a lot of fans who want to sit around and tell you how hard it is going to be to beat your opponents that day — a fact that you know, possibly, better than anyone.

The actual playing of the contest may be hard, but it is a pleasure compared to the waiting between games. Any warrior will tell you that he would rather be in the battle than be obliged to stand the suspense of waiting for the next day's contest.

This is what I meant when I wrote, in the section on "Baseball Humor," about Addie being a sensitive man. Pressure from the press and frustrated fans lasted through the Hot Stove months for a player like him. The Cleveland Press *version of the article cuts the opening paragraph. Attendance at League Park for 1908, the year of a memorable pennant race, was 422,262. That's about 5,484 in the house for the average home game, not a big crowd unless you're remembering Cleveland Municipal Stadium in 1983.*

(NOVEMBER 6, 1908, TNB)

Most everyone who is not familiar with the inside workings of baseball invariably have the impression that the manager of the club gives the players implicit instructions in regard to what to do when at the bat.

The idea is generally accepted when a man steps to the plate with runners on the bases and it is a question as to what course the batter is to pursue.

While it is true that the batter usually receives instructions before going to bat, it is also a fact that the nature of the play tried by him must often be changed after he has faced the pitcher.

This change is caused by something that may have occurred, which was not apparent when he first stepped into the box.

Usually the manager will say to the man going to bat: "Use your own judgment." In cases of this kind he is wholly dependent on the ability of the batter to do the right thing at the right time for the success of the play, and any time the man is fortunate enough to get a away with whatever he may try, the credit should go as much to the player as to his manager.

As a demonstration of this kind of work I can mention a play, which won the Cleveland club a game from Boston on the Red Sox's last trip to the Forest City.

With the score a tie in the last half of the ninth, Cleveland had men on first and second with no one out. The logical play seemed to be for [George] Stovall, who was at bat, to sacrifice.

Larry [Lajoie] was on first at the time and could not instruct the big first baseman as to what he wanted him to do.

The entire Boston infield was looking for a bunt and played accordingly. Third and first basemen were drawn way in while shortstop was over near second to take any throw that might come there and the second baseman was well over toward first to cover that base.

Instead of doing the conventional, Stovall swung hard on the first ball pitched and fouled it. The entire Boston team took it for granted he was merely doing this for a bluff and would lay down the next offering.

George crossed them again and this time instead of fouling the ball he planted a pretty single to center which scored [Bill] Hinchman from second with the winning run.

Somebody asked Stovall, in the clubhouse after the game, why he did not bunt and George replied that he did, but he also added, by way of explanation, "I had no chance to bunt in the infield because it was playing in so close, so I bunted to the outfield."

Since it's my call, I rule that Addie's inside analysis of the plate appearance is more relevant than George Stovall's quip—so this article is safe at home in "The Insider Game" section. The baseball game is Addie's shutout, over Cy Young and the Red Sox, on September 17. Outfielder Bill Hinchman's 16 triples in 1916 would lead the National League. Note that there is no mention of any system of hand signals from the bench or coaches' boxes in this Deadball game.

Next up, Addie considers the old practice of players taking turns as first and third base coaches.

(NOVEMBER 7, 1908, TNB AND CP)

Of all things a ball player is compelled to do, that to which he has the most aversion is to be sent out on the third base coaching line.

No one objects over going to first to coach, as there are very few plays that arise there which need much advice from the coacher. At third it is a different proposition.

On every play where a man is trying to score from second on a hit to the outfield, especially where it is going to be close at the plate, the base runner invariably relies on the coacher's judgment.

The runner is forced to seek advice in plays of this kind, as he is in no position to see the ball, when running as fast as he can with his back to the play.

Any time the play goes wrong, which it often does, the poor coacher is blamed by the fans for his apparent lack of judgment.

If he sends the base runner through and an out is recorded at the plate, he is blamed and on the other hand, if he stops him and the throw home happens to be a little bad, everyone in the stands will arise and yell "bonehead" at him.

Then again, if a man happens to be caught napping at second it's the coacher's fault. No matter how often he may have yelled to the base runner to get back to the bag and tried in every way to warn him of his danger. Still, if the opposition manage to nab the sleepy runner, it's all the fault of the man coaching at third.

With a crowd of 10,000 people all yelling as hard as they can, does anyone imagine it possible for the base runner to hear the coacher trying to advise him to be careful?

There are a good many times when it is only a question of judgment as to whether or not a coacher shall send a man home. The chances are that anyone else would have done the same thing, but if the runner is caught everybody can immediately see where it would have been better to have held him at third.

No matter what he does and it fails to go right, the coacher has to stand for a lot of criticism. Even should the man reach the plate in safety he (the coacher) is never even thought of as having had anything to do with the play.

The best he gets is the worst of it. Thus it can be seen that it is a task that every player hates to have assigned to him.

The Cleveland Press *version of this article was edited down to seven paragraphs. The decision to hire a professional coach was taken in 1909, when the Giants' John McGraw hired Arlie Latham. McGraw may have surprised baseball people: Latham's nickname was "The Freshest Man on Earth." (He could be a champion disrupter, from the coaching box. Spider Jimmy McAleer once became so enraged at Latham, then with the Reds, that he chased him across the field with a bat).[11] Latham was also the man who played forever. At age 49, he became the oldest player to steal a base. Early in Latham's mock-epic career, he earned a footnote in Cleveland baseball history when he hit the first home run in League Park. (He was awarded a box of cigars for the longest Reds hit of the day off Cy Young.)*

(NOVEMBER 11, 1908, CP)

Any time Clark Griffith, the ex-manager of the Highlanders, who seems certain to be manager of the Cincinnati team next season, commences to tell anything about the pitching end of the national game, everyone sits up and listens.

The "old fox" was one of the greatest pitchers the game ever saw, and, naturally, whatever he may say on the subject of pitching is always received with considerable attention.

"Griff," with a party of friends, was doing a little fanning [colloquial] at Chicago during the world's series, and during the course of the conversation the subject of pitching came up.

"Never let a weak hitter get away from you," was "Griff's" advice. "I found in my experience that it always pays to work your hardest on the fellow who is not supposed to hit. Don't make the mistake of holding him cheaply.

"If you do, he will sneak in a base hit on you, and, possibly, before you are aware of it, there will be a couple of men on the bases, with a good hitter coming up. Then you try to get the good hitter, and find that you have not enough stuff to put him on the shelf; and before you know what has happened they have you beaten."

"The same theory holds good when you are managing a club," continued Griffith. "Always make it a point to play your hardest against the weaker clubs. Those are the teams you are supposed to beat easily, and a game against them counts just as much as does one won from a team that is fighting you for the lead."

It seems that Addie's Cleveland editors are limiting him to five- or six-paragraph columns these weeks. Clark Griffith holding forth in a hotel lobby is a reliable Joss bromide, and he spends half of his allotted paragraphs clearing his throat.

(NOVEMBER 14, 1908, CP)

What probably wins more games than any other thing in baseball is the unexpected. By that is meant doing something for which the opposition is not looking.

Any club that plays a conventional style of a game never will win a pennant. If a club is playing the game "according to Hoyle" [colloquial] it won't be long before every other team around the circuit will be "wise" to the fact, and once this is known, good-by chances for the flag.

If a team bunts every time it gets a man on first with no one out early in the game, it's a cinch that it won't be long before the other clubs will be "laying for" just such a play.

Who would ever expect a pitcher to steal a base and thereby win a ball game? This is what "Dusty" Rhoads did against Philadelphia in a game at Cleveland a few seasons ago.

"Dusty" was on first, with one out, in the ninth. Cleveland was a run behind. The batter had two strikes and no balls. No one ever dreamed that Rhoads would try to steal.

Catcher [Ossee] Schreck[engost] of the Athletics must have figured the same way. On the next ball pitched, the Nap twirler made a break for second. The man at the bat swung and missed, and was out, but "Dusty" stole second easily, and scored the tying run a few moments later when [Harry] Bay singled to right.

Bob Rhoads' given name isn't what you'd expect, either: it's Barton Emory Rhoads. With Cleveland, the pitcher stole two bases a season, in 1905, 1907, and 1908; seven in his eight-year career. Addie is recalling the game of May 24, 1905. Joss is credited with 10 steals lifetime. Both Rhoads and Addie knew something about pitchers who stole bases. In the fifth inning of a game on May 7, 1906, Detroit pitcher Bill Donovan stole home against their Naps, after stealing second and third. "Wild Bill" had stolen home on Cleveland the previous season, too. Addie's friend Win Mercer was the first pitcher to swipe home in the twentieth century. Edmund Hoyle's (born 1672) book of rules for indoor games is the source for this colloquialism.

(November 20, 1908, TNB)

It takes a lot of nerve to play football; and it takes a little sand to play baseball, too.

One often reads about some gridiron warrior who played a part of a game, and sometimes the entire contest, with a broken rib, dislocated collar bone, or other painful and occasionally dangerous injuries.

There is no denying that it takes grit to do this, and the player who accomplishes feats of this kind is to be highly commended for the nerve he displays.

At the same time, the football player is not alone in the field when it comes to doing things along this line.

There are times during a season when ball players display an amount of nerve in staying at their posts which compares favorably with anything shown by their football brethren.

Very few cases of this nature ever come before the public, unless they are of a very serious nature, as the players' injuries are always kept within the secrecy of the clubhouse.

A grand example of grit on the ball field was shown by Billy Sullivan of the White Sox when he went to Cleveland and caught the last game of the season of 1908 there.

Bill stopped the slants and shoots of [Frank] Smith and [Ed] Walsh in that memorable battle with the thumb of his throwing hand split badly, and one could lay a lead pencil in the orifice of the wound.

In this game Sullivan hardly ever tried to catch a thrown ball unless there were men on the bases.

Harry Bemis caught a double-header for the Naps at New York the day [Bill] Bradley had his arm broken, a couple of seasons ago, when he should have been in bed instead.

All the Cleveland catchers were out of the game with the exception of Harry, and he gamely stuck on the job. His right leg was swollen so badly from bruises and bumps that he did most of the work on one leg.

He was in such bad shape that it was impossible for him to go ten feet away from the plate for foul flies.

Numerous instances of this kind could be mentioned, and nearly every player in the business has, at some time or other in his career, shown real grit.

This proved a decisive loss for Cleveland, before an overflow home crowd of 20,729, in the race for the 1908 pennant. On October 3, Ed Walsh relieved Frank Smith and won a 3 to 2 decision by striking out Lajoie. The bases were loaded with Naps, requiring poor Sullivan to catch the ball. Walsh had pitched a complete game on the previous day, as Addie's opponent in his perfecto. Addie Joss was sometimes accused of being on the fragile side, in the era when the Walshes and Chesbros and McGinnitys were setting the standard for starting pitchers. Frank Smith was a college boy from Grove City College, in western Pennsylvania. He pitched two no-hitters and led the American League in strikeouts in 1909. Neyer and James list Frank Smith's good curveball as his second pitch, after his spitter. All those spitballs dropping into the mud, from both Smith and Ed Walsh, would have been punishing on Billy Sullivan, or any catcher. Harry Bemis led the league's catchers in fielding percentage in 1903. An ailing Bemis caught both ends of a doubleheader in July 1906.

(November 24, 1908, TNB and November 26, 1908, CP)

In looking over the fielding averages of the American league pitchers, announced Monday, one noticeable feature is the number of put outs credited to the Chicago club's twirlers.

[Ed]Walsh had 41, White 28, [Frank] Smith 23 and [Nick] Altrock in 23 games had 21. Walsh led the league in this respect, having the advantage of participating in many more games than any other twirler. "Doc" White led the others and Smith was next, being tied with one man for third honors.

As a pitcher usually gets most of his put outs by covering first base, the Chicago twirlers seem to have a little something on their rivals in this department of the game.

In this day of baseball a pitcher is called upon to do something besides pitch. In order for him to get the best results when in the box, he must be able to field his position, and this carries with it the covering of first base.

[Charles] Comiskey, the owner of the Chicago club, was in his time, one of the greatest first basemen the game has ever seen and one of the first men who saw the advantages to be gained by having the pitcher cover first base on all drives towards right field.

Ever since he became a club owner, "Commy" has always had a first baseman who used this method and naturally, all the pitchers who expect to secure a permanent berth on the "Old Roman's" club are drilled to cover the bag until it has become almost second nature.

This important part of the defensive end of a club's play gets more results than show on the surface. When the first baseman is always sure that the pitcher will be on the bag he knows he can take chances on going after balls hit between first and second, which would otherwise elude the second baseman and go for hits.

It's a pitcher's duty to go to first base on all balls hit into right field and once a twirler gets in the habit of doing this, the covering of first base really becomes an easy matter.

A year earlier, Ed Walsh set a record with 12 assists in a 13-inning game on July 16. Addie also earned the reputation for being a fine fielder. His 3.0 assists per game ranks first all time for pitchers. For 1908, this modest sports editor is also credited with 23 putouts in 42 games on the mound. (His career high was 26, in only 34 games, back in 1906.) It was good-fielding first baseman George Stovall who was on the field with Joss in 1908. In three games at first base (in 1902, 1903, and 1905), Addie Joss made one error in 33 chances. This article was reduced to five paragraphs in the Cleveland Press.

(NOVEMBER 26, 1908, TNB AND DECEMBER 1, 1908, CP)

It is an established rule in baseball that when your team is ahead the proper thing to do is to make all plays safe; that is, to be sure and get one man, no matter if another scores.

This is the reason that one often sees an outfielder, who has a good chance to throw out a man trying to score on a hit, refusing to make the attempt. Instead, he will toss the ball to the second baseman, in order to prevent the man who hit the ball from going on to second.

Many a game is tossed away because an outfielder will try to get a man at the plate on a hit of this kind, and, by so doing, allow the batter to take an extra base.

There are times when it is a matter of judgment on the outfielder's part as to whether or not he can get the man at home. If he [lands?] him, well and good, but if he misses, which he often does, the result is dangerous.

A play of this kind came up at Cleveland last season in a game between the Naps and Boston. Cleveland was in the lead by a score of 3 to 1, when the Red Sox went to bat in the seventh inning. With two out and [Denny] Sullivan on first, ["Doc"] Gessler singled to left center.

[Left fielder] Josh Clarke fielded the ball in clever fashion, and, as he whirled to throw, someone yelled: "Third!" The throw was right on the bag but Sullivan, who is a fast man, beat the peg.

Gessler went to second. [Bill] Carrigan, the next man at bat, hit a ground ball to [David] Altizer which took a bad hop and rolled past him into center field, allowing both men to score. The next man went out, retiring the side. This tied up the game, and Boston finally scored the winning run in the eleventh inning.

It is evident that had Josh thrown the ball to second, holding Gessler on first, only one run would have scored on Altizer's error. This would have left Cleveland one run to the good, ensuring the win.

Josh was not at fault, as he had his back to the play, and only did what someone who could see advised him to do. Still, it illustrates the fact that it is not always the wise thing to try to get the man nearest the home plate, especially when you are far enough in the lead to play it safe.

Outfielder Denny Sullivan would finish the season in a Cleveland uniform. Harry Gessler, who answered to both "Doc" and "Brownie," led the league in on-base percentage in 1908. Bill Carrigan was a terrific defensive catcher whose style was reflected in his nickname, "Rough." He was a reserve catcher on the 1912 championship Red Sox and their playing-manager the next year. The sports editor has memorialized Dave Altizer playing one of his three games as the Naps' shortstop that season.

(November 28, 1908, TNB)

There is a lot of difference between being fresh on the ball field and having plenty of self-confidence. It's a pretty ticklish position for a young fellow, who is just breaking in, to be sent to bat in a pinch, and especially when there is a catcher behind the bat, who is trying to take advantage of the youngster's nervousness, by handing him a line of talk that is not calculated to steady his nerve.

Louis Evans, who finished the season with the Montreal Eastern league team, was taken south by McGraw last spring. He stayed with the Giants the early part of the season. He was also here with the Colts.

In a game the New York team was playing at Philadelphia, in which the score was close, McGraw found an opportunity to send Evans in to bat for someone, at a time when the Giants had a man on second and needed a run to win.

The youngster stepped to the plate and as he took his position, "Red" Dooin, the Phillies' star backstop, after looking Evans over from head to foot, let drop this remark:

"You had better be careful, young fellow. This pitcher is wilder than a hawk and is liable to cop you on the head any minute."

A moment later the twirler let go of a fast one that fairly whistled past Evans' face. Lou stepped back and as Dooin caught the ball, he remarked:

"I told you to be careful or he will get you."

The next ball pitched was closer to the youngster's head than the first one, and Evans, who was wise to Dooin's game, thought it was time to take a hand in the proceedings. Leaning over to Dooin he said:

"Tell that guy out there that if he ever expects to drive me away from the plate he had better pack that slow one in his grip."

Before Dooin could recover from his surprise at the remark he heard Evans say: "If he hands me up another one like that I will knock the button off his cap with a line drive. Tell him to duck. I don't want to kill him."

Then to make it good Evans drove a vicious liner through the box, scoring the man from second. He was not molested again.

Cleveland native Louis Richard Evans played under the name of Steve Evans. His debut, as a pinchhitter, was on April 16, 1908. (There is no record of Evans having recording an RBI in his two plate appearances that year.) He was a prankster to rival Germany Schaefer. That he was even on the New York roster was part of his continuously running comedy routine: he dodged John McGraw all spring training so the Giants' manager couldn't send him to Montreal to start 1908. Steve Evans played the 1907 season for the Dayton Colts. He established National League records for being hit by pitches, but his best years were in the Federal League. He retired his Louis and Steve act after two last seasons with Roger Bresnahan's Mud Hens. Charles Dooin led National League catchers in assists in 1908, and may have worn shin guards before Bresnahan did.

(NOVEMBER 30, 1908, TNB)

This thing of going towards first base to get a bunt, especially on a fast man, is about as hard a thing as a pitcher is called upon to do in the fielding line.

There is nothing that makes a twirler look so badly in the eye of the fans, than to see him stand in the box and let the runner scamper down the line for a base hit.

No one has ever been able to successfully invent a check for the play. It's simply a question of who shall run to cover the base, as there is absolutely no way to plan the play before it is made.

With a fast man at the bat, and one who is liable to bunt, the pitcher is always on the alert, but he is never able to tell exactly whether the batter will lay the ball down the first base line, or along the chalk mark running from home to third.

Both the first and second basemen must play back in their natural positions and if either come in to field the ball, it's better than an even bet, that the runner will beat the pitcher to the bag.

If the batter is lucky enough to get the ball past the pitcher, there is hardly any chance for the second sacker to field it in time to get his man.

Often spectators will see a pitcher stand flat-footed in the box, with a fast man hurrying down the base line, after a bunt of this kind.

This is really no fault of the twirler, as in nine cases out of ten he has been crossed. The moment he sees that the batter is going to bunt he naturally starts towards third and once he is on the move in that direction there is not a chance on earth for him to go towards first and field the ball.

Instead of the twirler being sound asleep on the play, as most people who do not know, imagine, he is wide awake, and simply because he is on the alert, is the reason why he is made to look bad.

If he were "smoking" on the play he would never be started in the wrong direction and it would be a good deal easier for him to get his man.

It's a mighty tough play for the box artist to get away with, and this probably accounts for the fact that so many of the fast men of today are successfully bunting in the first base direction so often.

"Smoking" is a particularly fine euphemism for loafing on the field. But Addie's tortured syntax in this article seems to mirror his pitcher's anxiety about bunts.

(November 30, 1908, CP and December 2, 1908, TNB)

About the hardest thing an infielder has to do is to learn to come in to handle slow-hit balls. At first glance this would appear a simple thing to acquire; but ask any infielder about it, and he will tell you this sort of ground ball gives him more trouble than the hard drives.

There are several reasons for this. In the first place, a hard-hit ball will invariably bound true; that is, it will hop along the ground, so that the infielder will be able to judge it with a degree of certainty.

A slow-hit ball invariably works just the opposite way. It is not hit hard enough to cause it to overcome any small obstacle that may be lodged in its way, and an infielder who is trying to field such a hit is merely taking a chance on where it will bound.

In this day, when speed is one of the most essential things to the successful player, there are usually a good many men on a team who can fairly make the dust fly in going down to first.

On a sharp hit ball by one of these sprinters, the infielder has a chance to knock down the drive, without getting it clean, and still has a chance to get his man. But if the ball is hit slowly and the infielder is forced to come in on it, there is never any chance to get the runner, unless the ball is handled without the semblance of a fumble.

Another thing that makes this sort of a drive hard to handle, is the fact that the inner works man [i.e., the infielder] is always forced to throw the ball while on the dead run and often when he is entirely out of position to make the peg.

This sort of a play, in order to be successful, must nearly always be made with one hand, as there is seldom time for the infielder to get two hands on the ball and still have margin enough to shift from one hand to the other for the throw.

While the going back of an infielder to get a hard drive and his handling and throwing of it makes it look a lot more spectacular, the short bounder is by far the harder play.

Bill Bradley is sometimes credited with popularizing the play whereby the third baseman picks up a slow-hit ball with his bare hand and throws it to first in one motion. Bradley was the anti–Mike Mowry, also a standout fielder at third base, whose unorthodox method was to box the ball hit to him, pick it up, and then throw it. The Cleveland Press *version of this article omits paragraphs six and seven.*

(NOVEMBER 27, 1908, CP AND DECEMBER 3, 1908, TNB)

The double steal, with men on first and third, is a play that is mighty hard for the man on third to make successfully. The runner at this station is always placed in a delicate position, and it is generally more of a failure than a success.

There is absolutely no chance for the man on third to get across the plate unless the runner at first goes through with his end. Catchers always bear in mind that when the play is attempted, nine times out of ten the opposition is trying to score a run, and act accordingly.

There are several ways the club on the defense have of check-mating the move. Sometimes either the shortstop or second baseman will cover the keystone position alone, but more often the shortstop takes the bag, while the second-sacker will come in about 20 feet ahead of second to take the short throw.

If he sees the man at third start for home he will grab the ball and relay it to the plate. But if he sees that the runner at third is staying close to the bag, he will let the toss go through to the shortstop.

This is where the man at first must get in the game. If he stops on his way to second, and shows the opposition that he is not going through with the play, it [sic] has plenty of time to make sure the man at third is not going home, and still have ample opportunity to catch him.

Then, again, the catcher may throw to the pitcher, instead of second, and woe unto the base runner who is led into this trap, as there is never a chance for him to get away from the twirler's relay to third.

There is still another method the catcher may employ to ensnare his man. This is by making a good bluff to throw the ball to second, enticing the runner to start for home, and then quickly tossing the ball to third.

It's a mighty tough place for a base runner, and about the only chance he has to get home is to have an error made by the opposition in handling the ball, or take a chance and start home as soon as the catcher makes a move to get rid of the ball.

In the latter case, it is a question of showing up the backstop or be shown up by him, with the chances all in favor of the man behind the bat.

He would have made a great pitching coach after a nice, long career in Cleveland. Think of Mel Harder. The Cleveland Press *did not print the last three paragraphs of this story.*

(DECEMBER 5, 1908, TNB)

One of the peculiar things in baseball is the condition where certain pitchers have "it" on certain clubs, and vice versa. Why this should be is one of the unexplainable things about the game. After a twirler has been defeating a club for a considerable length of time, he begins to feel that he has a little something on that team and this feeling makes him work with a good deal of confidence.

The same holds good in regard to the team, as the players seem to feel they are going to have a tough proposition on their hands the minute they see the pitcher take off his sweater, preparatory to warming up.

What luck is attached, to games of this kind always seems to break with the winner, and probably this, as much as the twirler's ability, helps him to down his foes.

The theory works the same way when it is a club that has "it" on a pitcher. It's an established fact that Harry Howell, [Jimmy] McAleer's star "spitball" pitcher, simply can't win a game from the Washington club. No matter how good he may be or how well he twirls, something always crops up that returns him on the loser's end of the score.

On the other hand, "Doc" White, of the [White] Sox, has merely to step on the rubber to beat Joe Cantillon's outfit. Tom Hughes has long been a Jonah to the Naps and has had such remarkable success against the Cleveland outfit that Cantillon worked him two games in as many days in Washington last fall. Hughes delivered in such fine shape that the Naps were unable to score a run in either contest.

"Dusty" Rhoads has always been a stumbling block in the path of the Philadelphia club. The Athletics, on the other hand, have a huge laugh to themselves every time Larry [Lajoie] sends the writer out on the rubber.

I was so successful, (?) against them during the season of 1907 that Lajoie decided to take no more chances on any of his infielders getting killed by getting in front of line drives and terrific grounders and as a consequence I braced the bench every time we played there last summer.

When Jesse Tannehill was a member of the old Boston team, under the management of Jimmy Collins, all "Tanny" had to do to beat the [Naps?] was to toss his glove out in [the box].

To show the luck that some twirlers play in when facing certain clubs, it is only necessary to relate an incident that happened in Cleveland a few seasons ago.

"Bill" Hogg, of the New York Americans, was seldom able to win in Cleveland; in fact, he has won [but?] two games from the Naps since becoming an American leaguer.

[One?] day at League park the Highlanders, with Hogg in the box, [were] playing the Naps to a stand[still]. The score was a tie at the [beginning] of the eighth inning. The [first] two men for Cleveland were [easi]ly retired.

[Lajoie], who was next at bat, drove a liner right over the shortstop's head and when Danny Hoffman gave chase, it looked as though Larry would have to sprint some to reach second.

The ball bounded against the screen in left field and much to the surprise of everyone in the grounds, stuck in the wire netting in such a manner that Hoffman was unable to get a firm grip on it.

Larry kept on going around the bases and finally when Dan saw the big fellow was going to score he gave the ball a vicious poke and knocked it through the screen, the ball falling on the outside. This run won the game and shows how Hogg's usual bad luck against us was still with him.

Statistics in baseball really do tend to even out over time. Here, Cleveland gets one back from Boston, who had won five years earlier when Cy Young, his hit finding a depression below the right-field wall, circled the bases. It was Harry Howell who offered to bribe the official scorer to rule Napoleon Lajoie's eighth bunt a hit, in the controversial doubleheader that decided the 1910 batting title. Howell, who loaded his pitches with the juice of the slippery elm, recorded the lowest career ERA (2.06 for over 1,580 innings pitched) for a Brown. "Long Tom" Hughes shut out Cleveland five times in 1905. The League Park game when center fielder Danny Hoffman couldn't retrieve the ball—Lajoie's hit, of course—was played on July 5, 1907. At the end of that year, on September 25, Hoffman got the only hit in Addie's twenty-seventh victory. Bill Hogg was, in fact, a hard-luck player and he died young. We may recall that he was the pitcher who broke Bill Bradley's wrist with a pitch.

(DECEMBER 7, 1908, TNB)

Fans generally seem to have a mistaken idea of what pitchers' control really means. The usual impression is that the fewer bases on balls a twirler hands out during a season, the better is his control.

While in a certain measure this is the truth, still there is something else than mere[ly] the ability of getting the ball over the plate between the shoulders and knees of the batter.

The successful twirler of the present day, in order to be a consistent winner, must be able to not only get the ball over the plate, but must also be able to put it where the batter is least liable to hit it safely.

Some batters are weak on a high ball, close to the handle, while others cannot hit a low, fast one pitched inside. The same is true of balls pitched on the outside, high or low, as may suit the occasion.

In order to get the ball in the places where the batter is weak the pitcher must possess great accuracy, which is the true test of control.

Again there are many occasions when the catcher has called for a waste ball, in order to try to stop a base runner from stealing a base. If the pitcher has not enough command of the ball to be able to hand it out where the batter cannot hit it and where the backstop can readily handle the sphere, it's going to be pretty tough for the pad artist to make his end of the play right.

Many a pitcher who gives quite a few bases on balls during a season really has better control than the averages show.

Twirlers of the type of "Buck" Orth, Ed Killian and "Dusty" Rhoads who depend for success on their ability to make the hitters swing at wide balls, are often forced to go a long ways to get their men.

That is, they will sometimes pitch up three bad balls in an endeavor to land men, before they see that he will not swing at bad ones and then rather than give him a chance to hit a "cripple," meaning one which the batter is reasonably sure will be right over, they will walk the batter to take a chance with the next one.

Of course, a walk at the beginning of an inning or when there is no one on the bases, is just as good as a base hit, still, the pitcher who is always trying to make a man hit at a bad ball, gets away with many a game for just this reason and they are the ones who are usually there with the control.

Over the seasons, baseball's strike zone has been variable, but the human anatomy that makes hitting and throwing possible is a constant. Al Orth and Ed Killian didn't strike out batters; they just won (over 300 games between them). Orth was called "The Curveless Wonder" for serving up pitches that only looked hittable. He changed up on his changeup. Edwin Killian served up only nine home runs over a 214-game career. The left-handed control freak was twice a 20-game winner. Killian was a rookie on the 1903 Naps.

Cleveland's League Park, viewed from center field, in 1909 (the final year for its original wooden grandstand). Shortstop Neal Ball is shown positioning center fielder Joe Birmingham, after the Athletics have scored a run. Napoleon Lajoie is left of second base, where George Stovall pounds his first-baseman's glove. The Naps' third baseman is George Perring. Connie Mack, wearing a boater, is seated on the visitors' bench (Library of Congress).

(DECEMBER 18, 1908, TNB EXPANDED FROM DECEMBER 7, 1908, CP)

The announcement made some time ago by President [Charles] Comiskey of the White Sox that he is going to build a new park, will be hailed with delight by every ball player in the American league.

It has long been conceded that the Sox grounds are the hardest in the league to hit on. This probably accounts for the fact that the White Sox are dubbed the "Hitless Wonders."

Being a hard ground to hit on, it is naturally a swell place for the pitcher. One of the principal reasons for this is a strong wind that is invariably blowing directly with the pitching.

Detroit, St. Louis and Cleveland have grounds where conditions are about even for the pitcher and hitter. There is seldom much wind blowing at these places, and, consequently, the pitcher is neither at an advantage or disadvantage.

The St. Louis Grounds are probably the best of the three for the pitcher, as, for some unaccountable reason, it always appears that the distance from the rubber to the home plate is short, making the twirler feel that he is right on top of the hitter.

Of course, this is only a case of imagination, as the distance is the same as in every other park. Still, it seems to help a pitcher a good deal to feel that way.

The New York American grounds are probably the worst in the league for the box artist. There is always a strong wind blowing there, which has a tendency to cool off the pitcher in a way that is not conducive to good arms.

Outside of the real hot months it is mighty hard for a pitcher to get up a good perspiration on [President Frank] Farrell's park and there is always the danger of catching cold in one's arm.

Another thing the pitcher has to contend with while on these grounds is the sun, which shines directly in the heaver's eyes when on the mound.

The same conditions in regard to the wind prevail at Boston, except that there it is usually damp and penetrating.

The fact that it is usually cool in Boston is one of the reasons why "Cy" Young pitches such great ball there. The big fellow does not care very much for the hot weather, but can fairly make them whistle across when the day is a trifle cool.

On the old grounds at Philadelphia it always seems that the slabber is pitching up hill and that the plate is a mile away.

In Washington it generally is so hot the twirler is "all in" along about the fifth inning. Early and late in the season the twirler finds himself looking right into the sun after every ball he has pitched in the Capital city and this does not make his work any easier.

The Cleveland Press *printed the initial three paragraphs of what Addie must have rewritten into the full article that appeared in the Toledo* News-Bee. *Addie takes us on a guided tour of the eight American League parks in use through the 1908 season. (The old term "grounds" is becoming an anachronism.) By 1909, even Toledo's minor league park was a new concrete-and-steel facility. Cleveland's League Park would be renovated, and brought more in line with these "Jewel Box" stadiums, in time for the 1910 schedule. Comiskey Park would open on July 1, 1910. By then, Philadelphia and St. Louis had been hosting baseball in new venues for a season and a half. Shibe Park and the new Sportsman's Park were under construction when Addie wrote this article.*[12]

For the upcoming 1909 season, the White Sox still call South Side Park home. The Browns play their final season in the old Sportsman's Park (new park, same name, constructed on the same site). The Highlanders make do with scruffy Hilltop Park until the Polo Grounds opens, in 1913. The Red Sox are located at the Huntington Avenue Grounds (Fenway dates from 1912). The Athletics' home is Columbia Park. President Taft will toss out the first ball for the Senators' last season at American League Park, in 1910 (they move into Griffith Stadium).

Disabled Charlie Bennett makes the ceremonial first pitch for the Tigers in Bennett Park (he will inaugurate Tiger Stadium in 1912).

It's hard to say how Addie's assessments of pitching/hitting advantages in these old ballparks stand up to SABR stats, but this time I'll go with the first-hand subjective report from the man on the mound.

(December 21, 1908, TNB)

When President ["Garry"] Herrmann of the Cincinnati club signed Clark Griffith to manage his Reds for next season, he made a move that brought him congratulations from the baseball world.

"Griff" did not win a pennant while in charge of the New York Americans, but this fact does not mean that he does not know how to handle the reins as a leader.

The "old fox" always had a team that was well up in the race until last season, and must be given a great deal of credit for finishing as well as he did, when it is considered that he never had a strong pitching staff.

It has been conceded by most every player in the American league that the club under the management of Griffith was about as tough a proposition to beat as any in the league.

"Griff" had his men playing the game to the limit at all times. Usually after a few series with any club it is possible for the opposition to be reasonably certain what that club will do under certain conditions, and, once knowing this, the system is always looked for.

Not so with the Highlanders. There never was a moment when the opposing team could be reasonably certain that the New Yorkers were going to attempt a certain play.

As for trying to get their signals, there never was a chance. "Griff" always had something up his sleeve to spring on you and above all things never knew what the word "quit" meant.

That the Highlanders under "Griff," were the first team to successfully pull off the "squeeze play," shows that the new Red manager is always keenly alive to the possibilities of the game.

Besides this, the New York club was the first team in the younger organization to play the "hit and run," when the batter had two strikes and no balls, and for a long time got away with the play, simply because no one ever figured the Highlanders would try anything so daring.

"Griff" may not turn out a pennant winner in Cincinnati this coming season; in fact the chances are he will have a tough time landing the club in a good first-division berth, but no matter where the outfit finishes the fans of Cincinnati can be assured he will give them the best he has.

The 1909 Reds did finish in the first division, but in fourth place. Addie pitched in the days when the hit-and-run play could be still considered part of the daring "scientific game." What was most adventurous about Griffith's years in Cincinnati was the introduction of the league's first Cuban players.

(December 22, 1908 TNB)

Many great batters are spoiled by being forced to play a sun-field. In most major league parks Old Sol is bad only early and late in the season, at a time when he gets low earlier in the day.

To anyone who has never experienced the sensation of trying to catch a ball, which soars directly into the sun, this would not seem such a difficult task, but when tried it soon becomes apparent that it is a matter of no small moment.

The sun-field that Willie Keeler has been forced to play in New York is probably one of the worst of its kind in the country.

Bill [Bradley] attributes his falling off in batting to the sun's glare, and, when it is considered that he usually hits well on the road, it is evident that there is something in his complaint.

The smoked glasses, which outfielders who are forced to play the sun-field usually wear, help somewhat, but the pasturer who is required to work in a field of this kind right along, is bound to sooner or later slump in his hitting.

Everyone knows how hard it is to see anything after emerging from a dark room into the blinding rays of the sun. The constant playing of a sun-field is a good deal like that.

Even though batters may not hit a ball into the sun during an inning, the fly chaser is constantly forced to look into the rays in order that when a drive is hit at him he will know just how to play it.

The only chance the fielder has to get any relief is to look down at the green grass, and while this eases the blinding effect somewhat, it far from leaves the eyesight as clear as it should be.

It's a mighty tough proposition, this playing of a sun field, and the wonder is that the men who toil in the glare of Old Sol are able to hit the ball at all.

One of a series of Addie's ruminations on ballpark conditions around the league. When he tries out a different angle for this article, the pitcher winds up sympathizing with the batters' handicap! Still team captain in 1909, Willie Keeler's hitting decline was probably more attributable to age (37) and the loss of the speed that had made him so effective for so long. Keeler still regularly patrolled right field in Hilltop Park, although the lefty was sometimes used at third or second base. Interesting to hear Bill Bradley's own reason for his diminished hitting skills. Of course, he would hit below .200 for the 1910 season, after League Park had been renovated.

(December 27, 1908, TNB)

There is nothing so hard on a twirler, especially on a hot day, as to have the opposing players make him pitch the limit on every batter.

By this is meant not hitting at the first ball offered. Instead the man at bat takes one or two and by so doing, makes the twirler go the limit to get him.

This applies especially when the game is close and the pitcher is obliged to go at top speed all through the contest to land a victory.

It's an old and established rule among players that on a day of this kind the best means of procedure against the pitcher is to make him pitch. This probably accounts for the fact that so often the spectators see the man at bat stand there and take one or two strikes without ever offering to hit.

At first glance this would seem almost like suicide for the club at bat, but where this is kept up all day it can readily be seen that in the end it more than pays.

It is a pretty tough job for any pitcher to stand on the rubber for nine long innings and be forced to pitch hard to every batter that steps to the plate.

Work of this kind is bound to tell on him and nine times out of ten the twirler, when forced to go the limit all day long, will show some signs of weakening before the game is over.

Probably the one great reason why more pitchers do not lose games on account of this fact is because the rest of the players are also affected by the heat, and in the closing innings of the game are not as strong and full of life as they were early in the game.

Many times during the season the pitcher begins to wobble along about the seventh inning and the only reason he gets "by" is because the opposing players are "all in" with him.

In cases of this kind about all the pitcher can do is to hand them over and trust to luck and his support to pull him through.

Another fine way to put a pitcher "all in" on a hot day, especially if he be a little portly, is to have a few fast men lay down some bunts.

It doesn't do a twirler a bit of good to be forced to chase over to the third base line a couple of times in an inning as fast as he can go and handle a few of these little rollers.

It's a tough enough job for the pitcher to go through a close game on a hot day without being forced to handle a lot of bunts, but when the opposition is also making you pitch the limit all the way, it gets doubly hard.

Not a hot afternoon in Cleveland on October 2, 1908—temperatures were in the 50s, with clear skies—but Addie took only 74 pitches to retire 27 batters in a row. Pitching in all manner of weather conditions—Cleveland in early spring and fall can be unpredictable—Addie completed 234 of his 260 career starts. (Carl Lundgren was named "The Human Icicle" for his effectiveness when pitching in the cold.) None of the men who did much pitching on the Naps' staffs would be considered to be portly. Six-footers, like Joss, Bob Rhoads and Bill Bernhard, could carry 200 pounds. Bill James lists 242-pounder Ed Walker, who threw 20 innings over two seasons with the Naps, as the heaviest player of the decade. An inch taller than the English-born Walker, Addie weighed 57 pounds less.[13] *Cleveland would have to wait, for its genuinely big pitcher, until the Indians' Garland Buckeye (he confessed to 269 pounds). "Gob" Walker died in Akron, Ohio, in 1947.*

(January 2, 1909, TNB)

The pinch hitter's life is far from being a continual bed of roses. To the casual observer it would seem that for a man to sit on the bench every afternoon for seven or eight innings, with nothing to do but watch the game and then be called on to step to the plate in a pinch, to hit for some weak sticker, would be pretty soft work.

Nothing of the kind. The man on a ball club that is kept on the pay roll to do stunts of this kind, has his work cut out for him and even though the rest of the regulars continually tell him what a snap he has, there is not a one of them who would willingly exchange places.

The pinch hitter holds his job mainly on the strength of his ability to swat the ball. Every time he is sent in to hit for someone he is fully aware of the fact that it's up to him to deliver with a safe drive.

He has been sitting on the bench possibly the greater part of the afternoon without getting a chance to see what sort of stuff the opposing pitcher is serving this day and knows that the moment he steps to the plate, the flinger will give him everything in his repertoire.

Then everyone in the stands is looking forward to his ability to clout and are banking on him to make good. The fans very seldom, if ever, take into consideration the fact that no matter how good a hitter a player may be, he only makes one base hit in about every three trips to the plate.

Then there is that degree of uncertainty as to when he may be called upon to get in the game, that constantly keeps the emergency swatter on the anxious seat all during contest.

He never knows what moment his manager will take out some weak batter that he can be substituted. About the only chance the pinch hitter has to feel jubilant is when he has been called on to perform the hitting stunt and drives out the base hit that returns his club the victor of the contest.

To have the cheers of the fans ringing in his ears at a time like that is a mighty fine thing, but does that atone for the number of times after he has failed to deliver the much-needed hit and on his way to the clubhouse hears some particularly rabid fan yell: "Get out, you big mutt. You couldn't fall out of a boat and hit the water!"

No Bluebird or Broncho or Nap recorded as many as 10 pinch hits in a season, although one of Addie's catchers, Ted Easterly, was a notable pinch hitter of the era. Indian Bibb Falk's 14, in 1931, was the standard for Cleveland teams for 29 years. According to hardballtimes.com, 86 percent of major league starts were complete games in 1901, but by 1909, Addie's last full season, the percentage of complete games was down to 65 percent. It follows that team managers' handling of pitchers created a need for the new pinch-hitting specialist.

John McGraw is said to have coined the term "pinch hitter" to describe Sammy Strange's coming through in the pinch, although Paul Dickson traces the term's first use to an article by Edward J. Nichols, in The Sporting Life, *April 26, 1902. Pittsburgh manager Fred Clarke turned his rookie "Ham" Hyatt, in 1909, into the National League's first professional pinch hitter. The Pirates won the World Series that year. Bill James identifies Dode Criss, a left-handed hitter, as baseball's first professional pinch hitter, and credits Jimmy McAleer with the idea. Criss' four-year career, all with the American League Browns (1908–11), was devoted almost entirely to pinch hitting. The first player to reach 40 pinch hits, Criss was a great minor league pitcher (he pitched in 30 games for St. Louis). The Naps deployed Jack Lelivelt, another left-handed pinch hitter, during the 1913 and 1914 seasons.*

(JANUARY 4, 1909, TNB)

It is an established fact that the left-hand hitter never makes many base hits when opposed by the southpaw twirler. One of the reasons for this is because of the fact that there are so many more right-handed pitchers in any league than side-wheelers.

Very seldom, if ever, is there more than one southpaw working regularly on any club. He toils on an average of once in four days, and only at that time do the left-hand hitters get a chance to go up against the offside heaver.

No matter how good a hitter one may be, it is natural for him to pull a little when the pitcher starts to deliver the ball.

By pulling, is meant stepping back a little. The left-hand batter does this just as much as his right-hand brother, and when the portside slugger is opposed by a southpaw, the tendency to do this is even greater.

Naturally, this makes him weak on a curve ball that is pitched low and on the outside. The left-hand batter, knowing he is weak on this sort of a ball, is constantly on the watch for it, and if the pitcher has steam enough to blaze a fast one through, the chances are better than even it will completely cross the man at bat.

In the American league there are a few left-hand hitters who can successfully gauge the southpaw's curves as well as they can the right-handers's.

Matty McIntyre of the Tigers hits left-hand pitchers as well, if not better, than he does right-handers, but, as a rule, the southpaw has it all over the heartside slugger.

Dick Cooley, who saw years of service in the major leagues, never was particularly fond of hitting against left-hand pitchers.

When Dick joined the Detroit club, in the first game he played at Bennett park he was called upon to face Otto Hess, who at that time was working splendidly for the Cleveland club. As a consequence, Dick's first appearance before the Detroit fans was far from being a howling success.

Hess is a pitcher who, when right, has as much speed as any man in the business. This, coupled with the fact that his curve ball breaks fast, and that he has one of those hip-pocket deliveries, makes it tough for anyone to hit him, particularly a lefthander.

Otto had Cooley scared from the moment he let go of the first ball, and it was laughable to see Dick, who was spiking the water bucket on every ball pitched, trying to meet one.

Dick struck out the first three trips to the plate, and, as he was going out to his position in the outfield at the close of the inning, ["Larry"] Lajoie softly remarked, just loud enough for Cooley to hear: "What's the matter, Dick? Are you afraid of this fellow?"

Cooley could not have hit Hess with a handful of shot that day.

"Matty" McIntyre is Addie's exemplar for the left-handed hitter in many stories. He shared the outfield with Sam Crawford and Ty Cobb on the pennant-winning Detroit teams of 1909 and 1910. All three men hit from the left side, but I wonder if they saw many southpaw pitching matchups, at the dawn of "inside baseball." "Duff" Cooley hit a touch under .300 in a 13-year career that started before the rules of 1893. He was a Tiger for his final season, 1905. Otto Hess' best season was 1906, when he won 20 games (and saved a league-high three) with Cleveland.

(JANUARY 5, 1909, TNB)

Have you ever noticed that when a pitcher, especially if he is new at the game, is getting his bumps, how much faster and harder he works?

Young twirlers seem to think that in order to stop a batting rally they are obliged to shut their eyes and just blaze every ball through.

It seems that in cases of this kind they entirely lose sight of the fact that there is something to the pitching game besides speed.

The one great thing that a twirler must always bear in mind is the fact that the man at bat is always just as anxious to make good as the pitcher. I know of a catcher whose ability to "kid" batters was recognized everywhere he had ever worked, and his old cry whenever a batter came to the plate in a pinch was: "Never mind, fellows; nobody is scared but the hitter."

While this may not hold good in all cases, it carries a good deal of truth, and no matter how much the pitcher may feel worried at the sight of a good hitter, he can rest assured that the batter is just as shaky.

If pitchers, especially youngsters, would only keep this in mind, and pitch accordingly, there would never be so many balloon ascensions during the season.

The minute the opposing players are wise to the fact that the pitcher is in the air, they commence to pull off things at the bat they would never think of doing under normal conditions.

One thing they always do is to make the twirler go the limit on every man. If he is a trifle wild, as is usually the case, they wait until they get him in the hole; in other words, until he is forced to put the ball over.

Usually the twirler who is ballooning will never think of such a thing as a change of pace, but just wheel them in as fast as he can, and, in the majority of cases, right through the middle of the plate.

No wonder he gets hit, and the real surprise is that he ever retires the side. Every pitcher gets a lacing once in a while, and sometimes oftener, but there is no excuse whatever for a man ever forgetting how to pitch in cases of this kind.

Add the term "ballooning" to the growing lexicon of lost baseball idioms. Today the word describes salaries, signing bonuses, ticket prices, ERAs, postseason games, and agents' egos.

(JANUARY 22, 1909, TNB)

Since the foul strike rule went into effect several years ago it has been the general [sic.] accepted theory among ball players that it does not pay to "wait out" a pitcher, as it formerly did.

The players work on the supposition that if he [sic.] takes the first ball pitched and it is a strike, which is the case a good many times, and then happens to foul the next one, he really has two strikes called on him before he gets set at the plate.

When opposed to a pitcher who has a reputation for having good command, this proves quite a handicap to the hitter. With this state of affairs most clubs have discarded the method of making the pitcher go the route and usually offer at the first good ball pitched.

While this system is generally used by all major league clubs, there is one team in the American league that still makes it a point to go the limit with all the pitchers it faces during the season. This team is the White Sox.

[Charles] Comiskey's club has been rightly dubbed the "hitless wonders," and to one who is not thoroughly conversant with its style of play, it is a constant source of wonder how the Sox are able to win games on so few hits.

In the first place Fielder Jones has always been fortunate enough to have had a grand pitching staff and this, coupled with [Billy] Sullivan's masterly work behind the bat, and the fact that the Sox are very good on the defense, makes it hard to score runs against them.

But how do they manage to score runs with so little damage with the bat? The first six men in the batting order, [Ed] Hahn, Jones, [Frank] Isbell, [Patrick "Patsy"] Dougherty, [George] Davis and [Freddy] Parent, certainly make a twirler pitch to the limit to get them. The first two always seem to have two strikes on them before they seriously think of offering at one.

While the other four may not be so adept at making the pitcher go the route, they are always trying to work him for a walk.

It is a well known fact that the team, headed by Jones, usually wins its games in one inning and this is the way it often comes about.

Hahn will get a walk. Jones will lay down a good bunt and the pitcher boots it. The next man sacrifices and then someone will come along with the hit that gives them two runs and usually the game.

Every pitcher who faces this club goes into the box, knowing that if he is a trifle wild, the chances are two to one that he will lose, and [this] doesn't help him a bit in his endeavors to make it hit [colloquial].

Making the pitcher go the limit at all times, may not prove successful to every club, but it surely pays the White Sox and in a good measure accounts, for the fact that they are always serious contenders for the American league championship.

The American League adopted the rule for its inaugural season, declaring that a batter's first two foul balls count for strikes. During the White Sox championship season of 1906, the third-place Naps outscored them by 93 runs and led the league in scoring. Right fielder Ed Hahn hailed from Nevada, Ohio. George Davis, playing second base at the end of his long career, was a rookie outfielder with the 1890 Spiders. He made Cooperstown as a shortstop, four times leading his league in fielding percentage and driving in 1,439 runs. Left fielder Patrick "Patsy" Dougherty led the American League in runs scored for two of its first three seasons.

(JANUARY 23, 1909, TNB)

"What constitutes team work," is a question often asked of anyone directly connected with the playing end of baseball. The fans are constantly reminded that this feature of a club's play is one of the most important essentials in its success.

Naturally they wonder what really constitutes team play and hence, the reason the above question is so often asked. Team work is nothing more than a perfect understanding between all the members of a club as to what is going to be done on any particular play.

For instance: There is a man on first with but one out. If the base runner decides to try for second he should first impart this information to the batter, so that the man at the plate can in any legitimate way, help him reach the base in safety. Or vice versa.

If the man at the bat doesn't know what the base runner is going to do, it can readily be seen that his chance of helping the runner advance to the next station is not near as sure of being successful, as if he were aware of his intention.

This same theory applies to every play a team may make, where there are two or more men connected with the play. We will say that with a man on first the guardian of the sack decides that there is a chance to catch the base runner napping.

The first sacker, accordingly, signals the catcher to throw down there on the next ball pitched. In order for the backstop to be sure that his end of the play is going to be made right, he must let the pitcher know what he is going to do, so that the box artist can hand the ball so wide of the plate that the batter will not have a chance to hit the ball and thus spoil the attempted play.

An[y] number of plays of this nature might be cited, but they all come back to the fundamental point of a thorough understanding between the players.

When this understanding is not thorough it certainly works havoc with a club's team play. With a man on first and one out, the hit and run play is attempted.

That is, the batter decides on that play and gives the signal. He takes it for granted the man at first is going down on the next ball pitched and to help him out swings at the ball, no matter where it is.

Instead of the base runner starting for second, he remains glued to the bag simply because he has missed the sign. The man at bat goes through with his end of the play and possibly misses hitting the ball.

When he looks around and sees that the base runner is still on first, his confidence is shaken and he is afraid to give the sign for fear the runner will miss it again. Consequently no play is attempted by them.

A play of this kind may easily lose a club the game and emphasizes the importance of having an understanding between every member of the club, if that team expects to be contender for the championship.

When base coaches were usually players, the sign that put on a hit-and-run play was given by the batter—not by the third base coach, and apparently not forthcoming from the dugout, either.

(January 25, 1909, TNB)

How many times during a season is a player asked, especially if he is a pitcher: "Who decides what you are to pitch to the batter, the catcher or the pitcher?"

Always comes the same answer: "The catcher." The next question the fan usually asks is: "Do you always have to pitch what the pad artist calls for?"

The fans seem to take it for granted that either the pitcher or his receiver depend entirely on the other man's judgment as to what is the proper thing to hand up to the batter.

The fact of the matter is, that they always try to work together. That is the catcher will call for a certain ball and if in the pitcher's judgment another kind would do better, he simply shakes his head, which tells the man behind the bat that he does not want to pitch that style of ball.

In reality the pitcher acts on his own judgment, because he is the one who is trying to deceive the batter. This holds good, especially where the man in the box is a player of considerable experience.

Many times when players have explained this to outsiders the question arises, "How does the catcher know what you want to pitch after you have shaken your head?"

The answer is simplicity itself. Among players there are but two things a pitcher is called upon to pitch. They are designated as fast ball and curve ball. This may seem a trifle surprising to the uninitiated, who hears about the wonderful and numerous curves possessed by the twirlers.

When a catcher calls upon his battery mate for a curve ball he is set to catch any kind of a curve that his pitcher may decide to pitch.

He can tell, already knowing a curve ball is coming, when the ball leaves the pitcher's hand, just about how much of a break it will take.

If the ball is thrown directly over-handed it takes a drop, while if it is pitched side arm, the ball will follow what is generally known as the out curve.

That is why among the players, there is no such thing as the in-curve. What the general public terms, an in shoot, is nothing more than a fast ball, that has enough speed to make it break a little.

It is thrown with all the speed at the command of the twirler and is allowed to slip out over the ends of the fingers. The break it takes never causes the catcher any trouble and is not termed as a curve ball.

A catcher may sometimes call for a slow ball, but not because he is afraid of being crossed. His judgment tells him this sort of ball will fool the batter and he is imparting his hunch to the pitcher.

We know that it was the pitcher in nineteenth-century "base ball" who gave his catcher the sign for his next pitch. Addie's repeated reduction of the pitcher's repertoire to fastball and curveball, one and two fingers, does suggest what an impact on the art of pitching the spitter must have had. But it doesn't account for the many other kinds of pitches that Deadball pitchers threw for outs: Three Finger Brown's or Guy Morton's or Earl Moore's curves; Eddie Cicotte's or "Nap" Rucker's or "Kickapoo Ed" Summers' knuckleballs; "Cy" Falkenberg's or George Kahler's emery ball). The Neyer/James Guide to Pitchers *rates Joss' fastball the third best in baseball for 1900–04 (behind those thrown by Jack Powell and Rube Waddell) and still sixth best (now Walter Johnson's is first; Waddell third) for 1905–09. Addie featured a good out-curve for his secondary pitch.*

(January 30, 1909, TNB)

It has long been conceded that one of the principal assets of the winning pitcher is control. The general understanding of this is the twirler's ability to get the ball over the plate. But there is something in control besides being able to split the plate.

The twirler who can work the corners and has the command to make the batter hit at balls that are not over the plate shows real control.

The fellow who has enough confidence in himself to take a shot at some batter's head a couple of times and then be able to come back and get two or three strikes over the plate, when he is forced to do so, is also there.

When a pitcher establishes a reputation for control and very seldom hits anyone, the players soon learn to feel that they need not be afraid of getting hit when facing him. Once let them get this idea and that particular box artist will find it pretty hard sledding.

The batters stand up at the plate and refuse to back away an inch. This practically makes the pitcher's curve ball of no good to him and he will be severely handicapped in his work.

The pitcher who is not afraid to drive one at the batter's head, once in a while, and by so doing let him know that he is not altogether safe, usually finds that he gets pretty good results.

Of course, there is no pitcher who would intentionally hit a batter, but as long as it's a case of dog eat dog, it is just as fair for the twirler to take advantage of those things as it is for the batter.

There is no team that particularly likes to face a pitcher who is there with the fast one and who is just wild enough to make the man at the bat be ready to jump out of the box on every ball pitched.

When Fred Glade set the strike-out record for the American league at Washington a few seasons ago, the big fellow was favored with a dark day. This, coupled with his tremendous speed, made him practically unhittable, but what probably helped him as much as anything, was the fact that early in the game he hit outfielder [Frank] Hulseman [sic.] on the head.

It was an awful jolt big "Hulse" received and no wonder the rest of the Washington players were going to bat the rest of the day with one foot in the batter's box and the other in the water bucket.

One of the greatest of all control pitchers is making the important distinction between control and command. His headline states it in a paradox: "Too Good Control Bad for Pitcher." Who remembers Fred Glade and his record game? The Browns rookie fanned 15 Senators on July 15, 1904, to set the American League record. (Glade did hit two batters that day.) The disappeared Glade set another record, again in a game against Washington, when he gave up the first walk-off home run hit by a pitcher (to Tom Hughes, August 3). Glade would pitch only 132 games in his career; his family was wealthy, so he didn't need the job. Washington's hit batsman Frank Huelsman was so marginal that Addie misspelled his name "Hulseman." He was the Senators' starting left fielder for 1905, his last year in the majors.

Fred Glade's nickname was "Lucky." Maybe thinking about him brought the sports editor back to one of his favorite topics, luck.

(February 2, 1909, TNB)

The pitching of a no-hit game by any pitcher is a rare thing and one of which any twirler may well be proud. At the same time the box artist who performs this feat is simply plastered with horseshoe luck.

To go through nine innings without a member of the opposition being able to hit one "where they ain't," certainly carries with it something besides mere ability on the part of the pitcher.

In games of this kind the pitcher must be favored with great support by his teammates. Nine times out of ten it is really their wonderful work which makes it possible for him to achieve such a feat.

How many times during a season does one see a twirler go along for seven or eight innings without the semblance of a hit being made against him? When everyone in the stands has settled back with the expectation of seeing the box artist accomplish the feat, somebody will swing wild on one and pop a little "Texas leaguer" over the head of one of the infielders.

No doubt many times during the game someone has hit the ball a good deal harder than did the man who made the hit, only to be unfortunate enough to have it go directly into the waiting hands of a fielder.

Without trying to take away any credit from the pitcher who has been fortunate enough to go through a game without anyone making a hit against him, the fact remains that it takes considerable luck to get away with a game of this kind.

Can anyone imagine a pitcher going through nine innings without a hit being made off him and still lose the contest? That is what happened to "Dusty" Rhoads in an exhibition contest in Albany, N. Y., a few seasons ago.

Rhoads lost his game, 1 to 0. He walked a man to start the sixth inning. The base runner was sacrificed to second and immediately stole third, by the grace of a bad decision by the umpire. He scored a moment later on a long fly to left field.

Addie overlooks Earl Moore's no-hit loss to Chicago, on May 9, 1901. Or was he discounting his longtime teammate's feat because "Crossfire" Moore gave up a hit in the tenth inning? Moore was still alive to hear about Harvey Haddix's extra-inning loss. Addie was to throw his second no-hit game on April 20, 1910. That milestone required a good bit of good luck too: Bill Bradley juggled an infield hit in the second inning that was later scored an error. Note that Addie doesn't associate the baseball phrase "hit 'em where they ain't" with Willie Keeler, as we do naturally. This is the second exhibition game Addie remembers Bob Rhoads (last noted in Minneapolis) pitching against a minor league team. This time, he's facing the Albany Senators of the New York State

League. In 1899, Connie Mack had offered to sign Addie to his first professional contract to pitch for the Albany club.

(February 4, 1909, TNB)

Clark Griffith, the new manager of the Reds, says he is not going to allow any member of his team to wear a glove the first week of the training session. "Griff" says that if the players are not allowed to wear gloves they will not be slamming the ball around hard enough to hurt their arms.

This applies particularly to younger players and if the "old fox" can get his men to adopt this rule in the right spirit, there is no question but it will have a beneficial effect.

The trouble with a good many youngsters who are taken south for a try out is that they seem to get the impression that to make good, it is necessary to show their manager all the speed and curves they have the first few days in the southland.

Many a promising youngster puts himself out of it in this manner. Not only does he do himself an injustice, but at the same time he is hurting the pennant chances of his club.

Of course, the veteran, who has gone through the mill a good many times, is not liable to hurt himself in this manner, but it's pretty hard even for him to keep from letting himself out, especially on a warm day.

With no catcher's gloves on the field it is going to be pretty hard to get anyone to handle speed and naturally there will be little "smoke" displayed until the big mitt makes its appearance.

The first week of a training trip should be more in the nature of a priming, for the harder weeks to follow, than a jumping-in on the work right off the reel.

Players have found that in order to get in shape for the strenuous work it is a good idea to try to get in shape the first week out.

Running around the park once or twice every day, develops the wind and strengthens the heart action wonderfully. This, coupled with picking up bunts for about ten or fifteen minutes, twice a day, soon gets the desired results.

This stunt of picking up bunts certainly is a wonderful help in getting one in shape. It carries with it several features.

In the first place, it teaches one to field, a department of the game in which no one is perfect or can get too much practice on. It also calls into play every muscle in the body.

If the player be afflicted with a little too much weight, he soon finds this sort of work will help him reduce the extra avoirdupois, as it keeps him constantly bending over to get the ball and then quickly straightening to toss it back to the hitter.

There is never any danger of the player, who is working in this manner, to hurt his arm as he never throws the ball hard. This in itself is a great help to him. By tossing the ball slowly, he soon gets his arm in such shape that it will stand a greater strain, without hurting it in the least.

Jerry Denny was the last position player to eschew a glove in a regular season game. Before he was "The Old Fox," Griffith was a young pup rookie in 1891, four seasons before Denny retired. ("Cannonball" Gus Weyhing, who played a few innings for Cleveland the year before Addie joined the club, was baseball's last barehanded pitcher.) Avoirdupois, *from the medieval French, is for "goods sold by weight." Addie arrived for spring training in 1910 about 20 pounds overweight, and nursing a sore pitching elbow.*

(FEBRUARY 11, 1909, TNB)

The unexpected in baseball is what wins. It doesn't make a bit of difference in what department of the game this is done, the result is always the same. Any time a club can turn a trick, or a play that is not looked for, the chances for getting good results are much better than when a conventional style of game is adopted.

This holds good for pitchers as well as any other player. One of the great essentials of the successful twirler is his ability to outguess the hitter, or in other words, pull something the batter is not looking for.

Players and managers are divided in regard to one play that is often presented to the box artist. This is where the batter has two strikes and no balls. Is it good policy to put the next one right over the plate, or should the pitcher hand up a couple of teasers before giving the batter another good one?

Of course, a good deal depends upon the man at bat. At the same time, as much depends upon the man pitching. Some twirlers work on the supposition, that if they have two strikes and no balls on the batter, they can afford to pitch a couple that are wide of the plate, figuring to cause the batter to hit at a bad one.

That system is all right if the batter will chase a bad one, but where the man at the plate is wise to this, as most every good hitter is, the slabbist after handing up a couple of bad ones, finds that the batter is then on even terms with him.

This is especially true where the box artist trying to get the swatter to go after a bad one, has pitched a couple so wide of the plate that there is absolutely no chance for any kind of a hitter to chase them. Trying to make a batter hit this kind of a pitch-out is suicidal and always fails to get the desired results.

Pitchers like "Cy" Young never waste any to get a batter, after he has two strikes and no balls. Of course, "Cy" is endowed with a tremendous amount of speed and can afford to take a chance on driving a fast one through, but at the same time he catches many a batter on this play and gets away with it, simply because the hitter is looking for him to waste one.

"Cyclone" Young was the master of the "hop ball," a pitch so fast that batters swore the ball rose in its last feet of flight.

(February 13, 1909, TNB)

The left hand hitter has a great advantage over the man who bats from the right side of the plate. No wonder there are so many port side clouters in the game today.

In the first place he is fully five feet nearer first base and besides, when hitting at the ball he swings directly into his stride.

The right hand hitter after taking a clout finds himself turned around, so that he is facing third base. He is then forced to turn again and start for the initial bag.

When it is considered that there are hundreds of decisions every season, where base runners lose hits, by just being beaten to first by infielders' throws, it can readily be seen that the man who bats from the left side of the plate stands a much better chance of accumulating a high average.

Ability to hustle down the first base line, is another great point in favor of the batter and swells many a batting average.

A fine illustration of this, is seen in the Detroit club. The Tigers have three great hitters in [Ty] Cobb, [Sam] Crawford and [Claude] Rossman.

For straight-away hitting ability it is a hard matter to choose between them, but Cobb, on account of his tremendous speed, generally outhits his team mates.

Ty is quite a bit faster on his feet than Crawford and this probably accounts for the difference in their averages. Cobb easily can out-run Rossman and naturally has a great advantage over him.

It is doubtful if either Crawford or Cobb have anything on the big first baseman when it comes to straight-away hitting, but when speed is taken into consideration, they lay over "Ross" quite a little [colloquial].

A typical middle batting order for Detroit had Crawford hitting third, Cobb cleanup, and then Rossman — three straight left-handed hitters.

(FEBRUARY 19, 1909, TNB)

One of the hardest things a pitcher is called upon to do is the task of finishing a game, which has been started by some other twirler.

Usually the pitcher sitting on the bench, is called upon to relieve his fellow twirler at a time when the opposition is hitting, with a considerable degree of regularity.

It is an established fact among the members of the profession, that once a team gets to clouting the ball, nothing short of a miracle will stop it.

When a club starts hitting this way, every member of the team becomes imbued with a certain feeling of confidence in his ability to hit anything pitched.

A good many times a change of pitchers will stop a batting rally, but just as often the new twirler is treated just as shabbily as the first one.

What makes it particularly hard for the second pitcher, is the fact that a good many times he is not really ready for such an arduous task, not having had time enough to get thoroughly warmed up before taking up the unfinished work.

It is mighty tough on a pitcher's arm, too, to be forced to leave the bench, practically cold, and then step into the box and be expected to work just as hard, if not a little harder, than if he had been carefully groomed for the occasion.

There are very few box artists who are blessed with the ability to successfully do this, and when a club is fortunate enough to have a man like this on its pay roll, it has added an inestimable asset to the team.

Relief pitching became a specialty late in the evolution of the game, and saves weren't even kept as a statistic—much less holds, blown saves, and games finished—until 1969. Famous starters like Mordecai Brown and Eddie Plank were still routinely sent in to close games. Addie tells us he'd be sitting on the bench, not warming up during a game he'd finish for the starter. Although Paul Dickson has discovered the term "relief pitcher" in use as far back as Peter Morris' June 17, 1885, story for The Sporting News, *the bullpen hasn't yet become an institution: John McGraw was employing the versatile "Doc" Crandall as a relief pitcher (mostly finishing games for the starters); and Clark Griffith was forced to rely on relief pitching because of his Highlanders' poor starting pitching. A history of Cleveland relievers might go back to Willie Mitchell (a good starter who, like Otis Crandall, was often called upon to relieve), later Clint Brown.*

(FEBRUARY 24, 1909, TNB)

There is nothing prettier, from the baseball fans' point of view, than to see an outfielder skim along the green, grab a fast bounding sphere and not stopping to straighten up, hurl the ball to some baseman, just the least bit ahead of some madly dashing base runner.

Nothing looks quite so spectacular and the high regard the public has for players of this kind, is always shown by the thunderous applause that greets such a feat.

The man making the throw is always the recipient of this applause and no credit is given the baseman who touches out the runner.

His task, while not so spectacular, is fully as important to the completion of the play. About half the time the runner and ball reach him at the same time. He not only has to catch the ball, but at the same time, put it on the runner.

If he be the least bit timid about getting cut, by spikes, it won't be long before every player around the circuit is wise to the fact. From that time on whenever a man slides into the timid player's base all he will see will be nice, long, sharp spikes.

There are so many ways that the baseman can help his club, in plays of this kind, that it is surprising the fans have not long ago recognized it and given the infielder proper credit.

Fred Beulow, when in the majors, pulled a play on Charley Hemphill, at that time with the Browns, that shows what a baseman can do in a play of this kind.

"Hemp" was on third with one out, when the batter hit a long fly to Harry Bay of the Naps. Bay hasn't the best arm in the business and Hemphill, after making sure the ball had been caught, started for the plate.

The center fielder whipped the ball in as fast as he could. Buelow stood at the plate with both hands resting on his hips looking out towards the outfield with an expression on his face saying as plainly as words, "no chance to get this fellow."

Hemphill must have taken it for granted, when he saw Buelow that Bay had not made a throw and naturally slowed up. In the meantime, Bay's throw had been hurrying to the plate. Buelow reached out, grabbed the ball and put it on the astonished St. Louis player.

It's interesting that Addie doesn't give his readers an anecdote of Ty Cobb running with sharpened spikes high. "Eagle Eye" Charley Hemphill was with the Browns from 1902 to 1907. He played partial seasons with both the hapless 1899 Spiders as well as the 1902 Bronchos. In between, he was the first right fielder in Boston Red Sox history. Hemphill was a good base runner: 42 stolen bases for the Highlanders in 1908.

(February 26, 1909, TNB)

One of the most dangerous things a base runner can do is to start to slide to a base and then just before he hits the dirt, try to stand up.

Often spectators see a player start to steal and after the catcher drops the ball notice him slide into the bag, when there is absolutely no chance of his being caught.

To the fans this sometimes looks like grand stand play or a foolish piece of work. In reality it is the only proper thing the base runner can do.

Here is the reason: A base runner starts for second and as he nears the base gathers himself for the slide. Maybe the catcher has let the ball get away from him and is not even going to make the peg.

Someone on the coaching lines, who has the best interests of the man going to second at heart, but fails to understand the danger of stopping, after once starting to slide, yells: "Stay up. He has dropped the ball."

The base runner tries to follow instructions, because he relies implicitly on the coacher for instructions. The result is, either a badly sprained ankle, or a broken bone.

Usually an accident of this kind is directly laid to the spikes a player wears, but in nine cases out of ten, it's the result of not going through with the slide, which has been started.

It's always a mighty good policy to slide to a base, especially when the player has already gathered himself for the effort.

Often a base runner is enticed to slide to a base through the shrewdness of the wise fellow who is covering. The runner watches the baseman to see where that individual is playing for the throw and slides accordingly.

Many a time the catcher lets the pitch get away from him and sometimes the ball goes clear back to the grand stand. If the man who is covering makes the bluff that he is waiting for the throw — standing there with outstretched hands as though he was momentarily expecting to catch the ball and put it on the runner — he can oftentimes cause the man to slide into second.

By the time the base runner gets up and sees that he has been tricked, it is too late to try for third. Consequently his team has been deprived of the extra base by the good judgment of the baseman.

Addie's conclusion, with the fielder who tricks a runner by pretending to be waiting to receive a throw, neatly complements his previous lesson, on the catcher who pretends the throw is not coming. These articles often venture beyond basic how-to-play instruction (found in manuals of the day) in their details of "inside baseball" that would add to his readers' enjoyment of a game at League or Armory parks. For now, they constitute the book he didn't live to write, perhaps something on the order of Christy Mathewson's Pitching in a Pinch *or Johnny Evers'* Touching Second.

6

Of Spiders and Colonels

THE NINETEENTH-CENTURY GAME

Adrian Joss' entire major league career happened within the first decade of the American League charter. Addie was a rookie pitching in League Park only half a dozen years after the Cleveland teams of Patsy Tebeau and Charles "Chief" Zimmer hosted the Temple Cup on the same grounds. Cy Young, Bobby Wallace, and Jesse Burkett were stars for the Spiders, and Addie Joss played with these men. His last manager in Toledo, Bob Gilks, filled in for the great Ed McKean. When he married, Addie chose to live in a city with a baseball tradition that reached far back from its Midwest sources, like the Maumee River that rushed by, in his days and in his sleep, endlessly.

In order to write the following stories, Addie made himself a student of the game's past. Make no mistake: He would never have presumed to write history. The man was a professional athlete, who found work as a sports editor only intermittently, for a few months at a time over a few years. But Addie did write a history, ipso facto, *as he witnessed it and heard it retold. And he knew that baseball is a game that remembers itself; stories about nineteenth-century players and teams were popular in the newspapers Addie read.*

Alfred H. Spink and Albert G. Spalding undertook separately their writing of official baseball history in 1907, the watershed year when Addie Joss became a newspaper journalist. Unlike either Spink or Spalding, he had no special agenda for his writing. Instead, he created an unburdened narrative—free from magazine formulas, dogmatic argument, and even innocent of most of the codes of his adopted profession—like good talk.

(JANUARY 20, 1907, TNB)

Very few if any of the theatergoers who attended the Valentine [theater] the past week were aware that in Lew Simmons, who with his partner Frank White, pleased all with their black face turn, they were watching a former manager of a famous pennant winning ball team.

Simmons is 68 years old and has been before the public both in a theatrical and baseball way many years. He occupied a prominent part in baseball affairs in 1882, where he, Bill Sharsig and Chas. Mason, took charge of the Philadelphia Athletics in what was then known as the American association.

The association was composed of Philadelphia, Baltimore and Pittsburg comprising the eastern division with Cincinnati, Louisville, and St. Louis forming the western half. That season Cincinnati won the pennant and the next year, the Metropolitan club of New York and the Columbus team were added making an 8-club league.

It was during this [1883] season that the Philadelphia club or the Athletics, as they were better known, did their great playing, which finally captured the pennant.

The personnel of this team were as follows:

Catchers — Edward Rohar [Rowen], Jack O'Brien.
Pitchers — Bob Mathews, George Washington Bradley, Jumping Jack Jones. [Also Fred Corey, Jersey Bakely, and Harry Stovey.]
First base — Harry Storey [Stovey].
Second base — Cub Stricker.
Third base — Fred Corey. [Corey was a pitcher and utility player; George Bradley played third.]
Short stop — Mike Monahan [Moynahan].
Left field — Judd Burchell [Birchall].
Center field — Bob Blakeson [Blakiston].
Right field — Bill Craven, Lou [Lon] Knight.

After a season of brilliant playing the race narrowed down to the Athletics and the St. Louis team then owned by the peculiar Chris Von Der Ahe. The situation finally came to this stage:

The Athletics had to win one game in Louisville out of a series of four in order to win the pennant, while St. Louis must win all four games from the Pittsburg team in order to tie the Athletics.

Simmons, as [general] manager of the Athletics, had offered every member of the Pittsburg team an overcoat should they win one game at St. Louis, and Von Der Ahe wired on and promised each man on the Louisville team a suit of clothes should they win all four games from the Athletics.

While St. Louis was winning the first two games of the series from Pittsburg, Louisville was doing the same with the Athletics and excitement was at fever heat.

Simmons was the recipient of innumerable communications from Philadelphia, all asking, "What's the matter?" The third day of the great series saw the two teams ready for action in plenty. The Athletics had "Jumping Jack" Jones, (a name he derived from his peculiar delivery) in the box and Louisville pinned faith in Guy Herker.

The home team went to bat first and when the ninth inning rolled around, the score stood 6 to 4 in favor of the Athletics. In the first half Louisville tied the score. The Athletics were then blanked in their half and so was Louisville in the beginning of the tenth.

For the Athletics in the eleventh, Storey [Stovey] the first man to bat got a base on balls. He stole second and went to third when Lon Knight hit a short single. Knight immediately stole second and with men on second and third, Mike Monahan [Moynahan] strode to the plate and hit the first ball pitched to center field winning the game and the championship.

In the meantime St. Louis won from Pittsburg again so the pennant was won by a half a game.

The players reached Philadelphia a few days following the last game and all the way through Pennsylvania were met by delegations of admiring citizens.

Upon their arrival in the Quaker City they were placed in carriages and headed by bands were paraded through the principal streets to the Mercantile club, where they banqueted.

Simmons retained control of the club until the close of the season of '87, at which time he disposed of his interests and took once more to his first love — the stage.

In commenting on the difference between those baseball days and the game today Simmons told me a few things about the spit-ball and handed out the information that Mathews used it in the 80's with as much success as the best of the present day spit-ball twirlers.

"No one seemed to know what he was doing with the ball but we always knew it was something new as the ball would be wet on one side," said Simmons Saturday.

Simmons tells some interesting news regarding his first visit to Toledo in 1871, at which time he was half owner of the Simmons and Slocum minstrel troupe.

The black face boys were coming in from Fort Wayne but were delayed by [railroad track] washouts and did not arrive until just a few moments before the time for the curtain to rise.

Simmons relates in order to keep the people in their seats the actors were compelled to go on the stage in their street clothes.

Although not connected with baseball at the present time Simmons is an ardent enthusiast and during his off-seasons can always be found at the American League park, Philadelphia, when the team which he originally helped put upon the baseball map, is playing at home.

Where Addie's spelling of a player's name disagrees with The Great Encyclopedia of 19th-Century Major League Baseball, *I have corrected it in brackets following. There is a chance that he took those names verbatim from the old trouper's mouth, and that should be recorded too. Or maybe the typesetter made his own spellings from Addie's copy. Among these players, only Harry Stovey (156 steals in 1888), "Cub" Stricker (second baseman for Cleveland A.A., N.L. and Players League teams) and Bobby Mathews (a 140-pounder, who won 30 games in three straight years) are much remembered today. Christian Frederick Wilhelm Von Der Ahe was a colorful man with a colorful name. His Browns played in a colorful league, too: in its inaugural season of 1882, American Association players wore nine different color-coded uniforms to designate positions. Team captain Lon Knight, who played every game in right field, was what we would call the manager; Lew Simmons was the GM.*

Notice that pitchers threw from an area designated as "the box," a term Addie still uses even after the official rule changed the term to "pitcher's plate," in 1904. And at the start of a game, the home team got to choose whether to bat first or second in innings. The spitball would be legal for all pitchers until the 1920 season. After the ruling, only "certified" players were permitted to continue to use the pitch. That short list included the pitching matchups for the 1920 World Series, Cleveland's Stan Coveleski and Brooklyn's Burleigh Grimes.

(FEBRUARY 3, 1907, TNB)

Of all the amateur teams Toledo boasts of, probably none was better known or established a more enviable record than did the Starrs. They were known in every part of the state and had the reputation of being a team that was worth going miles to see on account of their wonderful playing.

The president of the club was Charles Starr, at one time councilman from the Fourth ward, and well known about town. Starr organized the team during the season of 1889 and spent the rest of the season getting the bunch in good playing shape.

It may be imagined how much the team improved when it is stated that during the following year they lost but three games out of 35 played. But 1891 was the team's banner year, for during that season they played about 45 games without a defeat.

At this time the city had another organization called the Volunteers which had theretofore been the city champions. It was only natural that with two such strong teams in the same city a meeting to settle the question of supremacy should be arranged.

Amid great excitement the clubs met to settle the long-disputed question. While the Volunteers played a good game, they were no match for the fast-coming Starrs and were overwhelmingly beaten by a score of 16 to 0.

Another team called the "Browns" had aspirations for the championship and immediately challenged the Starrs to defend their newly acquired title, and on the following Sunday the teams locked horns. As with the Volunteers, so was it with the Browns, for they found the new champions too strong, being defeated 8 to 2.

The fame of the Starrs reached such proportions that the management of Presque Isle engaged them for the following season to play every Sunday as a special attraction.

The management of Metropolitan Park, then situated on Cherry street, also engaged the team for their weekday games.

In 1892 the Starrs lost four games, not because they were not playing as fast as during the previous year, but they were meeting teams of heavier caliber.

Of the four games lost, only one was to a local team, the Maroons. Two of the other three defeats were by the Pemberville club, who at that time had the well known local twirler, George Kelb. This was just prior to Kelb's Cleveland engagement. The other team to defeat them was Fremont, who had another well known ex–Toledo twirler, "Long John" Blue, pitching for them.

Prior to the Freemont game, in which the Starrs were defeated 8 to 6, the teams had met at Presque Isle and battled for supremacy for 14 long innings, at the end of which the game was called on account of darkness, the score standing 3 to 3.

About this time Starr disposed of his interests in the club and Sam Cohn, the politician, assumed the management. This was the last year the team remained intact, disbanding early the following year. Most of the members joined the latter day team, called the Ivys.

Charles Starr, president and manager, is well known by the older residents of the city. He conducted the finest barber shop in the city at that time and was state organizer of the Foresters. But it was as councilman of the Fourth ward that he became universally known. He is one of that organization whom the grim reaper has taken into his fold.

Frank McKinley, who was an honorary member of the club, is also dead.

Richard Ward, financial secretary, also official scorer, is now the manager of the American District, while Johnnie Russell, who was the mascot of the team, is now a well known theatrical mechanic.

Of the players, Fred Yeager, center fielder, is now foreman of the Claus Shear works, at Fremont. John Hannan, right fielder, is dead, but prior to his death held the position of city yardmaster of the Ann Arbor railroad.

Bill Smith, who at that early date delighted the crowds with his wonderful catches and marvelous throws which he continued to duplicate when a member of Strobel's team, was the club's regular left fielder and his baseball career is too well known to Toledo fans to need special mention. Suffice to say, he is now manager of the New Castle team in the O[hio]. and P[ennsylvania]. League.

New Castle is fortunate in securing his services and should his managerial ability equal his worth as a player, the fans need have no fear as to the outcome of the 1907 campaign.

Henry Gilday, sub outfielder, has charge of a machine shop on the north side of Chicago.

Ollie Pecord, the club's star batter, played first base, besides taking his turn in the box. Everyone knows Pecord through his connection with every sporting event pulled off in Toledo.

Ollie, after leaving the Starrs, filled an engagement with the Nashville club of the Southern league, which organization at that time had the world renowned "Tacks" Parrot as a pitcher. Parrot took an aversion to Pecord, which culminated in a mix-up, with the result that Parrot received a severe drubbing at the hands of the youngster.

Nashville was trying to sell Parrot to Cincinnati and when "Tacks" declared that the club was too small to hold both he and Pecord, the latter was released. He gave up the game after this and possibly the game lost a star, as his early work gave promise of a great future.

Few of Frank Kiley's friends who know him now as the genial freight agent of the T., & O. C. will recognize in him the slender youth who did such great work for the Starrs at the keystone station. In his present occupation Kiley is as successful as when a member of the Starrs.

John Degnan, who used to take in everything that came his way while playing shortstop, is now a member of the Toledo fire department, being captain of No. 9 engine house. The bravery, daring and nerve he now shows every day is no doubt due to his early training on the ball field, as at that time he was always at his best when the occasion required nerve and stamina.

Dudley Robinson, the Starr's crack third baseman, is foreman of the T. & O. C. car shops at Kenton, while Tim Russell, who did all the catching later played with Wheeling, is dead.

John Judge, one of the club's twirlers, is located at the Merchants hotel, at which place he holds a good position.

Lon McCree, the club's star pitcher, was one of the famous McCree boys and is now a tester of automobiles and is employed at one of the largest automobile factories in the country.

William Skelley, another honorary member of the team, is employed by the Blade as mailing clerk.

"Pugs" or "Lefty" Kelb started one game, and pitched in two others, for the 1898 Spiders. One memorable spring training game before the regular season, on March 25, he scored the run in Hot Springs, Arkansas, that beat the Pirates. Kelb died, in Toledo, in 1936. Bill Smith is probably the Cleveland Blues outfielder who played one game in 1884. Toledo's automobile manufacturing, for a time, rivaled nearby Detroit. The Pope Motor Car Company sold

its Pope-Toledo model for $3,000. Pope had various competitors in the city, including the De Lux Motor Cars. The Toledo & Ohio Central train station has been restored. Showboat "Tacky Tom" Parrot was the Reds' Opening Day pitcher for 1894.

Addie's friends and readers really did include the firemen, the post office employees, and the hotel workers that Billy Sunday alluded to in Addie's funeral sermon.

(FEBRUARY 24, 1907, TNB)

At Hot Springs, one day during the "boiling out" season Jack Taylor of the Cubs related to a few players in the lobby of the Majestic hotel his first experience with that great bunch of sluggers, who comprised the Philadelphia Nationals.

Jack broke in at Chicago, when the National league was the only major league organization, going up from Connie Mack's Milwaukee team. Chicago was at home playing the "Phillies."

Clark Griffith pitched the first game and anyone who doesn't know the secret of "Grif's" success may well wonder why the sluggers didn't tear down the fences.

Taylor had heard much about the hitting ability of ["Larry"] Lajoie, [Ed] Delahanty and the rest of the bunch, and when he saw how easy the "Old Fox" mowed them down, he told the rest of the team he didn't see where they had any license to be known as hard hitters.

Taylor was sent in to pitch the next day, and what happened is best told in his own words. "Thomas, the first man up, bunted safe," said Jack. "The next singled and then Delahanty, the greatest of them all, tore one down the third base line for three sacks. The big Frenchman [Lajoie] followed and drove the ball clear to the club house in center field for a circuit of the bases. When [Elmer] Flick nearly tore off my head with a line drive, I was glad to see [Tom] Loftus wave me in, as I knew the agony was over for that day at least.

"Oh, no, that bunch couldn't hit! Someone in a prize ring was doing the hitting, I guess."

The Naps were in Hot Springs, Arkansas, for spring training (the "boiling out" season) only for 1907. Jack Taylor once finished 187 consecutive games, including extra-inning contests and double-headers. He retired in 1907, with 152 career wins. The workhorse was born in New Straitsville, Ohio. Tom Loftus managed Cleveland teams in the American Association (1888) and the National League (1889).

(NOVEMBER 8, 1908, TNB AND NOVEMBER 9, 1908, CP)

The much mooted question [sic] often discussed of whether or not players of some years ago, would be able to deliver as high a standard of baseball now, as do the men in the game at the present time, is a pretty tough proposition.

There is absolutely no question but that the pastime is faster today than it ever was and for this reason alone it is safe to presume that the players of today must necessarily play a speedier game than did their brethren of years ago.

This does not mean to imply that the present day players are any better fit, physically, to perform things than were the old timers.

Occasionally baseball gets a chance to compare the merits of the older and younger generation, as in the case of Sam Thompson, who played a few games with the Tigers, a couple of seasons ago.

This was no fair criterion, as Sam was not in shape to play much and in addition is not as young as he used to be when he was such a terror to pitchers. Consequently very little could be gained by comparison with the rest of the Detroit players.

Emmet Heidrick, who joined the Browns near the middle of last season, was always considered a corking good hitter when playing regularly.

He laid off for a couple of years, just playing a few games during the summer months, more for exercise and the sport of it, than for anything else.

[Jimmy] McAleer persuaded him to join the Browns and finish out the season. Emmett came on and while his legs were not as strong as they might have been, thus interfering with his fielding and base running still there was no apparent reason why he should not be able to hit just as hard as ever.

The old-timers will tell you they know they can hit the "spitball." Well, here was Heidrick who had only been out a couple of years, a young man and one who had been playing quite a bit during his lay off, found the saliva slant almost impossible to hit.

If he could not successfully sole the damp fling, is it reasonable to suppose that old-timers would step to the plate and make a whole lot of base hits when opposed to a "spitball" pitcher?

When the star hitters who have remained in the game right along for a number of years, are finding it impossible to keep above the .300 mark, it seems more than likely that the old-timers would also experience some difficulty in doing a great deal of clouting.

The version of the article printed in the Cleveland Press *features an improved first sentence, beginning: "The question often discussed." At the end of the 1906 campaign, Sam Thompson came out of retirement to play eight games with Detroit, the team he started with in 1885. This isn't the humiliating Minnie Miñoso resurrection: The Tigers begged him to play because they needed a run producer. Thompson's record .92 RBIs per game has since been tied (Lou Gehrig and Hank Greenberg) but never broken. Elmer Flick began his career as the understudy to Thompson. Emmett Heidrick rejoined the Browns for 26 games in 1908, after retiring from the team four years before. He broke in with the 1898 Spiders. American League hitters in 1908 averaged just .239 combined with an anemic slugging percentage of .304. Comparable figures for big league batters in 1894, the year after the pitcher was paced off to 60 feet and six inches, were .309 and .435. In* Leveling the Field, *G. Scott Thomas' adjusted career stats for Addie come to 171 wins, 101 losses, 1763 strikeouts, and a 3.14 ERA.*

(December 31, 1908, TNB)

Jesse Hoffmeister, the Toledo ball player, who once received a trial with the Pittsburg club, was at one time considered one of the most promising young players in the country. Jesse had a great arm and was a fine fielder and strong hitter as well. Hoffmeister played a few games in the Smoky City aggregation and [he] got the fans wild with his [fielding?] and the way he shot them over from third, the position he was playing at the time.

The Philadelphia club, then managed by George Stallings, who [would take] charge of the Highlanders in coming seasons, came along and the rest of the story is better told in Stallings' own words.

"Our team at that time [boasted?] some of the greatest hitters in the country," he recently told the [unreadable text] opposing pitcher, his [unreadable] the time of their lives ducking the line drives [unreadable] whining grounders that were [bound?] to come their way.

"The minute we landed in Pittsburg, we were told what a [unreadable text] player Hoffmeister was, and naturally we were anxious to see him at work.

"The game started, and right off [unreadable] our gang started to hit. The first ball blasted at Hoffmeister went by him like a rifle shot and before he really knew what was happening it was on the way to the outfield.

"Then started a bombardment the like of which I have never seen. It seemed as though every hard-hit ball went straight down the third base line. Not one of them seemed to take a true bound, and this, coupled with the speed of the slams, made that afternoon one never to be forgotten by Hoffmeister.

"Then to make it still tougher for Jesse," continued Stallings, "we had a couple of pretty fast left-handers. And about the time Hoffmeister was backing out on the grass towards the outfield, trying to get away from some of the drives without getting killed, one of these fellows would lay down a bunt and be across the bag before Hoffmeister had a chance to field the ball.

"I believe that one afternoon had more to do with Jesse leaving the Pittsburg club than any other thing, and I don't know as I blame him any. I think I would have resigned myself."

Even though the newspaper page is badly damaged, the story Stallings relates, about Toledo-native Jesse Hoffmeister's perilous afternoon, comes through with the vividness of a nightmare. In his only major league season, Hoffmeister somehow survived 48 games at third base for the 1897 Pittsburgh Alleghenys. The likes of Napoleon Lajoie, Billy Nash, and Ed Delahanty would have been belting those line drives at poor, defenseless Hoffmeister. George "Tweedy" Stallings was managing in his first of 13 seasons. Next year, it would be his decision to move Lajoie from first to second base.

(FEBRUARY 9, 1909, TNB)

It is not always the fast man on his feet who makes the best base runner. Men like Ed Delahanty and "Big Bill" Lange, when in the hey-day of their career, were as good base runners as there were in the business. It was not their fleetness of foot that made them such wonders on the paths.

Both players were big men, who had the art of sliding to a base down to a science, and this, coupled with the fact that they always managed to get a good lead and took advantage of their bulk to intimidate the men covering second made it well nigh impossible for them to be caught.

Players of the stamp of Delahanty and Lange were always on the lookout for a chance to pilfer a base. In order for them to be successful it was necessary for them to get a good lead.

This was done by closely watching every move of the pitcher and acquainting themselves with all those little peculiarities, which by close observation are always manifested in the twirler's work.

Every box artist has some little peculiarity which he always discloses, letting the base runner know just about when he is going to let go of the ball. Once Lange or Delahanty were wise to this, they always took advantage of it.

Once under headway, these men always kept the man, who was covering, in view, and whichever way he went for the throw, they were sure to slide the opposite way. If the baseman stepped on the inside of the bag for the throw they slid on the outside of the base and vice versa.

Both men were big, powerful fellows, and whenever the baseman refused to give them the right of way, as a good many infielders do, they never hesitated about sliding into the player on the bag.

No wonder they were tough men to get. They easily led the old National league a few seasons, and when not leading were always well up.

Herein Addie supplies even further examples of big men base-runners. As he develops support for his Hot Stove argument, I imagine him bantering with fans over the direct line. Has it really taken till now to praise in print Cleveland-born Ed Delahanty, perhaps the premier slugger of his day? (Addie makes him sound like José Canseco without the juice.) "Big Ed" led the league with 58 stolen bases in 1898, and totaled 455 in a career abbreviated by his death on a railroad bridge at Niagara Falls. Bill Lange's nickname is usually given as "Little Eva." He led everybody in steals (73) the year before Delahanty did. Addie played against Ed, but Lange had retired after 1899. The record shows that Ed Delahanty had two hits in 11 career at-bats versus Addie Joss. Note that Addie published this piece, on the late Ed Delahanty, the same day that he wrote on the events surrounding Win Mercer's suicide.

7

"Is the American League a Minor League?"

WORLD SERIES REPORTS

Reporter Addie Joss covered three World Series, starting with the 1907 Classic, for the Cleveland Press. *His game-day reports (the only ones he ever wrote) were also syndicated and appeared in Scripps newspapers across the country, including the Toledo* News-Bee. *By the year of Addie's death, the practice of the $500 "player scribe" had become a problem, requiring the attention of the National Commission that ruled baseball before the commissioner system. During the World Series that year, for example, Giants teammates Christy Mathewson and Rube Marquard (or, at least, their ghostwriters, John N. Wheeler and Frank G. Menke) feuded, in their morning-after columns, over how to pitch Frank Baker. The National Commission prohibited, in 1913, World Series players from signing with ghostwriters.*

While the playoffs were dubbed, in those years, the "world's series," Addie traveled to just three cities—Chicago, Detroit, and Pittsburgh—and the games were played over a grand total of 18 days (including two scheduled offdays during the 1909 affair). In Addie's decade of baseball, Cleveland's regional postseason games with Cincinnati and Pittsburgh were taken as seriously by many fans: The first motion picture film of ball players was taken before a 1903 game for the so-called Ohio championship—not at the first World Series being played that same week.[1] *The World Series would not be filmed until 1908, the year 6,210 curious showed up in Detroit for the deciding game. It would take until the "Home Run" Baker Series of 1911, with its "player scribes" and their ghostwritten syndicated columns, before a Fall Classic would become a nationally popular event.*

From the 1907 World Series

The World Series of 1907 was only the fourth in modern history. But it's already a chance for the Chicago Cubs to redeem itself in postseason play: the team dons its gray road uniforms, for Game One, to break its home losing streak from last year's Series loss to the White Sox. This makes the first of three consecutive appearances for the Detroit Tigers, the only American League team Addie gets to observe from the press booth. Chicago takes the Series by winning four straight, after Detroit manages a tie in the first game (called for darkness at West Side Grounds, after 12 innings).

(DATELINE: OCTOBER 9, 1907)

The opening clash between the Cubs and the Tigers for the world's championship was one grand struggle, and, although the outcome leaves the strength of the teams as much a matter of conjecture now as it was Tuesday morning, the playing gives one something of a line on their respective merits.

The fielding of both clubs was nothing out of the ordinary, with the possible exception of two plays. One was made by [Johnny] Evers in the fourth. With [Sam] Crawford on second and [Claude] Rossman on first, he raced out into center and pulled down [Bill] Coughlin's short fly, doubling Sam who had started for the plate thinking the hit was going safe.

The other, and the play that wound up the game, was ["Germany"] Schaefer's catch of [Frank] Chance's awful smash. He got the ball with his gloved hand while running at full speed toward second, and doubled [Jimmy] Sheckard, who had been hit by a pitched ball.

[Bill] Donovan's pitching on the whole was much better than [Orval] Overall's, while in the few innings that [Ed] Ruelbach was on the slab, he was invincible. "Wild Bill'"s work was brilliant, because he was continually pulling himself out of tight holes, especially during the later innings. His judgment all day seemed perfect.

A striking example of this was shown when ["Heinie"] Zimmerman, who replaced [Joe] Tinker after the ninth, came to bat in the eleventh with bases full and one out. Bill put on a little extra steam, getting two strikes and no balls with two fast ones. The third ball he pitched was at the batter's head, driving him away, while the last one started right for the middle of the plate but took a quick break and the youngster missed it by a foot.

[Orval] Overall, while he pitched a good game, didn't seem to have near the things at his command that Donovan used so well.

Kling out caught ["Boss"] Schmidt, and to this fact can be attributed the Cub's numerous stolen bases. The Detroit backstop was far from being in his usual form. It was the missing of a third strike by him that let [Harry] Steinfeldt romp across the plate with the tying run in the ninth, when, had he held it, the game would have been over.

"Johnny" Kling gave a grand exhibition of catching and general all-around playing.

The Cubs had a golden opportunity to win in the tenth, but Steinfeldt threw it away. With [Jimmy] Slagle on third and Chance on second, Schmidt had a short passed ball, "Jimmy" came tearing for the plate at top speed as Schmidt ran to recover the ball, while Donovan hustled in to cover the plate.

"Jimmy" seemed to have the throw beaten, but as Schmidt drew back his arm to make the throw, Steinfeldt got in his way, blocking the throw. Slagle crossed the plate amid wild excitement, and the crowd, thinking the game over, started to pour on the field, but on Donovan's protest. [Hank] O'Day promptly called Slagle out for Steinfeldt's interference and the Tigers were saved.

"Steiny's" judgment on the play looked very bad.

Both clubs showed gameness that proves conclusively that the series will be fought to the bitter end. Both teams came from behind, the Tigers in the eighth, when they scored three runs, and the Cubs when they tied the score in the ninth, in each case overcoming a handicap that would have disheartened less worthy opponents.

If Tuesday's game can be taken as a criterion of the clubs' playing ability, then it can be safely said that the series will equal, if not excel, that one of last year that made the "Sox" world's champions.

At age 34, Cubs center fielder and leadoff hitter Jimmy "Rabbit" Slagle was probably the best offensive performer (four RBIs, six stolen bases) in this World Series. He was the first player to swipe two bases in one inning in a Series. The Cubs ruled the base paths, stealing 16 bases in the five games. Gerald "Heinie" Zimmerman had an undistinguished Series—his only at-bat was the strikeout Addie records — but he later fashioned an outstanding 13-year career as a National League second and third baseman. His best year was with the Cubs, in 1912, when he was league leader in hits, doubles, home runs, batting average and slugging. He returned to the World Series with the Giants, in 1917, the year he won the National League RBI title for the second consecutive time.

The News-Bee *also printed two boxes, in addition to the article above, under Addie's by-line.*

[Ed] Ruelbach or [Jack] Pfeister will pitch for the Cubs today. It will probably be [Jack] Pfeister with [Johnny] Kling at backstop. [George] Mullin or [Ed] Seiver — probably Mullin — will handle the pill for Detroit, and ["Boss"] Schmidt will catch.

The game will start at 2:00 p.m., instead of 2:30, to prevent another game being called on account of darkness. Yesterday's tie will be played off in Chicago Thursday.

The players originally scheduled to cut in on the receipts of only the first four games will now share the fifth. Just before the series started, ["Germany"] Schaefer, of the Tigers, happened to think that no provision had been made for the division in case of a tie, and the players got the national commission to agree to their share of the fifth.

The Game One tie was not completed on the following day, so the players' cut needed to be negotiated. The World Series players' regular agreement with the National Commission was to take a share in gate receipts for first four games of the Series; thus, only the two leagues and the club owners would profit from an extended playoff. Germany Schaefer is usually cast as a baseball clown, but here the Tigers' team captain is acting as player representative. He was a smart player on the field, too, pulling off a hidden-ball trick in Game Two. Schaefer was also known as an effective sign-stealing base coach and expert heckler.

Both the Cubs and Tigers had chances galore to break up yesterday's 12-inning tie, but something always came up to spoil the opportunities. In the first inning [Jimmy] Scheckard reached third on a single, a steal and a wild heave, but could not get home.

Detroit got two hits and a sacrifice in the third, but no runs. Two hits and an out put ["Boss"] Schmidt on third in the fifth, but [Johnny] Kling caught him napping on an attempted double steal. The same thing happened to ["Germany"] Schaefer in the sixth.

[Jimmy] Slagle scored the winning run in the tenth, but was declared out on [Harry] Steinfeldt's interference with [Bill] Donovan, who received Schmidt's throw after a passed ball. With one out and the bases full in the eleventh, ["Heinie"] Zimmerman fanned, and [Ed] Ruelbach forced ["Wildfire"] Schulte.

Detroit's two-run lead in the ninth inning of Game One was its biggest margin in the five-game Series. And the Tigers' three runs in the eighth represented precisely half of all the runs (four earned) they would tally against the Cubs in this World Series. Jimmy Slagle had stolen third base in the tenth inning, when Charles Schmidt let a pitch from Donovan get past him. His mad dash for the plate was, in its way, as daring a play as Ty Cobb's steal of home in the 1909 World Series. The only member of the Cubs' infield who is not in Cooperstown, Harry Steinfeldt led his team with eight hits in the Series, including its only triple. He was coming off a career year, in which he led the National League in hits and RBIs, and fielding percentage for third basemen.

(DATELINE: OCTOBER 10, 1907)

The second game of the world's series was in many respects a great improvement over the first, and while it resulted in a victory for the Cubs, the game itself showed that the clubs are evenly matched. The Detroit sluggers, [Sam] Crawford and [Ty] Cobb, were handicapped by being forced to hit against a southpaw, which partially accounts for the Tigers' low score, while the Cubs' two runs, scored in the fourth, were helped along by good base running.

[Hughie] Jennings' change of catchers didn't stop [Frank] Chance's men on the paths at all, and they ran wild every time they got on.

["Germany"] Schaefer hit in tough luck. Twice with [Davy] Jones on first, he and Davy tried the hit and run play, and both times "Germany" hit right over the [second base] bag, forcing Jones the first time, and being thrown out himself the second.

The first time they tried it, "Dutch" had [Jack] Pfeister three and two but [Joe] Tinker covered anyway.

[Claude] Rossman certainly did clout the ball, getting three hits for five bases out of four times at bat. They were all good hard drives.

Claud[e] really had four hits, but lost the second in a peculiar way. Cobb opened the inning with a single and "Ross," after two attempts to bunt, hit a short fly to right. It looked as if ["Wildfire"] Schulte was going to get it, so Cobb went down about half way. Schulte saw he couldn't quite make the catch and stopped short, getting the ball on a short bound, and threw to second, just beating "Ty" to the bag.

[Shortstop Charlie] O'Leary was the bright star in a fielding way. His chances were all hard, but the one that looked great was his one-hand stab of [Johnny] Kling's hit over second. He and [first baseman] Rossman both made fine plays on [Harry] Steinfeldt's hit, just previous to this, Rossman getting the putout by reaching high and taking the throw with his gloved hand.

Crawford made a fine play on Kling's line drive, which looked good for three bases. The ball was hit dead straight over his head, but Sam jumped while running back and pulled it down, doubling Chance off second.

[Jimmy] Scheckard's contribution was a shoestring affair, a beauty. He came tearing in on [Fred] Payne's line drive to left, getting the ball about six inches from the ground.

Johnny Kling again demonstrated what a wonderful catcher he is. His throwing was superb and general all around work perfect.

Tinker's steal of third, which gave the Cubs what proved to be the winning run, was a clever piece of work, by both him and [Jimmy] Slagle, who was at the bat. As Tinker started to steal, Slagle made a bluff to bunt, which pulled [Bill] Coughlin in just far enough so he could not get back fast enough to touch Joe as he slid to the bag.

The work of both pitchers was good, Pfeister twirling a steady game. While [George] Mullin was a trifle unsteady at times, he performed brilliantly in the second inning, when, after forcing in a run with no one out, he struck out Pfeister and Slagle and made Scheckard hit a grounder to Schaefer.

Schaefer pulled Mullin out of a close fix in the first inning. Slagle had reached third with none out when Schekard hit a high fly to Dutch, who caught the ball. As Slagle worked back to the bag, Germany hid the ball under his arm and when Jimmy stepped off the bag Schaefer snapped it to Coughlin, who touched the "Rabbit" as he made a desperate effort to slide back in safety.

If [Jimmy] Archer, who is likely to catch today, can stop the Cubs on the bases, the Tigers look to have an even break yet, as outside of this department of the game they seem to be the better team.

Tigers shortstop Charley O'Leary managed one hit in five World Series games. He was Germany Schaefer's co-star on vaudeville. Manager Hughie Jennings' platoon at catcher couldn't contain Cubs base stealers in next year's championship rematch of the two clubs, either: in 1908, they swiped another 15 bags. Detroit's trio of equally ineffective catchers were "Boss" Schmidt, Jimmy Archer, and Fred Payne. Claude Rossman's eight hits led the Tigers, but his fielding hurt them. We usually think of Sam Crawford as a model right fielder, but he made his fine catch playing center field. Ty Cobb patrolled right field in 1907.

Chicago's slugging right fielder, Frank Schulte, was nicknamed "Wildfire" after he and his teammates, before this 1908 season, saw a Lillian Russell play by that title. In 1911, the year he won the Chalmers auto (the ur–MVP), he was the first player in history to record 20 doubles, 20 triples, 20 home runs, and 20 stolen bases), and the first to hit four grand slams, in a year. (Cleveland's Jeff Heath, also a right fielder, was a 20–20–20 man in 1941.) Samuel James Tilden Sheckard was the left fielder in the famous "S" outfield (with Slagle in center and Schulte). A notorious streak hitter, he'd gone 0-for-21 in the 1906 World Series, but had five hits in five games in 1907 Series. In his best years, he led the league in runs, triples, home runs, walks (twice), stolen bases, on base percentage, and slugging; in his off years, he would hit in the .230s. He was named after Governor James Tilden.

(DATELINE: OCTOBER 11, 1907)

The third game of the world's series developed nothing startling in the general all-around play of either club. The Cubs won solely because they hit when hits meant runs, while the Tigers couldn't get the hit that would send home the base runners.

[Ed] Ruelbach pitched a very good game and had the Tigers helpless for the first four innings, but from then on they were hitting him quite hard, especially in the fifth and sixth innings, great fielding and a few horseshoes getting him out of ticklish places.

With [Claude] Rossman on third and [Bill] Coughlin at second and one out in the fifth, Charley O'Leary stepped into a curve ball and met it full on the nose. The ball was hit directly over [Joe] Tinker's head, and, had it got by, would have gone to the fence, but Joe, jumping as high as he could, managed to spear it, doubling Coughlin at second.

In the sixth [Ed] Killian, the first man at bat, singled, and [Davy] Jones walked. ["Germany"] Schaefer hit a fast bounder to the left of [Harry] Steinfeldt, on which the Cubs' third sacker made a great play, doubling Jones and Schaefer by throwing to [Johnny] Evers, who tossed to [Frank] Chance. Sam Crawford and [Ty] Cobb followed with singles. This play broke up what might have been a great batting rally. [Ed] Siever, on the other hand, was hit steadily.

What seems strange was the fact that it was the Cubs' left-hand hitters that were driving in all the runs. Evers duplicated Rossman's feat of getting three hits out of four times at bat. Two of John's were two-base hits. Both Rossman and Evers are left-hand hitters, and made their hits off south paw twirlers.

Killian's work, after the first inning he was in, was fully as good as any twirling that has been done in the series: his judgment on the Cubs' heavy hitters being fine, while his speed and curves were good. His change of pace is really what made him so effective.

["Boss"] Schmidt's work behind the bat was all that could be desired. No one attempted to steal clean on him. In fact, the Cubs were playing the hit and run game all day, and invariably when a man started down the batter would hit safe.

[Johnny] Kling's work, while not so spectacular as during the other games, was just as good. To really appreciate a ball player's worth, it is generally conceded, one must see him work quite a number of games. From what I have seen of Kling, I must say he is a wonder, and lives up to his reputation.

The Tigers' outfield was a bit wobbly Thursday, not so much in that Jones missed Tinker's long fly after a stern chase, but in that Dave [Jones] and Crawford nearly collided in going after Chance's fly in the fifth giving the batter a double on a hit that should have been an out.

The scene of today's battle shifts to Detroit, which will give the Tigers a slight advantage. [Hughie] Jennings' men are by no means disheartened, and will fight all the harder. In a series like this that means a whole lot. With an even break in the luck [Bill] Donovan should win today, as "Wild Bill" is right at his best now, and all American league rooters know what that means.

Cubs' starter Ed Reulbach was born in Detroit. His one-hitter against the White Sox in the 1906 World Series started a personal winning streak that lasted until June 29, 1907. (He would put together a 14-game winning streak in 1909.) He led the league in winning percentage in the Cubs' three consecutive pennant years. Reulbach first achieved fame as a college player, at the University of Vermont, after attending the University of Notre Dame.

The News-Bee *also ran a game summary in a box under Addie's byline.*

The Cubs blossomed out as run getters yesterday in the second round. [Harry] Steinfeldt leaned against a[n Ed] Siever offering, and whaled the ball over Bill Coughlin's head for two sacks. [Johnny] Kling moved him up, and [Johnny] Evers allowed him to walk home with a double over first.

The Cubs did a big business in the fourth and in addition laid Siever away. With one hand gone, Kling singled. Evers followed suit and ["Wildfire"] Schulte placed a safety in center. Kling scored, but Evers was nailed at third.

Schulte scored when Davy Jones dropped Tinker's long fly; and the shortstopper bounded over the pan when [Ed] Ruelbach pounded out a single. [Ed] Killian faced the Cubs in the fifth and got a warm reception. [Jimmy] Sheckard died, but [Frank] Chance got a Texas league two bagger and came home when Steinfeldt singled.

The Tigers' only run was made in the sixth. Killian opened with a single and moved along on Jones' walk. ["Germany"] Schaefer hit into a double play, but [Sam] Crawford was there with the pinch biff, and the slabber trotted home. The remainder of the contest was runless.

Ed Killian had the only hit in Addie's September 5, 1907, shutout in Detroit.

(DATELINE: OCTOBER 12, 1907)

Yesterday's game at Bennett park proved conclusively that if the Tigers expect to be in at the finish they will have to show much improvement over the day's play, as, in comparison with the Cubs, their general all-around play was bad.

The game was featured by good pitching on the part of [Orval] Overall, who after the fifth inning never seemed in danger. On the other hand, "Wild Bill" [Donovan] was hit steadily and at opportune moments.

The Tigers' only run was earned. The Cubs' first two runs were the result of an error, a walk, a sacrifice, a single and a long fly. This came right after the game had been delayed for about 15 minutes on account of rain, and possibly therein lies the explanation, as up to that time Wild Bill seemed to have the Cubs at his command.

The more glaring offense by the Tigers — and the one that practically lost the game, happened in the seventh inning, which opened by ["Wildfire"] Schulte beating out a hit to Donovan. On the next play someone's judgment went wrong. [Joe] Tinker bunted to Wild Bill, and someone in the infield yelled to Bill to throw to second. He did, trying to force Schulte, when it seemed that even with a perfect throw his chances for getting his man were slim. Overall sacrificed, and [Charley] O'Leary threw badly to the plate on [Jimmy] Slagle's grounder, Schulte scoring.

Had Donovan thrown to first on Tinker's bunt he would have retired the side without a run and possibly this would have changed the entire aspect of the game.

Another bad piece of work by the Tigers happened in this same inning, when [Claude] Rossman found no one covering first after he had picked up [Jimmy] Scheckard's bunt.

The fielding star for Detroit was [Ty] Cobb, when he made a couple of fine catches on line hits and long flies, an especially fine one on [Johnny] Evers' drive; while for Chicago, no one starred, all working in first-class form.

The Tigers were a trifle unlucky in the early stages of the game, in the fact that their line hits, as a rule, invariably found someone standing in front of them, this being especially true when they had men on bases.

Schulte contributed a fine piece of work when he threw out Wild Bill on the latter's clean single to right in the third inning. Schulte's handling of the ball and throw to [Frank] Chance were perfect.

Considerable feeling was shown by members of both teams toward each other. This fact was noticeable when Cobb slid into Chance at first on his hit to Tinker in the first inning.

Nothing short of a wonderful spurt and great improved form by the Tigers will ever give them a look-in [colloquial] from now on, as with the

Cubs three games to the good, they will enter into the rest of the contest with that confidence which always goes to a winning team. This in itself is practically enough to assure them the world's championship.

The News-Bee *report has "toil" for "play" in the first sentence. For the sake of clarity, I adopt the* News-Bee *spelling, "look-in," in the final paragraph, instead of the* Press' *"lookin." "Double-O" Overall's other nickname was "The Big Groundhog" because he was born on February 2. The Tigers never could hit him in World Series play: He won three straight against them, including two games in the 1908 Series, when he struck out a record four batters in an inning. In a silent comment on the poor fielding in the game, Addie cites for commendation only the game's right fielders, Schulte and Cobb. Detroit gave away eight unearned runs in this Series. Tigers kranks and kickers must have been as unenthusiastic about their team's chances as Addie sounds. A franchise record 297,079 attended regular season games at Bennett Park, but only 7,370 witnessed the decisive Game Five the next day.*

Game Five, the final game of the 1907 World Series, was played on Saturday, October 13. Two factors conspire so that we don't have a Joss report. The Cleveland Press *printed no Sunday edition, and Toledo* News-Bee *Sunday editions have not survived. If Addie was paid by the weekly* Press *to publish reports, under his name, in Sunday newspapers that subscribed to the Scripps syndicate, I am unaware of their existence.*[2]

From the 1908 World Series

This rematch of the Cubs and Tigers is the result of an anything but routine regular seasons for both teams. This is the year that the Merkle Boner keeps the Giants from the World Series. To win the National League pennant, Chicago has to defeat New York in the replay of a tie game. Detroit wins the American League championship in the final game of the season. The outcome of the Series is a repeat, but it's the last World Series title in Cubs' franchise history.

The opening game of this World Series was played on October 11, a Sunday. I am not aware of a report by Addie on Chicago's 10 to 6 victory. The game summary he offers his Cleveland readers, in the last three paragraphs of his report on Game Two, suggests that he didn't file a report on the first game.

(DATELINE: OCTOBER 12, 1908)

The second game of the world's series was won in handy fashion by the Cubs. After trying in vain for seven innings to solve Wild Bill Donovan's delivery they fell on him in the eighth, and when the smoke of the battle had cleared the Cubs were six runs to the good. Detroit's lone score came in the ninth at a time when [Frank] Chance's men had the game clinched.

For seven innings the contest was as fine a pitchers' battle as one would care to see, and from the way both twirlers were going it seemed sure the game would go into extra innings.

"FIELDING IS FAST"

In the eighth after [Harry] Steinfedt had fanned, and ["Solly"] Hofman made what is termed a "swinging bunt" down the third base line, ["Germany"] Schaefer fielded the ball too late to get the speedy center fielder.

With [Joe] Tinker at bat, Hofman started to steal. The ball was high and wide. Joe hit it high in the air toward right field. The wind got under the pill and [Ty] Cobb, who was sent to make the catch, was forced to see the ball drop in the bleachers. For the rest of the inning Bill was hit hard.

The fielding on both sides was wonderfully clean and fast, with [Johnny] Evers and [Jerry] Downs starring. Downs twice went to his left to get hard hit ground balls that were labeled base hits, and each time came up with the ball.

The one particular play which made Evers look good was on [Sam] Crawford's slow roller in the sixth, which he was forced to play with one hand while on the dead run toward the plate. Both the pickup and throw were perfect.

"EVERS A GREAT STAR"

You have to give it to Johnny. He is certainly in the game at all times. With Schaefer on first and ["Boss"] Schmidt at bat in the fifth, the hit and run play was tried. The Tiger backstop lined a beauty to right, on which Germany could have gone to third. The minute Evers saw the ball going safe, he ran over to second and acted as though he was waiting for a grounder. This caused Schaefer to stop, and when he saw it was a bluff, it was too late to go on to third.

The little fellow also crossed the Tiger infield when he beat out a bunt with [Jimmy] Sheckard on second and two out in the eighth.

Both Evers and Chance ran the bases splendidly in the fatal eighth inning. Chance worked the delayed stead once, while Evers went to second once while [first baseman Claude] Rossman tossed the ball to Donovan.

Bill was afraid to throw to second as there was no one covering third, and Sheckard was half way up the line to the plate, just waiting to score if the ball was thrown to second. Schaefer left third unguarded to cover the plate on this play, as Schmidt had fielded the bunt.

The umpiring of [Bill] Klem and [Tom] Connolly was excellent.

The opening game of the world's series at Detroit Saturday can be called nothing but a swatfest.

Both teams clearly demonstrated the fact that they can come from behind. This is one of the essentials of a pennant-winning cub, and both clubs showed gameness in the rain at Bennett park Saturday.

The fielding was what was to be reasonably expected with the grounds in such slippery condition.

Arthur Hofman earned the nickname "Circus Solly" for his circus catches in center field, or from his resemblance to a newspaper comic strip character. Manager Frank Chance had forbidden Hofman to marry and "distract" the team before this 1908 World Series. Following the victory over the Tigers, however, husband and wife moved to Akron, Ohio, where they ran a restaurant. It was Hofman who fielded the ball Fred Merkle hit into infamy. That's Germany Schaefer, who was the regular second baseman in the previous World Series, in one of his two games at third base in the 1908 Series. Being out of his usual position might account for his bad play in the eighth inning. He was back at second baseman for three other games. (Ironically, Tigers second baseman Jerome "Red" Downs filled in for an injured Johnny Evers, on the 1912 Cubs.) Tinker's wind-blown home run was the first in a World Series since 1903, and the only one in 1908. In spite of the rainy conditions, the box score shows that Game Two was played in a trim 84 minutes.

(DATELINE: OCTOBER 13, 1908)

The third game of the world's series emphasized the fact that the American league champions can come from behind.

This necessary attribute, coupled with "Ty" Cobb's great hitting and [George] Mullin's fine pitching, downed the Cubs at a time when it seemed they were sure winners of the day's game and gave Detroit its first victory over the pride of the National league.

From a playing standpoint, Cobb's hitting and base running, Mullin's pitching and Manager [Frank] Chance's work on the paths stand out conspicuously.

Mullin's pitching was of the very finest. George had everything. His speed was fine, control good, and, coupled with this, his curve ball broke fast and true.

"Entitled to Shutout"

The big fellow was entitled to a shutout, had the Tigers played flawless ball. Chicago's three runs were scored after a chance had been offered to retire the side.

With one out in Chicago's half of the fourth, [Johnny] Evers walked. He started to steal and George, calling the turn, threw to [Claude] Rossman.

Claude's throw to ["Germany"] Schaefer at second was high and wide, and Evers was safe. ["Wildfire"] Schulte fouled out to [catcher Ira] Thomas, which would have retired the side without a run. But Chance came along with a hit, which scored Evers, and before the inning was over the Cubs had scored two more. [Jack] Pfeister was hit hard throughout the game. [Ed] Reulbach allowed one hit and a pass, but as they came after two were out, no runs resulted.

"Hitting Was Great"

Cobb's hitting was great. His first single was a "Texas leaguer" over [Joe] Tinker's head, which scored [Charley] O'Leary with the first run of the game. His next was a slow bounder over Pfeister's head which he easily beat to first. The third a slashing double to left, and on his last trip to the plate, he singled sharply between [Harry] Steinfeldt and Tinker.

He immediately stole second in handy fashion and then, on the third pitched ball, broke for third. [Johnny] Kling's throw had him nailed, but "Steiny" dropped the ball.

Manager Chance did some great work on the bases, stealing second twice. The work that made him look great was when he scored from second while Rossman was trying to get [Bill] Coughlin's low throw on Steinfeldt's grounder.

"Ross" juggled the ball long enough to let "Steiny" reach first. Chance rounded third and, seeing the ball fumbled, kept on going to the plate.

Rossman's throw home was bad, but Chance would have beaten it in had it been perfect. Manager [Hughie] Jennings shifted his infield, putting Coughlin on third and Schaefer back at second.

[Hank] O'Day's ruling on balls and strikes was fine, while [Jack] Sheridan gave entire satisfaction on all base decisions.

In the Johnny Evers and Hugh S. Fullerton book, Touching Second, *published only two years after this World Series, George Mullin's curveball is described as a "meteoric shoot." Cobb improved on his performance from the last World Series, batting .365 and leading the Tigers in hits. But he managed only three hits in the four other games in the Series, none for extra bases. The two stolen bases that Addie reports were Cobb's only steals for the week. Detroit swiped six bags in the Series; the Cubs' manager stole five himself.*

(DATELINE: OCTOBER 14, 1908)

Today's game at Bennett park was far and away the best game of the world's series played up to the present time.

Both teams played grand ball in the field, [Ty] Cobb making the only error, which came on [Frank] Chance's line drive in the ninth, and was really an excusable muff, as Ty was running at full speed when he reached for the ball.

He overestimated his own speed and overran it, else the great outfielder would have made the catch.

By all odds the feature of the contest was the wonderful work of [Mordecai] Brown, both in the box and in his fielding. His control was perfect.

"MADE ONE SLIP"

The three-fingered wonder walked no one and his only slip was when he [plunked] [Bill] Coughlin with a curve ball.

Brownie was never in danger but once, and this came in Detroit's half of the fourth. [Charley] O'Leary and [Sam] Crawford had singled with no one out. With but a two-run lead the situation looked a trifle threatening.

Manager Chance, [Harry] Steinfeldt and Brown held a conference in the center of the diamond and the means of procedure were there decided upon. On the first ball pitched Cobb laid down what looked like a perfect bunt.

Brown came in on the ball like a flash, and fielding it perfectly whirled and threw to Steinfeldt, getting the ball there just as O'Leary was sliding into the bag. The play was executed perfectly, and looked as though it had been prearranged, as the moment Cobb bunted Steinfeldt went back to third to take Brown's throw.

"Shows He's A Wonder."

It was simply a marvelous play on the Cub twirler's part, and demonstrated conclusively that the great pitcher is a wonder in more ways than one.

On the next ball pitched [Johnny] Kling and [Joe] Tinker caught Crawford off second by another grand play. Brown pitched out and Tinker covered second.

Kling made a perfect throw to the bag and Sam was out by inches. The play was made absolutely perfect and with lightning-like rapidity.

This was Detroit's one and only chance. From that time on Brown was complete master of the game. Chance and Tinker also starred in the field for the Cubs.

The Chicago shortstop made a great play on ["Boss"] Schmidt's grounder through the box, which took a bad bound to Joe's right, as he was about to field it. He grabbed the ball with his bare hand and got his man by a stride.

"Tinker's Fine Play."

Tinker also made a fine play on Davy Jones' sharp drive to [the] left [side of the infield?], in the eighth. It required perfect handling and a good long throw to get Dave, but Tinker was equal to the task.

Manager Chance's work on the initial sack was great. He saved a run in the first inning by digging up a low throw from Tinker on Cobb's grounder. Crawford was on third at the time, and had the ball gotten away, it would have meant a run for the Tigers.

Crawford and O'Leary shone at bat for Detroit, while Chance, ["Wildfire"] Schulte and Kling made two hits each for the Cubs.

Crawford's first drive went into the [overflow] crowd in left field, and would have been an easy three-base hit, or possibly a home run. Schmidt's throwing to bases was poor, and this indirectly gave Chicago all its runs. Had he thrown out Schulte in the third and [Johnny] Evers in the ninth, the Cubs would have failed to score. It seemed as though he had ample time to get both men. [Ed] Summers, barring his wildness, pitched a fine game.

Both Press *and* News-Bee *articles on microfilm are badly damaged. The Cleveland paper announces this report with a box, titled "Joss Says," that contains three one-sentence paragraphs (only partially readable). The first repeats the lead sentence from the article, and the other two generalize about Three Finger Brown's pitching and fielding. Insiders will notice the clash of strategies here: Hughie Jennings has Cobb, the best player on the field, bunting with two men on base and his team desperately behind in the World Series; Frank Chance would probably have called for the hit and run. Addie's description makes me wonder if the Cubs stole the bunt sign (and the pitchout following). Also, Chance's great play around first base, and Rossman's poor glove work for Detroit, might be considered game-changers in these reports. But Addie sticks with what has become the historical view and blames the loss of Detroit's second straight Series on the inability of Tigers catchers to throw out Cubs base stealers.*

"Kickapoo" Ed Summers lost two games in the 1908 Series, on a staff with pitcher-first baseman George Winter. Summers went 0–4 with the Tigers in two World Series. The overflow crowd standing along the left-field foul line were among the 12,907 who attended the game at Bennett Park (10,500 was capacity). Only 6,210 showed up for the final game on the following day, still the poorest house in World Series history.

(DATELINE: OCTOBER 15, 1908)

When Johnny Kling camped under ["Boss"] Schmidt's high foul in the ninth inning of the last world's series game and as the ball fell easily in the great catcher's mitt for the last out of the big baseball show, it was apparent to every unprejudiced spectator who had seen all the contests that the team that had played the better ball was again world's champions.

A more finished article of baseball than was furnished by the Cubs in every game of the series has seldom been seen.

It is one grand baseball machine, and after watching the team play, one wonders how it loses as many games as it does.

Yesterday's game was only a repetition of the one preceding it. The Tigers were unable to hit when hits meant runs, and though [Bill] Donovan pitched a game which would bring home the bacon a majority of times his work went for naught.

The American league champions simply batter their way through their own league and when they failed to hit the Cub pitchers they looked just as any other slugging aggregation does when it is not hitting.

In the one game [Game Three] where the Tigers batted up to their true form they looked like the goods. On the other hand, the Cubs hit hard, ran bases cleverly, fielded well and looked like a great club all the time.

The umpiring all during the series was perfect, [Jack] Sheridan, [Hank] O'Day, [Tom] Connolly and [Bill] Klem doing the high class work that was expected of them.

From 1906 to 1910, the Cubs missed out on World Series play only once, a year when they still won 94 regular season games.

(October 16, 1908, CP)

Is the American league a minor league?

Following the second humiliating defeat of the Detroit Tigers by the Chicago Cubs, this is a natural query, and one that will be thrashed out in sport pages during the off-season of baseball.

Twice in succession the Tigers have theoretically proved themselves superior of all other American league teams, and then been made to look like novices by the champions of the National league. The natural assumption is that the American league as a whole is not in the same class with the National.

This is not true. There is on the whole no such difference in class as the victories of the Cubs over the Tigers would seem to indicate.

Here is the explanation, as nearly as it can be doped out: The Tigers are not the best all-around team in the American league. They have a splendid outfield, several great pitchers, a good catcher and a punk infield. They have won the pennant these past two seasons by the fine pitching of [Bill] Donovan, [Ed] Killian and [Ed] Summers, the good catching of ["Boss"] Schmidt, and their great batting.

Each time they have gone into the world's series they have lost their nerve completely. Schmidt isn't the same man. He can't throw, he can't hit. Nobody can hit. The infield is a little worse in its fielding. In their post-season form, the Tigers would be easy picking not alone for the Cubs, but for any club in the American league except perhaps New York or Philadelphia, and for any club in the National league except Boston or St. Louis.

The Cubs are undoubtedly the fastest, classiest, strongest club in baseball today. They play beautiful, wonderful ball. But they are not unbeatable. The White Sox showed that when they cleaned them up two years ago. [Frank] Chance's team was about as good then as it is now. There is no team in the American league, except possibly the New York Highlanders, which would not in all likelihood have won more than one game from the Cubs in the world's series this fall. That is, provided the said team did not completely lose its nerve and its speed, as Detroit did. On their all-season form, the Naps, White Sox or St. Louis Browns would have given the Cubs a terrific battle for the world's championship, and with some "breaks" of luck any one of those teams would have won out, as did the Sox in 1906.

If the long run of accidents and illnesses which kept the Cubs back all summer had finally given the National league flag to New York or Pittsburg, while Chicago, Cleveland or St. Louis had won out in the American, I think the odds would have been in favor of the American league winner in the post-season series. The Giants have only one real pitcher, [Christy] Mathewson, and unless he unaided could have won, New York would have had a desperate time to beat the Naps, Sox or Browns. The Pirate pitchers class pretty evenly with the mound workers of the American league's best teams, and battles between Pittsburg and any of the American league leaders would have been interesting.

As for "tail-end" teams, those of the A. L. outclass those of the N. L., as has been proven for several seasons past by the way the former consistently beat the leaders, while the Giants, Pirates and Cubs as a rule find the weaker clubs very easy picking.

No, the American league is not a minor league. [Jimmy] Collins' Boston bunch showed that when they took the world's honors from the Pirates five years ago. The White Sox showed it when they cleaned up the Cubs two years ago. The Athletics took a good beating from Mathewson, assisted by the Giants, in 1905. It is a sad thing for the American league that the Tigers "drop dead" after their regular season is over, and play like old women for the world's honors.

The appended figures of the recent series[3] show the Tigers' post-season form pretty clearly. They are nothing like their records for the regular season:

CUBS			TIGERS		
Player.	H.	Av.	Thomas	2	500
Chance	9	473	Cobb	7	369
Schulte	7	389	Mullin	1	333
Evers	7	350	O'Leary	5	250
Overall	2	333	Crawford	5	238
Hofman	6	316	McIntyre	4	222
Kling	4	250	Rossman	4	211
Steinfeldt	4	250	Summers	1	200
Scheckard	5	238	Downs	1	167
Tinker	4	211	Schaefer	2	125
Brown	0	000	Coughlin	1	111
Pfeister	0	000	Schmidt	1	072
Howard	0	000	Jones	0	000
Reulbach	0	000	Donovan	0	000
			Winter	0	000
Team	48	300	Killian	0	000
			Team	34	218

Two-base hits — Scheckard 2, Kling, Downs, Thomas, Cobb, Crawford, McIntyre. Three-base hits — Schulte, Hofman. Home run — Tinker. Extra bases on hits — Cubs 11, Tigers 8. Total bases on hits — Cubs 59, Tigers 40. Stolen bases — Cubs 16, Tigers 5. Sacrifice hits — Cubs 9, Tigers 3.

The Tigers completely rebuilt their infield for 1909 — plugging in Donie Bush at short, Jim Delahanty at second base, Tom Jones at first, and George Moriarty at third base — but still lost the World Series in seven games. Addie snubs George Mullin on his staff of Detroit pitchers. New York's Highlanders went 51–103 for 1908. Addie might have included the hapless Brooklyn Superbas among his National League cellar dwellers. An incomplete roll call from the Cubs' infirmary would include: Jack Pfiester (thumb), Joe Tinker (hand),

Jimmy Scheckard (eyes), Pat Moran (spiking), "Chick" Fraser (hand), Orval Overall (back), Johnny Evers (hip), and Frank Chance (back). When he writes that "The Giants have only one real pitcher," Addie is dismissing the contributions of northeast Ohioans Rube Marquard and "Red" Ames to Giants staffs. Marquard's qualifications for the Hall of Fame are still debated. Ames died in an accident in a Warren, Ohio, dairy.

(October 17, 1908, CP and TNB)

While the individual work of the various members of the world's champion Cubs, in the series just closed, was almost perfect in every respect and the manner in which they executed their plays was a revelation, still, in an organization like the Cubs there are always a few of the men who are the power behind the throne.

This is especially true of the defensive end of the game. The three men who stood out most prominently in this particular department for the Cubs were [Joe] Tinker, [Johnny] Evers and [Johnny] Kling.

Each of these three men are [sic] players of the highest order and usually do everything which great players must be able to do.

The more one sees of Johnny Kling the more you have to give it to him for being one of the greatest catchers the game has ever produced. He has all the natural ability which is such an essential factor and is a great baseball general as well.

No doubt most of the success of the Chicago club's pitchers is more than half due to the manner in which they are handled by the wonderful backstop.

He watches every move of the opposition and anytime he sees anything which he thinks is liable to come off he always has a move up his sleeve to stop the play.

Tinker and Evers are on the alert all the time. They watch Kling like a hawk for his signs to the pitcher and know what ball is going to be handed to the batter all the time.

This, no doubt, is principally the reason why they are able to cover so much ground on sharp-hit balls through the infield.

For instance: With a left hand hitter at the plate the signal for a fast ball is given by Kling. If the ball starts for the outside of the plate it is almost a sure thing that the sticker will not be able to hit the ball in any direction but left field and consequently both of these men are on their toes to start in this direction.

The very fact that an infielder is started in the right direction, no matter how small may be that start, often times gives the inner worker a chance to get in front of a hard-hit ball, which would otherwise get by him for a base hit.

The wonderful pair understand each other perfectly and there is never a slip-up in their work around the bag. Every trick of the game is right at their fingers' end. [Ty] Cobb stole second on Kling in the ninth inning of the only game Detroit won and as Johnny's throw was a little low the ball bounded far enough away from Evers to allow Cobb to go to third.

Ty slid for the bag and naturally did not see where the ball had gone. Evers, instead of jumping up and running for the ball, sat on Cobb and pretended to reach for it in a leisurely sort of a way, while Tinker sprinted into short right field for the ball.

Just such plays as these are what make this pair about as fine a combination as there is in the business and their work, as much as anything else, makes the Cubs the grand ball club they are.

It might amuse Addie to learn that Franklin P. Adams' "Tinker to Evers to Chance" (from the poem "Baseball's Sad Lexicon") is what we still remember, instead of his own trio with catcher Johnny Kling. According to the Reach Guide, *and like baseball publications of his era, Johnny Kling was enshrined alive in the catchers' pantheon. Kling operated a pool hall and a café in his native Kansas City after his playing days. Johnny was probably great in his new line of work, having earned the nickname "Noisy" for his constant chatter behind the plate.*

(OCTOBER 19, 1908, CP AND TNB)

WHILE there can be no denial of the fact that the throwing of Catcher ["Boss"] Schmidt, of the Tigers, in the world's series, was far from being perfect, still he was not altogether to blame for the way the Cubs ran bases on him.

Every member of the Chicago club, with the possible exception of [Harry] Steinfeldt, are wonderfully fast men on the paths and this, coupled with the fact that they have made the art of base running one of the features of their wonderful team play, makes them hard to stop on the lines.

The one great secret of their ability to run the bases so successfully comes from the fact that they are constantly on the alert.

They seem to make a study of the opposing pitcher and the manner in which he delivers the ball. As soon as one of them reaches first he immediately makes a bluff to start for second on the first ball pitched and by so doing causes the other team to disclose who is to cover second on the throw.

If the hit and run play is tried then the batter knows who is to take the throw and he can try to hit through the spot vacated.

When a clean steal is attempted the base runner always gets a flying lead. From their work on the paths it is safe to presume that the Cubs figure this way: Better to be caught off first a few times during a series than to get a bad start and always be thrown out at second.

There is a good deal of logic in this and right here, let it be said, that many a time when a player is censured for what is generally thought to be his failure to be wide awake on the paths, and he is nipped off first, it is really because he is trying to get a good lead to steal and is only caught because the opposing pitcher has called the turn on him.

Coupled with their ability to get a good start and their natural speed the world's champions have all mastered the art of sliding into a base.

With the exception of [Johnny] Kling, who always slides head first, the Cubs all slide feet first and can go into a bag either way. That is if the throw happens to be on the inside of the bag they slide on the outside, and vice versa.

This leaves nothing for the infielder to touch but the spikes, which in no way lessens his none too easy task.

One peculiarly [text creased here] thing about their base running was the fact that most of the time they started to steal when the batter had two strikes on him.

Several times during the series they attempted this, probably figuring that it would be the unexpected and that the pitcher, not looking for such a move, would put the ball where the batter had a chance to hit it.

This was tried a couple of times in the game that [Ira] Thomas caught. Evidently the Cubs did not know that the Highlanders used to work this all the time, and as Thomas was once a member of that club, it was just what he was looking for and in each instance he threw out the would-be base runner easily.

Baseball games are saved in the field and won at bat and on the bases. No matter how good a team may be in the field or clever may be their twirlers, few games will be won if they can't hit or run the bases.

The Cubs seem to get lots of runs for the number of base hits they make and this is only due to the fact that they are one of the grandest base running clubs ever put on any field.

First-decade Cubs teams ran. Catcher Johnny Kling stole more than 20 bases in consecutive seasons, apparently indifferent to the dangers of his head-first slides. Harry Steinfeldt, always Chicago's odd man out in the Tinker-to-Evers-to-Chance infield, was the slow player on a fleet team. But he had seasons of 29 and 22 stolen bases.

(October 31, 1908, TNB)

No matter how successful a baseball manager may be, or how good are the results he gets from his players, there will always be many who are ready to criticize him on the slightest provocation.

No matter how conservative the enthusiast may be in his own line of business, the minute he becomes an ardent admirer of a certain club, and roots hard for that team to win, he develops into a rabid fan.

When the club is winning and everything is going along in apple pie order he bubbles over with enthusiasm and praises for the players and manager. But as soon as things begin to look a little bad and the club starts to lose he begins to offer suggestions and tells what he would do if he were running the club.

There was considerable comment in Chicago during the third game of the world's series because Manager [Frank] Chance let [Jack] Pfeister finish out the inning in which Detroit hit him hard and scored the winning runs. On the face of it one would naturally think that Chance was making a mistake in allowing Pfeister to remain, when up to this time Chicago was leading by a score of 3 to 1.

But a little thought will show that the manager of the Cubs was only doing what any other leader would have done under similar circumstances.

[George] Mullin opened Detroit's half by drawing a pass, the only one Pfeister had issued. [Matty] McIntyre followed with a single, and when the big southpaw threw [Charlie] O'Leary's bunt to [Harry] Steinfeldt too late to get Mullin, the bases were filled with no one out.

With three left-hand batters—[Sam] Crawford, [Ty] Cobb and [Claude] Rossman—coming up, would it have been policy to take out a left-hand pitcher and substitute a right-hander?

Hardly. This is no doubt the way Chance figured it, and so he let Pfeister continue. Crawford hit one at Chance that he knocked down, but could not recover in time to get anyone.

Cobb beat out a slow bounder to [Joe] Tinker and when [Claude] Rossman singled to right Detroit was two runs to the good. It would have been suicide to burn up another pitcher at this stage of the game, as Mullin was holding the Cubs safe and it did not look as though they had a chance to score on him.

This is only one instance of how the manager is oftentimes criticized for doing just what he thought was right, and which was about the only course to pursue.

Of course, after it is all over the manager, as well as anyone, can see where he might have done differently, and possibly with better results, but it is a cinch that he was doing just what he thought best at the time, and if everyone would take that feature of it into consideration there would be less criticism.

Fans and newspaper writers who criticized their home teams were called "kickers." I don't know if John Albert (Hagenbush) Pfeister got his nickname "The Giant Killer" for his mastery over the New York club (15–5 lifetime) or the pun on the Jack of "Fee, Fie, Foe, Fum" fame. Probably both. To Frank "The Peerless Leader" Chance's chagrin, Detroit scored five runs in that sixth inning, the margin of victory in Game Three of the recently completed 1908 World Series. "Wabash George" Mullin, the pitcher who worked the walk that Addie remembers, also had a base hit in the Series.

From the 1909 World Series

The 1909 season marked several beginnings and endings. The Pirates' home, Forbes Field, is in only its fourth month of occupancy when the 27-year-old rookie Babe Adams pitches them to their first Series title. The 1909 championship is the first to be decided in seven games, a Deadball Era epic. Surely, the ordinarily short train rides between Detroit and Pittsburgh must seem an odyssey to Ty Cobb: A warrant is out in Ohio, for his arrest in the George Stansfield knifing. This is the last World Series that Addie covered. Instead, after the Naps' 1910 season, he joins an all-star team of mostly National League players (plus umpire Hank O'Day) on a 12-game barnstorming tour of Cuba. This World Series is especially hard fought: Three players are knocked out, six suffer spike wounds, three leave the field with injuries, and six players are fined for game infractions. Bobby Byrne, leading off Game Seven for the Pirates, slides into the Tigers' George Moriarty, and both third basemen have to be replaced. Detroit is keen to win a World Series, having lost the previous two to the Cubs. The Tigers had to work hard for this return trip to the play-offs: Ed Killian needed to win both games of a doubleheader—he rested for only 20 minutes in between—to clinch the pennant. Pittsburgh's postseason play was dedicated, in part, to avenge their loss to the American League in the inaugural World Series.

In the newspapers, the Series is billed as a clash of Titans, Johannes Peter Wagner versus Tyrus Raymond Cobb, the two best all-around players in baseball. It marks the first of only three World Series that headline the batting champs of both leagues.[4] *Six years earlier, Wagner had played poorly. Now "The Flying Dutchman" is 35 years old, and his critics are wondering if he's slowed. For his part, Cobb is fresh off a regular season in which he won the Triple Crown.*[5] *Cobb wastes no time to improve on his performances in previous World Series—and promptly steals home in Game Two. After seven games, Wagner vindicates himself by outhitting "The Georgia Peach" by .100 points and stealing a record six bases. But the 1909 World Series proves to be an unlikely hero's spotlight: Babe Adams wins three games, including the opener and the finale.*

(DATELINE: OCTOBER 9, 1909)

While it would be manifestly unfair to the Detroit team to say that the better club won the opening game of the world's series, it was plain to everyone who saw the contest that the team headed by [Fred] Clarke won because it played the better game.

Not a fielding slip of any kind marred the Pirates' work, and this in view of the fact that the Tigers hit the ball fairly hard all through the nine innings, makes their performance all the more creditable.

Pitchers [George] Mullin and ["Babe"] Adams pitched grand ball.

Barring the first and seventh innings, the Pirate twirler never was in grave danger. His two passes in the opener paved the way for the Detroit team's only run. That the Tigers did not score more runs then was only because he made a good play on [Sam] Crawford's sharp drive through the box. [Jim] Delahanty followed with a single, and had Sam's drive gone by Adams, there is no telling how many runs might have resulted.

"CLARKE'S GREAT DRIVE."

But one man reached first on Mullin up to the time Clarke drove out his home run with two down in the fourth. The Pirate manager had George two balls and no strikes. The next ball cut the heart of the plate about waist high and Fred, meeting the ball fair, drove it into the right field bleachers.

[Bill] Abstein opened the National league champions' half of the fifth with a mean bounder to Delahanty. The ball got by the second sacker and before [Ty] Cobb, who had failed to back up the play [in right field], could run it down, the first sacker was resting on third. [George] Gibson's double to right center scored Abstein.

[Shortstop Donie] Bush fumbled Adams' drive and when [Bobby] Byrne was hit in the head with a fast one, the bases were filled so that it was a comparatively easy thing for Gibson to score on [Tommy] Leach's fly to Davy Jones [in left].

"SCHMIDT'S LOW THROW."

Wagner doubled to the left field fence as a starter in the sixth, and went to third on ["Boss"] Schmidt's low throw to Bush in a vain attempt to catch the big Dutchman napping. ["Dots"] Miller fouled to Schmidt and then Abstein hit a swinging bunt down the first base line. The Tiger backstop made a rattling good play to get his man at first, while Wagner cantered across the plate with the Pirates' last run.

The one grand chance the American league leaders had to get back in the game was in the seventh. With two gone, Davy Jones shot a single to left, Bush walked, and, with the count standing three balls and two strikes on Cobb, the great right fielder got hold of the next one.

"LOOKED LIKE A TRIPLE."

The ball was hit hard, and directly between Leach and [right fielder John "Chief"] Wilson. It looked like a cleanup and a three-base hit for Ty sure [idiomatic], with a possible chance for a home run. Leach nearly flew across the field in his pursuit of the ball, and, judging the drive to a nicety, set himself for the catch. Tommy must have stumbled just a little, as for a moment he seemed to lose his balance, but, recovering himself, he grabbed the ball. It was easily the outstanding feature of the contest. The little fellow also made a very fine play on Jones' short fly earlier in the game.

Gibson's one chance to catch a base runner resulted in a short throw, on which Wagner made a wonderful play by getting it with his gloved hand, on a mean, nasty pickup, but too late to tag the flying Cobb. From the stands it looked as though Cobb was out, but ["Silk"] O'Loughlin, who was directly over the play, ruled otherwise.

Playing-manager "Cap" Clarke was one of the best left fielders (2,678 hits and 509 stolen bases career) and most successful managers (1,602 wins, four pennants) of the Deadball Era. Clarke's two home runs—both of them into the temporary seats at Forbes Field—and seven RBIs led all hitters in the Series; his four walks set a World Series record. His brother-in-law, "Chick" Fraser, pitched for the Cubs in the previous two World Series. Only the Pirates' "fifth starter," Charles Benjamin Adams' major league experience prior to the 1909 season totaled 26 innings. His opponent, George Mullin, led the American League in wins during the regular season. Jim Delahanty's single in the first inning would be followed by eight more in the seven-game Series, best on the team, and tied him with Tommy Leach for best in the Series.

Bill Abstein fanned 10 times in his 26 World Series at-bats, made five errors at first base, and ran the bases erratically. From 1909 to 1921, Owen J. Bush was an institution at the shortstop position for the Tigers. And the minor league field in Indianapolis (now Victory Field) was named after this favorite son. There was an Owen on the Pirates' roster, too. Owen Wilson hit a record 36 triples in 1912, many of them into the far reaches of Forbes Field. (Honus Wagner stroked the only three-base hit in the Series.) The Texan Wilson looked to Fred Clarke like a chief in the Texas rangers.

Davy "Kangaroo" Jones ended his baseball career in Pittsburgh, with the Federal League Rebels, before becoming a full-time pharmacist in Detroit. After his first practice session in Forbes Field, he bought sunglasses for the sun field. (Clarke's flip-down sunglasses were still in the future.) Note Addie's use of the word "cleanup" before the term "cleanup hitter" (not unlike the evolution of "pinch" into "pinch hitter"). Notably, there is no mention here of a legendary play. Cobb, standing at first base, is said to have challenged Wagner, declaring his intention to run on the next pitch—and the shortstop is supposed to have tagged Cobb on the mouth. Addie would probably have been in a good position to notice.

(DATELINE: OCTOBER 11, 1909)

Ever since the Detroit team has been battling with the pennant winners of the National league for the highest honors in baseball it has been the earnest desire of their many admirers to see the Tigers true to the form they have so consistently shown in the regular American league championship seasons for the past three years.

In Saturday's game at Pittsburg the American league adherents were treated to the gratifying spectacle. This, added to the fact that Wild Bill Donovan was going in grand form made it a comparatively easy matter for Detroit to win.

Bill certainly pitched a magnificent game, and barring the first inning when the Pirates scored their only runs, held the National league champions in the hollow of his hand.

A base on balls as a starter to [Bobby] Byrne, followed by [Tommy] Leach's two-base hit down the right field foul line, after two unsuccessful attempts to advance the Pirates third sacker, scored the first run.

[Fred] Clarke sacrificed Tommy to third. [Honus] Wagner had the Detroit twirler three balls and no strikes. He fouled off the next ball pitched. [Billy] Evans called the next one a strike and Honus swung and missed the third.

With two strikes and no balls on ["Dots"] Miller, Donovan pitched a high fast one on the outside, and the youngster drove a long fly to right, which bounded into the bleachers, scoring Leach.

"COBB STEALS HOME"

From then on the meeting was out [colloquial] as far as scoring any more runs was concerned for Pittsburg. Leach opened the third with a double to left, but Bill tightened up and Clarke, Wagner and Miller were unable to score Tommy or even move him up a base.

The spectacular feature came in the third inning, when [Ty] Cobb stole home. He was on third when [Vic] Willis replaced ["Howie"] Camnitz.

As Willis prepared to pitch Ty started up the line. He ran up about half way home, just as he usually does in plays of this kind, making it look as though he wanted to detract the pitcher's attention from the batter to him.

No doubt Willis thought this was his intention, and kept right on with his delivery to the hitter. Cobb hesitated just for the fraction of a second and then gathering himself, made a mad dash for the plate.

The Pirate pitcher whipped the ball to [George] Gibson low and on the inside, just in the proper place to give Gibson a good chance to tag the flying Georgian.

"Drove Fans Crazy."

It looked as though the Pirate catcher had the ball before Ty reached the plate, and Evans first called Cobb out, but immediately reversed the decision when he saw that Gibson had failed to touch the great outfielder.

It was a daring piece of baseball and drove the Detroit rooters to a state of wild frenzy. At the same time [George] Moriarty, who was at the bat, comes in for a large share of credit on the play, as he never moved out of the box, in this way making it hard for Gibson to see Ty coming, and this probably as much as Cobb's great slide caused the backstop to miss his man.

"Ty's Second Stunt."

Cobb gave the National league rooters another demonstration of his wonderful base running ability. He opened the eighth with a single to center. On the first ball pitched he and [Sam] Crawford played the hit and run. Sam drove a grounder at Miller, which the Pirate second sacker handled fast and clean to first.

Cobb never hesitated at second, keeping right on for third. [First baseman Bill] Abstein's throw was a trifle high and Byrne made a nice play in getting the peg, but too late to nail the flying Georgian.

Ty beat the play easily, but failed to hook the bag properly on his slide and over-slid the bag, Byrne touching him before he could recover.

"Moriarty's Great Work."

Moriarty's third-base play will long live in the memory of those who saw the contest. His gloved-hand catch of ["Boss"] Schmidt's throw to get

Wagner trying to steal third and his touching of the runner on that play was a masterpiece.

Addie's report on Saturday's game was wired on October 11, a Monday, for the Cleveland Press *edition. Bobby Byrne is at third base, not the better-known Tommy Leach (though Leach would eventually be moved in to replace an injured Byrne). Byrne's best year would be his next one with the Pirates, when he led the league in hits and doubles. He also boasted the best fielding percentage among National League third basemen for two seasons. Leach shaved his head before the World Series. His 49 career inside-the-park home runs rank second behind Tigers center fielder Sam Crawford's 51. Leach scored 1,355 runs in his career.*

Second baseman John "Dots" Miller regularly hit fifth in the powerful Pittsburgh lineup. In his rookie season of 1909, Miller led the league's second basemen in fielding percentage. Ty Cobb led the American League in stolen bases in 1909. He stole home a record 54 times in his career, but this is his most famous one. The rare and daring play was perhaps a defining characteristic of Cobb's attack game. Vic Willis was "The Delaware Peach," so we have him on the same field as "The Georgia Peach"; both are Hall of Famers. He appears here in a relief role, but his 45 complete games, in 1902, are the all-time record. The workhorse was a 20-game winner eight times (22 in 1909), and a 20-game loser in three seasons. Samuel Camnitz's best season was 1909, when he won 25 games for the Pirates and led the league's pitchers with an .806 winning percentage. Amazingly, the Pirates' outstanding starters, Willis, Camnitz, and "Lefty" Leifield, each went 0–1—and Pittsburgh still won the title.

The Tigers' tough third baseman George Moriarty went to five more World Series—as an umpire. The seating capacity for Forbes Field was 23,000 during the regular season. Attendance at Game Two reached 30,915. After the fine fall weather for the first two games in Pittsburgh, afternoons turned cold and windy, in both cities, for the rest of the Series. (Fred Clarke designed and patented a machine to deploy and remove the rain tarpaulin for the Forbes Field infield.)

(DATELINE: OCTOBER 12, 1909)

The one consolation American league fans got out of Monday's game at Bennett park was the fact that the Tigers conclusively showed that they are a game bunch of players.

Facing a handicap of six runs, until the seventh inning they came across with a bunch of four, and threatened seriously to make it a tie series.

That they did not eventually get on even terms, or possibly win out in the last inning, was only due to the fact that the Pirates had a mighty fast man on third when [Fred] Clarke drove a line drive at [Ty] Cobb in Pittsburg's half of that inning. The Georgia Peach made a fine throw to the plate to get [Bobby] Byrne, who was on third, but the Pirate third sacker with a good burst of speed and a fine slide just managed to elude ["Boss"] Schmidt as the Tiger backstop went to tag him.

"[Ed] Willett Fails to Do His Duty"

[Honus] Wagner followed with his fourth hit, scoring [Tommy] Leach with the second run of the inning. The Pirates put themselves five runs to the good in the first inning by hitting the ball hard. The run they scored in the next inning could have been prevented had Willett properly covered the plate when, on an attempted double steal, Schmidt caught Leach off third.

Both outfields played magnificent ball. The manner in which Clarke and Leach covered the ground intervening between their respective positions was wonderful. Clarke took most of the putouts, but a good many of the catches could have been made by either man. This necessitated a perfect understanding between them as to who was to make the catch.

Both Cobb's and Clarke's catches on low line hits, which peculiarly retired the last man for both teams, were beauties. [Sam] Crawford played a swell game in the field, showing exceptionally fine judgment on two or three drives.

Wagner, [Jim] Delahanty and ["Donie"] Bush starred with the stick. "Del" hit the ball on the nose all day, while Bush delivered with three nice singles.

"Wagner's Field Day—Four Hits, Three Thefts"

The great Pirate shortstop had a field day, making four hits and stealing three bases. His single to right in the fifth just goes to show what a hard man he is to pitch to. Clarke was on first with none out when the hit and run play was attempted. Schmidt called the turn on the play and had Willett pitch out. The ball must have been easily two feet on the outside, but Honus reached over and managed to drive the ball just out of Tom Jones' reach.

Someone must have gone wrong when [George] Moriarty attempted to steal second in the eighth. Morry had received transportation [slang, for a base on balls] with a ball having been called. The first two balls on [Tom] Jones were wide of the plate. The next one was a strike, and on the following ball Moriarty went down. Jones let the ball go by and [George] Gibson hurled it down to Wagner, who made a swell pickup and tagged George out.

If they were playing hit and run the ball was pitched just right for Jones to pull it toward short, the position left vacant by Wagner. The chances are that someone got crossed on the sign.

Robert Edgar Willett didn't give up a run in his 7 2/3 innings (two appearances) against Pittsburgh. He was coming off his career-best season, posting 21 wins for the Tigers. "Ed" was known for his fielding. Drawings, which adorn the page below this article in the Cleveland Press, *appear to undercut Addie's paragraph on Honus Wagner's "field day": "Cartoonist Stanley" depicts the shortstop falling over his own big feet. First baseman Tom Jones came to Detroit from the Browns, in a trade for Claude Rossman. Fred Clarke was fined $25 for abusing the umpire after Jim Johnstone called Abstein for interfering with base runner Moriarty.*

(DATELINE: OCTOBER 13, 1909)

[George] Mullin's great pitching was too much for the Pirates in yesterday's game, and this, added to the fact that the Tigers hit the ball hard at opportune moments, sent the two champion teams to Pittsburg on even terms.

This year's premier twirler of the American league held the heavy-hitting Pirates to four very widely scattered hits. Added to this, his control, in the face of weather conditions, was great, making a mighty hard combination for the National league champions to overcome.

George was never in danger but once, when he found himself facing [Honus] Wagner at the bat with two out and men on third and second. He rose nobly to the occasion. He curved over the last ball with the count three balls and two strikes, and when [Bill] Klem called it a strike the joy of the Detroit contingent knew no bounds.

Detroit's first run was in a good measure due to a hit and run play engineered by [George] Moriarty and [Jim] Delahanty. When "Del" started to steal, Wagner covered the bag. "Morry" reached over the plate and pulled a short fly back of third which no one but Wagner could have fielded. Honus could not recover in time, and the drive went for a hit. [Tom] Jones' hit to ["Lefty"] Leifield gave "Morry" and Tom a chance to move up while "Del" was being thrown out.

["Dots"] Miller partially stopped [Oscar] Stanage's hit, and might have held it had he not moved in a few feet just before the ball was pitched. Instead of the infielders coming in on the grass, they moved in half way, and had they been playing back naturally Miller would, no doubt, have caught the drive.

"Morry on the Job"

As it was, he partially stopped and Moriarty, who easily crossed the plate on the play, showed excellent judgment by remaining right on the job, and when Tom Jones neared the counting station [slang, for home plate], "Morry" gave him the office to slide, as he could see better than Jones how close [right fielder John "Chief"] Wilson's good throw was going to make the play.

Detroit sewed up the game in the fourth. [Tom] Jones beat out a bunt. Stanage tried to cross the Pirates by hitting, but Wagner made a nice play on his grounder over the bag and easily doubled the Tiger backstop at first. Mullin's walk, followed by hits by [Davy] Jones and Bush, scored a run and left men on sec[ond] and third with [Ty] Cobb at the bat.

"Cobb the Boy"

Leifield had Ty two strikes and one ball, all on fast balls, when he broke up [coloquial] a nice curve ball on the outside, the first one he had pitched the Tiger star during the game. Cobb drove it down the left field foul line for two bases, putting the game on ice for fair.

Mullin showed excellent judgment in the ninth when, after Miller had beaten out a bunt, [Bill] Abstein hit sharply to George.

"Mullin Cool"

The Detroit twirler paid no attention to Miller, but let him reach second while he played it safe by easily throwing out his man at first.

Fielding features were few. Mullin made a nice play on [George] Gibson's high bounder in the second, and [Sam] Crawford made a nice catch of [Bobby] Byrne's short fly in the eighth. Leifield's play on [Tom] Jones in the second was a nice piece of work.

George Mullin won two games in the Series. He fanned 10 Pirates in Game Four, and 20 for the World Series (the most since 1903). Before Game Five, the National Commission met at the Schenley Hotel, across the street from Forbes Field, and determined that a seventh game, if necessary, would be played in Detroit. As it happened, this was the first time a Game Seven would decide a championship. The coin toss also made it three years in a row that the Tigers would lose the World Series in front of the home crowd.

The young Bill Klem was friends, in Rochester, with "Silk" O'Loughlin. Klem umpired in 18 World Series and "never missed a call." A staff writer for the Press *noted "[t]he spectacle of four umpires doing duty in a ball game." He offered that "O'Loughlin and [Jim] Johnstone had little to do" on the foul lines, but "Klem had a hard day behind the bat, all protests [coming] from the players in the league he represents." "Dots" Miller was fined for arguing with Klem. Addie records Oscar Stanage's only hit in the games. The catcher's American League records for assists (212) and errors (41), in the 1911 season, still stand. He later coached for both the Tigers and Pirates. Albert Leifield wound up as a Tigers coach too. His 103 wins were the most by a Pirates pitcher from 1906 to 1911, but "Lefty" had only 19 other career victories.*

(DATELINE: OCTOBER 14, 1909)

[Fred] Clarke's band of National league pennant winners put themselves one game nearer the coveted title of world's champions at Forbes field Wednesday by hitting the ball hard at opportune moments.

[Ed] Summers was hit hard in the inning [the seventh] that Pittsburg scored four runs, and his own wildness, coupled with a few hits, scored the three runs earlier in the game [one run in each of the first three innings].

["Babe"] Adams was not hit very hard, but most of the drives were good, legitimate base hits. [Sam] Crawford starred with the stick. His first hit was a single through short on a successful hit and run play. Sam certainly got hold of the next one he hit safe. [Ty] Cobb, who was on first, started down. Adams handed up a fast one on the outside, and Crawford drove a vicious liner straight to the left field fence.

Crawford's home run went into the bleachers directly over [Tommy] Leach's head, and Tommy was about as far as he could get. Leach made a great try for the ball, tearing down a part of the fence in his mad pursuit of the pill.

[Honus] Wagner and Clarke pulled off the hit and run play to perfection in the third. The "Dutchman" pushed the ball through short in fine style. After [Bobby] Byrne singled in the seventh he and Leach worked it again.

[Jim] Delahanty and Wagner starred in the field. "Del" made a great play on Byrne's low line drive to right, the second baseman being forced to go quite a ways to his left to grab the sphere with his gloved hand just as it hopped up on a nasty bound.

"[George] Moriarty Starred"

Moriarty played the game to the limit when [George] Gibson attempted to steal in the eighth. Leach took a swing at the ball as the Pirate catcher started over. "Morry" saw him coming, but stayed in his regular position until he saw Leach had missed, and then hustled to the bag in time to get ["Boss"] Schmidt's throw and nail his man.

Davy Jones never saw ["Chief"] Wilson's drive which went for two bases in the eighth, and it is doubtful whether or not he would have been able to pull it down had he seen it.

Gibson followed with a "Texas leaguer" to right, which was the result of being fooled on a curve ball which he was just able to meet hard enough to drive over Tom Jones' head, scoring Wilson from second with the last run of the game.

Knuckleballer Ed Summers was hit hard in both of his World Series starts. He surrendered 13 hits and four walks in 7 1/3 innings (a 2.33 WHIP), losing Games Three and Five to the Pirates. Curveballing Babe Adams was touched for a lead-off homer by Davy Jones, in addition to the blast by Crawford that Addie remembers. They represented the only home runs by Detroit in the Series. All three round-trippers on the day caught the temporary bleachers installed at Forbes Field for the overflow crowds. Tommy Leach crashed through the two-foot wooden fence thrown up in front of the new center field bleachers and had to be revived. Babe Adams and Deacon Phillippe, a star of the 1903 Series and now reduced to two games in relief, were hired by a Pittsburgh newspaper to write game reports of this World Series. Cleveland-born Jim Delahanty joined the Tigers, coming over from the Senators, for the final third of the regular season in 1909. He enjoyed his best years at the plate in a Detroit uniform (.339 with 94 RBIs in 1911), before winding down his career in the Federal League. Catcher George Gibson was successful on two other stolen base attempts in the series (as many as Ty Cobb).

(DATELINE: OCTOBER 15, 1909)

It was proved conclusively in Thursday's game at Bennett park that the Tigers can come from behind.

That they kept plugging away in the face of th[ese] odds, and finally managed to gain a lead that returned them winners and gave them an even chance for the big title, surely proves that they are game, which, in itself, is no little factor in a team's success.

Several fine bits of baseball were played by members of both teams. [Honus] Wagner, in particular, did some grand work. ["Boss"] Schmidt opened the Tigers' half of the sixth with a drive into right which ["Chief"] Wilson let go by him for two bases. [George] Mullin bunted to ["Howie"] Camnitz. [Third baseman Bobby] Byrne came in from his position with the pitch, but Wagner sneaked over to third, and was there in plenty of time to get "Cammy's" throw before the Detroit catcher could slide into the bag.

"WAGNER DOES WELL"

Wagner also covered third in fine style when [Jim] Delahanty attempted to go from first to third on Moriarty's drive into right: Wilson making a fine throw to get Del.

Byrne's catch of Tom Jones' high fly at a time when a boot would have caused much damage was a fine play. The ball was hit a mile high between home plate and third base. It started to foul and looked as though it would be an easy out for the Pirate third baseman. The wind kept blowing the ball toward the home plate, and Byrne eased up for a moment, acting as though he thought [catcher George] Gibson would make the catch. Gibson stayed away and at the last moment Byrne came charging in and just managed to make the play.

This seems an oddly foreshortened picture of a dramatic game, which required a ninth-inning tag at home plate and a game-ending double play for the Tigers to avoid elimination. Winning pitcher Bill Donovan notched his second game of the Series, after suffering from a sore arm all regular season. Canadian-born "Moon" Gibson caught 150 games that season for Pittsburgh (134 consecutive), plus all seven Series games. He averaged 145 games behind the plate from 1908 to 1910, and three times led National League catchers in fielding percentage. Meanwhile, the Tigers were managed by Ned Hanlon–mentored Hughie Jennings, who platooned at catcher—and Detroit catching still couldn't control the opposition's running game. Game Six saw the biggest crowd for the Series: 30,915, packed Forbes Field. (Only 18,277 would turn up for Game Seven in Bennett Park, played under wintery conditions.)

The concluding Game Seven of the World Series was played in Detroit on October 16, 1909, a Saturday. Game reports were routinely wired to Cleveland on the mornings after the late-afternoon games, so it's probable that Addie Joss never filed one on the Pittsburgh Pirates' shutout win over the Detroit Tigers.

8

"I Should Suggest"

VIEWS FROM TOLEDO

Following are the considered views of a good citizen of baseball. Before the institutionalization of players' unions and agents, blogging and tweets, a ball player could make his own direct line: Herein, Addie enjoys audiences with the mayor of Toledo, and Charlie Hickman petitions American League owners. One hundred years ago, the professional game must have seemed already tradition bound to a man like Addie Joss. Perhaps it is mostly sentimental to think that Addie inherited the voice we hear in these editorials from his father, who had lost himself in local Republican politics.[1]

In early January 1907, the National Commission, chaired by Garry Herrmann, held its winter meetings in Chicago, and the News-Bee *sports editor was in attendance.*

(JANUARY 20, 1907, NB)

President [Charles] Murphy of the "Cubs" brings forth the argument that a series of seven games for the world's baseball championship is too short to determine the ability of the contesting teams.

Perhaps this was induced by the fact that the Cubs were beaten by the [White] Sox in the 1906 championship; nevertheless a majority of the sporting authorities all over the land agree with him.

Everyone who follows baseball is aware that an important factor in baseball is the way the luck of the game breaks and it can readily be appreciated, that in a series of so few games, this will have much to do with the winning of a championship.

Then, again, if only seven games are played, one club may have one

The Toledo residence (now demolished) of Addie Joss, 2440 Fulton Street. The pitcher died here, April 14, 1911 **(courtesy Toledo-Lucas County Public Library, obtained from http://images2.toledolibrary.org/).**

particular pitcher upon whom the manager depends to bring home the games and he may be able to do it; for example, [Christy] Mathewson of the Giants, who won all three games he pitched against the Athletics a year ago last fall.

But should the teams play 11 or 15 games it would be scarcely possible for one man to work successfully in six or eight of the games in such a short time.

President Murphy's suggestion, in my opinion, should meet with the approval of the national commission, which body governs all world's series.

The World Series was still in its experimental stages, and the number of wins required for the championship had not been settled until 1905, when the National Commission went with Giants owner John T. Brush's best-of-seven format. (The first World Series, in 1903, was a best-of-nine contest.) The Temple Cup, and more recently the Chronicle-Telegraph *Cup, had failed to establish a tradition of play and never caught on with the nation's fans. There had always been local and state champions to be determined by exhibition series after the regular seasons.*

Charles Webb Murphy (a prominent citizen of Wilmington, Ohio) and John McGraw were the most hated men in baseball, but Addie's treatment of them in his columns is equitable.

(FEBRUARY 10, 1907, TNB)

Charley Hickman's suggestion to the club owners of the American league regarding the painting of center field fences green, should meet with universal approval and will no doubt be carried out.

The one feature of the game that all the patrons like, is the hitting and with the foul strike rule and spit ball it is impossible for the good hitters to connect as frequently as they formerly did.

While great pitching feats are always admired, still the base ball loving public would rather hear the sound of a three base hit any time than witness a few hit struggle between two pitchers. There is something wonderfully exciting in seeing a batter drive the ball to the fence and the race between the runner and ball.

There is something about this feature of the game that no feat of great pitching or fielding can dim.

The reason for "Hick's" suggestion is that, whenever a center-field fence is covered with glaring signs, as so many are, the sun shining upon them casts a strong reflection in the batter's eyes, making it hard to see the ball from the moment it leaves the pitcher's hand.

Another bad feature is that when the ball is first put in play, it is as white as chalk and with a light background is hard to gauge accurately.

"Connie" Mack has taken up "Hick's" suggestion and has the fence to center field at Philadelphia painted dark green. As far as the pitchers are concerned no change need be made and as for myself the managers could put a large mirror on the fence and not offend me in the least, but for the good of the game the league should take favorable action on the proposal.

Dead center field in Philadelphia's Columbia Park was 440 feet, so maybe owner Ben Shibe figured the grandstand crowd couldn't read the ads from that distance anyway? I'm not sure Charlie Hickman's call—for organized baseball to strike a balance between the needs of advertising revenue and the creation of a playing field that promoted the spectacle of hitting—caught on, beyond Philadelphia. We do know that green, advertising-free center field walls were mandated by the National Commission for the 1914 season (a concession to the Baseball Players' Fraternity).[2]

(FEBRUARY 10, 1907, TNB)

Recently, while discussing the world's championship series between the White Sox and Cubs with Mayor Whitlock, the city's chief executive brought up the old question, "are baseball games fixed?"

The reason for the query was the fact that the rival teams won alternately upon each other's grounds. In fact, as may be remembered, the final game, which was played upon the south side grounds, and was won by the Sox, was the first game either team had won upon its own diamond.

While this was remarkable, it had no significance. There are always a few people who see things in the wrong light and it is the minority, always, which is loudest in its denunciation of the honesty of baseball.

"CAN'T THROW BALL GAMES"

As a matter of fact it is impossible to fix a game of baseball. That uncertain element, enters too prominently into every game to permit of it being thrown.

Suppose some pitcher was induced to throw a game. It would be hard for him to deliver the goods. He might give bases on balls, make wild pitches, or hit batsmen until the bases were filled, but he couldn't do much of this before he would be taken out of the box.

Or a pitcher might put them straight across the pan so his opponents would have no trouble connecting and hitting them to all corners of the lot, but his own team might come right back in the next inning and do the same thing.

But the best argument to prove that baseball games cannot be fixed is that a majority of the spectators are as conversant with the playing end of the game as the players are, and it would take them but a few minutes to discover that a game was not upon the level.

Then there is that inherent desire to win in every American's makeup, which of itself is difficult to overcome and which in the heat of a close contest, might make even a man despicable enough to permit himself to be bought, forget the sale and do his level best to beat the other fellow.

"STARTED IN FUN, BUT—"

On our trip to the coast in 1902, when the All American and All Nationals were playing exhibition games, it was understood that the trip was for pleasure, and while we were to play as good ball as we knew how, yet it was not a matter of life or death which team won.

Playing upon this basis we started for California. Up to the time we reached St. Joseph, Mo., the Nationals had put it on us with persistent regularity and were beginning to kid us about our inferior team.

This made us feel that we were being made sport of and it was but a few days before both teams were sliding into each other with spikes up, calling the umpire for alleged bad decisions and fighting tooth and nail for every game.

What started as a pleasure trip developed into a series of games as hard fought as any regular campaign.

The reason for the popularity of baseball is that its fairness is above suspicion, and as long as it remains so, it will hold its present high place in the esteem of the public.

Toledo's mayor Brand Whitlock, a former journalist, was the author of 18 books. As a reporter for the Chicago Herald, *he became close to Cap Anson. This time, Addie does not appear to be an especially good baseball historian, as he overlooks the betting scandal that determined the 1877 National League pennant; nor particularly prophetic, when we look ahead in time to the Black Sox. However, Addie's dismissal of corruption in the game is characteristic of the journalism of the day.*[3] *Rumors of game fixing, usually focused on ownership bribing players to extend the money-making World Series, followed in the wake of the 1906 Series, when the superior Cubs didn't sweep the White Sox. Addie's pet theme of luck is stressed in the story's subhead, "Luck, Desire to Excel and the Fans' Intimate Knowledge of the Game Honesty's Guarantee." In the close, he sticks to his point like a good journalist, and doesn't revisit his earlier tribute to Win Mercer, a man whose luck had run out (February 1, 1907, in Chapter 1).*

(February 17, 1907, TNB)

It may seem strange that after established methods have been accepted for years, without a protest, that I should suggest a new way to get at the true worth of a pitcher, but I never did believe there was "nothing new under the sun," and I think I have worked out a system whereby a pitcher's value may be ascertained more correctly than heretofore.

Many a pitcher finishes the season with a mediocre average [i.e., winning percentage] who is just as able a performer as some other man who may have a much better average.

One vitally important item to be considered when comparing the merits of pitchers, is the position of their respective teams at the end of the season.

The best twirler in the game may be upon a team that finished last in 1906, and his average suffers accordingly.

I believe that the most equitable solution of the problem would be to take the difference between the club's percentage and the pitcher's percentage, as the boxman's standing.

For example: A pitcher who averages .700 on a team that finishes the season with a percentage of .500 will have, under this scheme, a percentage of .200 better than his club has played.

A pitcher on a club which, we will say, won the pennant with a standing of .650, who has won .800 per cent of his games, would be credited with an average of .150.

The argument is advanced that the pitcher who had an average of .700 may have had all the luck his club experienced, which accounts for his showing. But it is an established fact that the higher the team in the race, the better the luck breaks.

While this may not be a popular means to determine a pitcher's worth, it seems to me to be the only way to accurately estimate the pitcher's value to his team.

Present-day managers realize this more than the public, which as a rule looks only at the figures compiles at the end of the season.

It only feels as if we're in on the origins of Bill James' Win Shares system. Of course, there was a practical motivation behind Addie's statistical analysis: He is negotiating his contract with the Cleveland front office—and negotiating in public! Addie, still a hold-out, continues to plead his case in the next column.

(February 24, 1907, TNB)

Many a pitcher is credited with winning a game when he doesn't officiate in more than one inning or may be charged with a loss when it's scarcely his fault. The ruling covering the derricking of one pitcher and the substitution of another is peculiar.

If the club is ahead when a pitcher is taken out and the man who replaces him loses the game, he gets credit for the loss, but if he wins, the man who was taken out gets credit for the victory. If, on the other hand, the team is behind, the twirler who is substituted gets credit for the win.

For example, say the score is 2 to 0, when the pitcher is taken out, for instance in the third inning. If the opposing team ties the score or goes ahead, but is finally beaten, the pitcher who took the other man's place loses the game. If the score is a tie the man who finishes the game gets credit for the victory or defeat.

It frequently happens that a man will pitch one or perhaps but part of an inning and still get credit for the victory. [Otto] Hess finished a game for me at Washington last season that caused a lot of controversy over awarding the credit.

Washington had us beaten 4 to 1 in the ninth. Then we made five runs, but during the batting rally "Larry" [Lajoie] sent [Claude] Rossman in to hit for me. This took me out of the game and Hess was sent in to finish it. He blanked the Nationals in the ninth and Ban Johnson decided Hess should be given credit for the game.

The same conditions, reversed, occurred at Cleveland. New York had us 2 to 0 in the eighth, with the bases full and one out with one run scored. Lajoie sent [George] Stovall to bat for Hess and he scored two runs. I was sent in to finish the game. The Highlanders failed to score and the credit of the victory went to me.

President [Bill] Armour is the only manager I ever saw take a man out of the box before a run had been scored on him. It happened at Detroit during the early part of the season of 1904.

Jack Hickey, who has been in the American association since, was pitching and about the fifth inning, with the score 2 to 0 in our favor, he developed a streak of wildness, walking three men in succession.

Bill took out Hickey and sent me in to finish. Charley Carr was next up and the first ball I pitched he souzed [soused] against the right field fence, driving in three runs before he pulled up at [third baseman Bill] Bradley's corner.

The score remained 3 to 2 and I got credit for losing a game in which I really pitched but one ball.

To me it appears an injustice for a pitcher to take up the running with his team behind and then be credited with a loss when, after holding down the opposition while his team ties the score, he is scored upon.

The argument is that the pitcher is scored upon but once, while his team has virtually won a game back of him, but, through the inability of the man he relieved, the game is lost.

Soused is a verb, meaning "thumped." It was American League president Ban Johnson who decided credit for a winning pitcher before there was the official rule. (Has somebody checked the box scores to give Addie another win?) The game in Washington was played on May 26, 1906. Toledo sports page readers would have been aware that current Mud Hens president Armour was formerly the manager at Cleveland. We have already met Claude Rossman, when he was a Tigers' star. But he broke in with Cleveland, and was the Naps' regular first baseman during its 1906 campaign.

(February 24, 1908, TNB)

The proposed Northwestern Ohio league looks good. Lima, Sandusky, Findlay, Fostoria, Bowling Green, Fremont, Tiffin, Defiance, Bryan, Wauseon and Napoleon are all good baseball towns and would make a strong circuit.

The cities are conveniently located and the cost of transportation would be reduced to the minimum. If Sandusky can be taken as a fair sample I can say from personal experience that the league would be a success. We played two exhibition games there last fall after the season closed and both were well attended. In fact the total attendance exceeded 6,000.

The population of these towns is sufficient to warrant a good attendance at each game and the promoters should have no trouble in framing up a first-class organization.

No trouble would be experienced in getting players. There are enough amateurs in Cleveland, Cincinnati, Toledo and Columbus to assure the league plenty of high grade talent.

It would certainly be a boom [sic] for local baseball talent and would mean the making of many a future great. A league of this class always develops men who eventually become major league stars. Considerable interest is being shown at this early date in the proposed organization, which augurs well for its ultimate success.

The Class D Ohio State League began operations with the 1908 season, fielding teams in Lancaster, Lima (the Cigarmakers), Mansfield, Marion, Newark, and Springfield/Portsmouth. After coming close to the American League pennant in 1908, Cleveland built a farm system. Somers and Barnard oversaw franchises in Toledo and Ironton, Ohio; Waterbury, Connecticut; Portland, Oregon; and New Orleans. (It was to a cottage on the beach at Sandusky, during the 1910 season, that Dr. Morrison Castle would send an ailing Addie, hoping for recuperation of his pitching elbow. He did return to the team, on October 13, to start a game in the state series against Cincinnati.)

(OCTOBER 26, 1908, CP)

The proposed abolition of the "spit ball" by certain members of the rules committee is causing much speculation among fans and players as to whether or not such a move would be advisable.

The general impression seems to prevail that it will not be done. Even though the "spitter" is abolished, the chances are it will not be done away with until the pitchers who use it have had at least a year in which to become proficient in the common or garden variety of foolers [slang].

There is no question but what this form of delivery has had, and always will have, a bad effect on the hitting end of the game. Any time a pitcher has the "spit ball" working, and by that is meant having it break low and fast, he is practically unhittable.

The "saliva slant" takes more of a break than an ordinary curve ball, and what is more, when handled by an expert, it can be made to break either in or out.

It is practically impossible for the batter to follow this break in the ball, and hence his inability to hit it successfully.

Fans seem to have taken a dislike to this form of pitching, particularly when the opposing flinger has the home batters on the run with it.

When the home twirler is making monkeys of the opposition with the "spitter," there is very little said against it.

Another reason given for its abolition is that it causes the fielders to make errors which otherwise would not have occurred.

This is especially true where an infielder who is obliged to make a hurried play grabs the ball on the moistened side. A wild peg is the usual result.

But after all is said and done, it is unlikely that the "spitter" will be abolished, for it would hardly be fair to the men who depend on this form of delivery for their success.

The pitcher who uses the "damp shoot" is only taking advantage of his peculiar skill in this line, investigation having shown that there is something besides merely wetting the ball which makes it so hard to hit.

It took Ed Walsh, [Charles] Comisky's great pitcher, a couple of years to acquire the "spitter," and it would surely be a hardship to deprive him of the use of it after he has worked it to a point where it is a near-science.

If it is abolished, plenty of time should be given to the "spit ballers" to acquire some other form of delivery with which they can retain their effectiveness. One season will surely not be too long.

"Heinie" Berger threw the best spitball on Addie's pitching staffs with the Naps. The hardest one he had to face as a batter must have been Ed Walsh's. Walsh learned the pitch from Elmer Stricklett, during spring training in 1904, but didn't throw it until the 1906 season. He was right about the grandfather clause. Cleveland's great Stanley Coveleski and a list of fellow spitballers were allowed to continue to use the otherwise illegal pitch after 1920. Addie's contemporary, Alta Weiss, a female pitcher, may have had the best spitball in northern Ohio. She traveled with the Weiss All-Stars of Cleveland, starting in 1908. The future physician once pitched an exhibition game at League Park that drew 3,000 spectators.

(DECEMBER 12, 1908, TNB)

When the rules committee of the major leagues saw fit to do away with the privilege formerly extended to twirlers, whereby they were allowed to discolor a new ball during a game, it inflicted a more severe penalty than the majority of fans realize.

The main reason for the elimination of this privilege was because it became tiresome for the spectators to continually watch the pitcher take a new ball and get down on his hands and knees and rub the sphere in the dirt and grass until it was partially or wholly discolored. This ruling made the work of the pitcher a much different proposition last season.

Any time a club was ahead, especially if along in the closing innings of the game, it used to be a mighty good thing to always discolor a new ball. If the ball was not rubbed in the dirt, it loomed up as large as a barrel when pitched against a dark background.

The batter had a much better chance to see and hit a new ball on a dark day. That's one reason why the pitchers always rubbed it in the dirt before handing it up to the plate.

Since the new rule went into effect, it is practically impossible to get a good grip on a new ball. It is absolutely necessary for a pitcher to have a firm hold on the ball when pitching a curve.

To show this works to the twirler's disadvantage, we'll say, for an illustration, that the man at bat is weak on a curve ball. The count stands two balls and two strikes on him, when he fouls off the next one pitched. The umpire tosses out a new ball to the pitcher, and right here is where the box artist is placed at a disadvantage.

He knows the batter is weak on a good curve ball, but he also knows that, with a new ball to handle, he is going to have considerable trouble in making it break just where he wants it to.

He tries to bend up one, and, nine times out of ten, it does not break just right, and the batter whales it good and hard.

Many a game is lost because the pitcher is not allowed to discolor the ball any more. The hit that started Chicago's batting rally in the last game of the season at New York, which won the National league pennant for the Cubs, according to one who should know, was secured in this manner.

[Joe] Tinker, who was at bat, is supposed to be weak on a curve. [Christy] Mathewson tried to curve a new ball, failed, and Joe laced it out for a three-base hit. That started the trouble, and it never stopped until the Cubs had enough runs to cinch the game and championship.

Had Tinker failed to get on, there is no telling but what Matty might have gone through the inning without being scored on.

Rules for 1908 made it illegal for a pitcher to intentionally deface a ball. (The fine for the offense was $5.) The official game ball was still "dirty" a dozen years into baseball's future, when one thrown by Carl Mays hit Cleveland's Ray Chapman. Before Mike Hargrove and Gaylord Perry would make the time between each pitch into a prisoner's dental appointment, there was Eddie Plank—and, before him, Clark Griffith. However, Deadball Era rules allowed for up to 20 seconds between pitches. Wonder who was Addie's informant for the inside dish on the deciding game? Sounds suspiciously like some Giant Addie knew, perhaps Roger Bresnahan? The Toledo celebrity was *behind the plate that game, but the journalist's friend Fred Merkle was on the field, and his acquaintance Rube Marquard was close by, on the bench.*

(DECEMBER 16, 1908, TNB)

The day of the successful high-ball pitching is a thing of the past. There was a time, and not so very far distant, when it was the generally-accepted theory among players and spectators that one of the necessary requisites of the successful twirler was the ability to keep the ball high, and around the batter's neck.

For a long time this proved successful, but, when the batters became accustomed to this style of pitching, and learned to keep away from it, the slabber found himself up against it every time he resorted to the high fast one.

With the advent of the "spit-ball" it became apparent to all that the low ball was much harder to hit, and, naturally, all the present-day twirlers soon adapted themselves to this style of delivery.

The one great reason for the inability to hit the low ball successfully, as given by all players of experience, is the fact that it is much harder to gauge properly.

This is especially true when the man at the bat is trying to pull off the hit-and-run play. Formerly, when the twirlers kept their fast balls high, it was pie for the batter to either step back or in, as the occasion required, and push or pull the ball in the direction which he wished it to go.

With the low ball, it is entirely different, as the batter does not gauge the ball any too well, and finds it a difficult matter to place it where he wants it to go.

It is particularly hard for the batter to follow a low ball on a dark day, as can be cited in many instances, especially in the second game of the first world's series between the New York and the Athletics on the Polo grounds.

"Chief" Bender, who was on the mound for Connie Mack's men that day, is a pitcher who, when right, has a tremendous amount of speed. Philadelphia managed to score a few runs for Bender early in the game, and, with this lead, there was no chance for the Giants to catch up.

Bender had the advantage of the gathering gloom in his favor, and this, coupled with his ability to keep the fast ball low, proved a huge stumbling block in the path of the aggressive Giants.

Members of both teams say the big fellow was unhittable on account of this, which goes to show how much harder it is to hit the low ball than the high one.

On October 10, 1905, Charles Albert "Chief" Bender shut out the Giants on four hits. His catcher that day, Ossee Schrecongost, a familiar figure in these columns, scored twice. It was the only game of the Series in which the Athletics were not themselves shut out. Bender kept the ball low. He was a master of the "fast curve" and a changeup that acted like a knuckleball. Charles Albert Bender was a graduate of the Carlisle Indian School, where Jim Thorpe would distinguish himself. Mel Harder's slider would be the next revolution in pitching, followed much later by the Elroy Face forkball.

(DECEMBER 29, 1908, TNB)

It's an established fact that it is almost impossible for a batter to successfully gauge the "spit-ball" when handed up to him by an expert damp finger; but it is not generally known that, at times, it is almost impossible for the catcher to properly handle this sort of delivery.

For some unaccountable reason, the pitchers who use the "spitter" are unable to tell exactly where the ball is going to break, or how much of a shoot it will take.

One time the ball will break out, another time the sphere takes an inward shoot, but most of the time it breaks down, just like a drop curve.

These queer pranks are the bane of every catcher. [Jack] Chesbro's wild pitch at New York, which gave Boston the American league championship a few seasons ago [1904], caused by a "spitter" getting away from the big fellow's control, has already been made famous.

"Buck" Orth, who until the middle of last season, served up "spit-ball" slants and shoots for the Highlanders, nearly put Harry Bay out of the business for good at Cleveland one day during the summer of 1906.

"Buck" has a "spitter" that breaks like an outcurve, only a good deal faster. Bay, who crowds the plate when hitting, and who grasps the bat with hands spread quite a ways apart, swung hard on one of Orth's offerings.

The ball, instead of going where Harry thought it would, took one of those crazy shoots toward Bay and struck him on the forefinger of his left hand.

Naturally the ball did not travel very far, just going over Orth's head and so slow that it was an easy matter for the fleet-footed outfielder to easily beat the throw to first.

Bay's finger received the full force of the blow and he was out of the game for a couple of weeks. This was one of the times where a man made a base hit with his finger.

Probably no pitcher in the business has a better "spitter" than big Ed Walsh, the famous White Sox twirler. Ed gets a wonderful break on his "spitball" and this very fact caused him to lose a game at Cleveland last fall.

The Naps had a man on third in the third inning, with two out. [Wilbur] Goode [sic] was at bat and Walsh had two strikes and no balls on him. [Ossee] Schreck[enghost] called for a "spitball" and the big twirler let drive.

It was a little high and wide and Goode let it go. Schreck set himself for just about where the ball should have gone, but instead of coming true, the little pill took one of those crazy shoots and dropped fully a foot lower than the ordinary "spitball" would have done, with the result that it barely touched the catcher's mitt and, glancing from the glove, shot into the crowd, allowing the runner on third to trot home with the only run of the contest.

We left Ossee Schrecongost scoring in the 1905 World Series. Now Addie remembers him behind the plate, in one of his last half-dozen games, at the end of the 1908 season. Wilbur Good (like Schrecongost's best friend, Rube Waddell, a denizen of Punxsutawney, Pennsylvania) played 42 games in the Naps outfield in 1908. "Lucky" Good's best season was with the Cubs, in 1914, when he played every day. Al Orth won 203 games by throwing an improbable slow ball, and a submarine spitter (he called it a "thumb ball") which broke away, not down, at the plate. To boot, Orth was the consummate pinch hitter.

(JANUARY 11, 1909, TNB)

In looking over the averages of the American and National league players for the past few seasons one is impressed with the fact that the number of bases stolen by the cleverest runners in both organizations, is far less than it used to be.

Any major league player nowadays who can steal 50 bases during a season is considered some pumpkins on the paths.

Not so many years ago, it was considered nothing at all for a good base runner to purloin anywhere from 50 to 75 bases a year and Big Bill Lange, in the heyday of his career as a member of the old Chicago Nationals, set the mark at something over a hundred.

Naturally the question arises, were the men of those days faster on their feet than are the players of this generation, or did they have the art of pilfering bases perfected to a more finished degree than their later brethren?

It is hardly likely that in either of these things did they excel. What probably causes less base stealing now is due to the change in the style of the game.

In the old days when a fast man got to first it was the usual policy to let the man steal at the first good opportunity.

Now a different system is pursued. The minute a man reaches first, he is either sacrificed to second, or the man at bat tries in every legitimate way he can to help him reach second.

The hit and run play has become universally adopted and this does away with a good deal of clean stealing.

Any time a fast base runner reaches first the opposing catcher, figuring that he will attempt to steal, is constantly on the look-out for this move, and in order to prevent the runner from going through with the play, has the pitcher not only hold the runner very close to the bag, but also has him pitch out whenever his judgment tells him the attempt is to be made.

This practically kills off any chance there is to steal clean and forces the opposition to resort to the hit and run.

Probably the one great reason, though, why the number of stolen bases become less every year lies in the fact that in order to steal bases the runner must first get on.

In the days when it was nothing to steal 50 or more bases, the feat was usually accomplished by men, who never hit under .300 and who often clouted the sphere at a .350 or .375 clip.

Naturally these men, hitting at that pace, reached first quite a few times during the season and this gave them a great advantage over the players today.

When a man has a tough time hitting .275, as a good many of the present-day stars do, it is only natural that he will not steal quite as many bases as he would were he slugging the ball for a percentage of 100 points better.

This view from the Hot Stove League was printed under a headline asking, "Is Baserunning Lost Art?" It may be read as a response to a Henry Chadwick piece in the Spalding Guide for 1906, *where he pronounces the decline in stolen bases to be a disaster for the game. Addie and Chadwick would have been shocked at the stolen base figures for MLB by mid-century. In 1950, Dom DiMaggio's 15 steals were good enough to lead the American League by a safe margin; in 1957, the entire Senators team stole only 13 times all year (the all-time record low).*

But Addie's analysis of baserunning stats doesn't hold up unless he is using league figures only from the previous two seasons. And his observations hold true more for individual trends than for league results. Going back to 1901, the National League reached its highest total for stolen bases in the 1905 season (1,601); the American League peak was in 1906 (1,533). Individually, the only 50-base stealer in the big leagues for 1908 was Honus Wagner, who led the N.L. with 53 bags; Chicago's Pat Dougherty led all the A.L. with 47 swipes. Figures for the upcoming 1909 season would be significantly up. Today we consider "Little Eva" Lang's 73 steals in 1897 to be below 110th place all time. And we recognize Cincinnati's Hugh Nicol's 138 stolen bases in 1887 to be the record for one season. There were six 100-plus base stealers in the major leagues in 1887.

The first Cleveland player in the twentieth century to steal at least 50 bases and lead the league was Kenny Lofton, in 1992, a feat he repeated for the next four seasons. The first to lead the American League was Harry Bay (1903), although Ollie Pickering stole the league's high in 1900. In 1904, Elmer Flick shared the title with teammate Bay (38 steals), and then won it outright in 1906 (39). When Addie wrote this article, the last Cleveland player to record at least 50 stolen bases in a season was his old friend Jimmy McAleer, who stole 51 bases (while hitting only .237), in 1891.

Addie was right about the decline in hitting. American League batters for the 1908 season struggled along with a .239 average, and an anemic .304 slugging percentage. The comparable figures for major league hitters in 1894 were a lusty .309 and .435. To enliven the offensive side of the sport, the cork-centered ball was introduced in 1911.

(JANUARY 12, 1909, TNB)

There was a time, not so very long ago, that all managers were under the impression that in order to have a good infield it was necessary to get small men to play the inner works positions.

In those days it was rarity to see a large man playing on the infield, unless he was stationed at first base, but now there is hardly a team in the country but has two or three big men on the close defense.

The general supposition, in this day of the game, has come to be that a good big man is just a little better than a good little man.

While the little fellow may seem to be doing a lot more work and makes it look more spectacular, he is hardly, if ever, doing one bit more than the big fellow.

The good sized man has all the advantage, when it comes to pulling down high or wide throws.

Everyone seems to take it for granted that the little fellows are always faster than the big men. In some cases this may be true, but there are any number of big men who can give anyone in the country a fine chase when it comes to getting over the ground in a hurry.

The big fellow does not appear to be going as fast as the little man, because he is taking so much more of a stride.

On first sight no one would think Pat Dougherty of the [White] Sox was a speed marvel, but if you were out there pitching and the big fellow dropped a bunt in front of the plate, it would not take long to discover that Pat can cover the distance from the plate to first base about as fast as anyone in the business.

Men such as [Ty] Cobb, [Sam] Crawford, [Honus] Wagner, [Elmer] Flick, [Larry] Lajoie, [Bill] Bradley and a host of others of about their size don't look so very fast, but run them along side of such men as ["Donie"] Bush, [Harry] Bay, [Billy] Maloney, [Johnny] Evers and [Terry] Turner and they would show just as much speed as the little fellows.

This piece is perhaps less a viewpoint than the Deadball equivalent of a satellite-radio topic to prompt call-ins. Its provocative headline read: "Big Men Are Speedier / Can Get Over the Ground Faster Than Small Chap." Addie's specimen of the speedy big man, Patrick "Patsy" Dougherty (6 feet, 2 inches, 190 pounds), led the American League in steals for 1908. He collected 261 steals over his 10-year career as an outfielder. Five-foot-ten Billy Maloney stole a National League best 59 bases for the Cubs in 1905, his career year.

(February 22, 1909, TNB)

One thing baseball fans like more than anything else in a game except to see the home team win, is ginger.

By this is meant life or action. Nothing is more tiresome to spectators and players than to be forced to watch a contest that drags.

This is one of the reasons why all managers always instruct their players to keep moving and lively on the field, either by their actions or talk.

A lively, hustling, gingery ball club is always a favorite with the patrons of the game and it's very seldom that a team of this caliber is not a top notcher.

The same thing holds good of the individual player. Any time you see a man, who is constantly talking on the field and giving his pitcher encouragement, you are seeing a player who is always in the game and one who is a great help to his club.

Addie Joss, author of sports columns and 160 major league wins **(Cleveland Public Library Photograph Collection).**

It's mighty encouraging to the pitcher to have a team behind him, with every member constantly chattering during the game. It makes the twirler feel sure that everybody is working just as hard for a victory as he is.

The effect this has on the opposing club is hard to estimate, but it gets the desired results. It rather gets on one's nerve to be forced to listen to this constant talk from the opposition, no matter what the score may be.

If a gingery player's team is behind and he still keeps it up, it makes you sore to think that you can't keep him still, even though his club is getting a good beating.

On the other hand, if the conditions are reversed, it galls a little to hear this line of talk and doesn't tend to take away any of the sting of the coming defeat.

The American public likes ginger of life, in any line of sport. It appeals to them more forcibly in baseball than in any other pastime.

"The American public likes ginger of life" is an insightful observation of popular culture as it was rapidly inventing itself, and being invented by "Teddy" Roosevelt and others, at the launch of the American Century. An infamous instance of a teammate failing to hustle may have kept Cleveland out of the World Series in 1908, and Addie was part of the play. In the ninth inning of the October 4 game, Bill Hinchman was slow to run out a grounder to Bobby Wallace, and the Naps' runner on third base did not score. The runner at third was Addie Joss.

Toledo editors intended the following to be Addie's so-long-till-fall column before he jumped on the train for Macon, Georgia, where he would rejoin the Naps for his eighth season. As it turned out, this is the last story he ever wrote for the News-Bee.

(FEBRUARY 27, 1909, TNB)

"ADDIE JOSS' FAREWELL STORY ON OLD MEN AND THE NOVICES"

There seems to be an impression among the fans that the early career of the youngster, especially on a southern training trip, is made precarious by the treatment he receives at the hands of the older men on the team. This is all tommy rot.

Of course, it is only natural that if there is going to be any preference shown by the management, the older men, who have earned this distinction, should get it. But as this is seldom if ever done, it can readily be seen that from this standpoint, the youngster is on a par with the veteran.

In a good many respects the newcomer gets a little the best of it, on account of the fact that the older fellows are supposed to know what to do. Little attention is ever paid them by the manager. On the other hand, knowing that the youngster has a good deal to learn, most of the manager's instruction is given to the beginner.

He is looked after and watched all the time and when he makes a mistake, is soon informed of his error in a quiet way.

This holds good with the older men as well. On most clubs there are a number of players who have no fear of losing their positions and are always ready to do anything to help the youngster.

They do this, not alone from a tendency to see the young fellow get along, but by helping him develop they add that much strength to their club.

The idea that on every major league club there are numerous cliques, especially one grand one, directed by the older men against the new comers, is all a mistake. Could any of the home fans see the youngsters sitting around in front of the hotel, mixing in with the older men every evening, this idea would soon become a thing of the past.

The 1909 edition of the Naps was a mix of rookies and immortals. The team was even more optimistic than most are in spring; it had nearly won the pennant the previous season, the best finish in Cleveland's brief American League history. Addie could look forward to a spring training with Cy Young, and no one could know that this was to be Lajoie's last season as the manager. Counted in the rookie class of '09 were two good catching prospects, Steve O'Neill, who didn't make the cut but would be back with the team for good in September, and good-hitting Ted Easterly; solid "Ivy" Olson, Casey Stengel's grammar school mate and the Dodgers' shortstop in 1920, when the Indians won the World Series; outfielder Tom Rafter; and pitchers Gene Krapp, who would win 13 games in his first season, Carl Sitton, and "Lucky" Wright. Addie by now was a game-tempered veteran, a world removed from the hazing he wrote about in his first newspaper column. He must have relished his role of joshing and mentoring this newest bunch of yannigans.

Endgame

Addie Joss would report to this spring training camp, and two more, with Cleveland. His last was at Alexandria, Louisiana, in 1911. He was too weak to pitch at all that spring. Instead, Addie sat on the bench and wondered at the new kids. There was Vean Gregg, fresh off a season in the Northwest when he'd thrown an impossible 14 shutouts. And there was that left-handed hitter, a Deep South boy, already beginning to catch up with major league pitching. That old bat—"Black Betsy" he called it—was always in his hands. The new rabbit ball really jumped off that big wagon tongue, and he swung harder and smoother than any. For the state championship the previous fall, when Addie came back to win a game against the Reds, the kid had played a good center field behind him. That bat was his spoon and his pillow. They called him "Shoeless Joe."

Appendix: Contributions by Joss to Other Newspapers and Periodicals

We first find Addie among the respondents, printed above Jake Beckley and John H. Hart, who are contributing to The Sporting News*' regular column Gossip of the Players. He tells his fans the story of his joining the Toledo Mud Hens, just half a dozen years earlier. This string of sports clichés is a sample of Addie's early prose, at least a year before it came under the scrutiny, sometimes careful, of newspaper editors.*

(*The Sporting News*, NOVEMBER 17, 1906)

Addie Joss: "I was living up in Juneau when I got a chance to get into the professional game. I received a letter from Charley Strobel offering me a place and I accepted just as quick as I could. I never thought for an instant that I would not make good. Why, I packed everything that I had in a trunk and took it all along with me when I went to Toledo. When I went into the box for the first game I was sure I would win. I don't believe that I ever had better speed or control and I got away with flying colors. I made good from the start and it was because I had confidence in myself. I am probably an exception to the rule, but I was never afraid and I never felt particularly green, though I probably was."

Addie must be remembering his successful debut, in the spring training game of April 17, 1900, against the Detroit Tigers. He pitched well enough that day, and in the April 23 exhibition game against the Negro League Columbus Giants, to make the Mud Hens' roster. But his Opening Day start, against Mansfield, resulted in a less-than-stellar 16 to 8 win.

The following feature article is another source for the legend that Addie

Joss was a correspondent for The Sporting News. *It is our only surviving example of what might be called Addie's mature prose in a deliberate attempt by the newspaperman to write for a magazine. The result is mixed: He tries out lofty stylings (the biblical "woe be unto him" and "is as nothing"), but overall he sounds defensive and exhausted. We might remember that Addie wrote this article in the weeks of self-questioning and public accusations following his Naps' failure to win a close pennant race.*

(*The Baseball Magazine*, VOL. 1, NO. 6, 1908)

"THE STRENUOSITY OF PITCHING"

To the casual observer it would seem that a major league pitcher's life is one continual bed of roses, especially if he be fortunate enough to be successful in winning a good percentage of the games in which he officiates. At first this seems a fair conclusion to draw, but when one delves a little farther into the matter, it soon becomes evident that this is an erroneous impression. It is true that pitching today and then resting for the next three or four days has its advantages, but the acquiring of this privilege also carries with it a few things that, as a rule, seldom, if ever, come to the minds of the baseball loving public.

In the first place, the pitcher must work as a minor league apprentice some years before he is even given so much as a chance to show his major league ability. Once this privilege is granted him, it's better than an even bet that he will find innumerable difficulties with which to contend before he wins a permanent berth on his club's pitching staff. A sore arm in the spring, or a little bad luck in the club's Southern exhibition games, all tend to make his none-too-light task even harder. With all these obstacles overcome, and secure in the knowledge that he is considered one of the regulars, he still has numerous difficulties to face.

In this day and age of baseball, when the game has practically developed into a one man game, that man being the pitcher, no pitcher walks out on the diamond without knowing that the winning of the ball game in a large measure depends on his individual efforts. He knows only too well that the least slip-up on his part will invariably spell defeat for his team.

Then he must be able to hold his own under fire. The young pitcher is a mark for the coaches of the opposing side, and woe be unto him if he shows by any sign that what they say makes any impression upon him.

It is not at all wonderful that so few can stand the terrific strain to which they are subjected. No player in [sic] the team is called upon to go through such a baptism as he. What the other players of a team have to go through is as nothing compared to the initiation of a pitcher. Theirs is comparatively an easy thing.

Not only must a pitcher be cool, collected, fearless, with a strong arm and good command, but he must be an adept fielder, able to handle the most difficult of bunts and to throw the ball to any of the bases according to the emergency. A miss in any instance is apt to be fatal to his success in the game. Then not only must he be able to do this part of the work correctly, but on all bunts to the first baseman he must cover the bag himself. Then he is expected to back up every base in case of throws from the in and out fielders. If any player in the team has a busy time of it from the time he steps on the field till the game is over, it is the pitcher.

The mere physical exertion required of a pitcher is little indeed compared with the strain on his nerves. In order for a pitcher to do his best, in any contest, he must be keyed up to about ninety-nine per cent of his energy; and when one is forced to [do] this more than once every three days, something is bound to give way. One often is told how they used to pitch in the olden day, when a club had but one pitcher; and of the wonderful record of [Charley] Radbourn, who landed the pennant for Providence almost single-handed. In the beginnings of professional leagues there w[as] not the number of games that there are today. The clubs did not play more than four games a week at most, filling in the open dates with exhibition games. Now it is an every-day affair. Again, there was not the strain of pitching in days gone by that there is today. A man may be perfectly willing to go in and pitch as often as he is requested, but he is bound to conserve his forces and if he overworks disastrous consequences will be sure to follow. It generally happens, when a man works twice in the same series, that he will lose the second game. He needs just about three days' rest, and if he does not get it he is taking great risk. Occasionally a pitcher will work in both games of a double header. If his arm is in good shape and he is feeling right, there is no reason why he should not do it. It is no worse than working in a protracted game: pitchers have worked for twenty-four hours without feeling any ill results at all. Such great pitchers as [Christy] Mathewson and [Cy] Young have been obliged to succumb to the strain of working too frequently, without a sufficient rest between working days. A pitcher is no mere machine.

Besides the constant strain to which a pitcher is subjected, there are some other matters that must not be forgotten. Long railroad rides, especially in hot weather, are most tiresome and fatiguing to all players, but especially to the pitcher who is booked to work the next day. Take, for example, such a trip as that from St. Louis to Boston, which requires two nights and a day on the road. It takes a little time to rest from such an arduous journey, and if the train is late matters are worse: for there is hurry to get to the hotel, take a bath, partake of a meal in haste and then hustle for the ball ground. A man is then incapable of his best work.

It has happened in case of a delay in traveling that the ball player goes directly from the train to the ball ground, and is obliged to don his uniform on the train — something that is altogether too strenuous. This does not occur very often; but, when it does, it is a tired lot of ball players that gathers on the field: and if the game is won, it is a wonder indeed. Yet I have known a team completely fagged and travel-worn to go on the field and give a sound drubbing to a club that had the benefit of a night's rest. You can never tell what may happen. In such a case sleep is not beautiful after such an experience. I am of the opinion that a pitcher — a battery if possible — ought to be sent ahead so as to obtain a rest of [sic] the night. This is sometimes done, but it is exceptional.

Probably the greatest handicap to a pitcher is the weather. This is especially true of the early days of the spring. Very few of the major league pitchers come north after their spring trip in July condition. Should a man go in to work on a cold spring day, there is more or less danger of ruining his arm for the remainder of the season, if not for all time. The pitcher must go in and pitch just as hard as if the month was July: he cannot refuse to work. Some clubs refuse to work their best pitchers under such conditions; I consider this very good policy indeed. Good pitchers are scarce, and it is very foolish to take the least chance with a man who is sure to do good sustained work after the seasonable weather arrives.

A pitcher naturally becomes heated while at work, and perspires more or less freely. If he does not take great care of his arm between innings, by keeping it well protected, he is liable to suffer. This is especially true on a cold or rainy spring day.

So, from beginning to end, the pitcher's life is a round of hard work, trouble and care. All is not roses. But still the life is worthwhile.

"Strenuosity" was a popular term in pre-war America for the organized recreational exercise which was acquiring the status of a cult. Writers had begun to explain the value of baseball as an "Americanizing" agency. But Addie has appropriated the word for his defense of pitching as strenuous labor. Old Hoss Radbourn pitched in 75 of Providence's 114 games in their pennant year of 1884. In Addie's American League, four pitchers won two complete games in one day (Ed Walsh twice). Cleveland's "Dutch" Levsen was the last to pull off the feat, in a doubleheader on August 28, 1926. In the modern era, Wilbur Wood won two games on May 28, 1973, and later that summer became the last pitcher to start both ends of a double header, on July 20. Contemporaries sometimes debated Addie's durability, but he completed all 31 of his starts in 1903.

(THE WASHINGTON *Post*, APRIL 6, 1911)

"JOSS TALKS IN EPIGRAMS"

Addie Joss, star pitcher of the Naps, has written a few baseball epigrams for fandom's benefit. They read as follows:

Pitchers are 80 per cent of a baseball club.

Without a good pitching staff a club cannot win, even though it be strong at the bat and in the field.

More games are won and lost in the third-base coaching box than any other position on the field.

The third-base coacher has the toughest job of the entire team. He has to suffer for the mistakes of the base runners, as well as any he may make himself.

The fans can make or break a baseball club.

They can kill a young pitcher by yelling "Take him out!" if he happens to have a bad inning. The manager may win that particular ball game by listening to the cries of the crowd, but lose a lot of others by thus destroying that pitcher's confidence in himself.

Baseball fans are too grasping. They want their team to win every game. They forget that the opposing teams are strong outfits, perhaps stronger than their own club. They seem to think that the opposing club should be just strong enough to be beaten. Consequently they don't give the opposing teams credit for pulling off stuff that circumvents their own favorites and causes victory to go the other way.

Young pitchers must learn sooner or later how to pull themselves out of bad situations. They will not learn if they are sent to the bench every time they get to going bad. There is not a star pitcher in the country today but had to take some terrific beatings before he acquired the wisdom that has make him a star.

This piece was published just six days before Addie's death. The observations make epigrams in the sense that they are distillations of many of the stances Addie took in his newswriting, including his thinking about the new role of third base coaches, the nature of confidence, and the distraction of fans. Bill James has credited Addie for originating what has become baseball wisdom, in the first epigram.

(*The Baseball Magazine*, VOL. 7, NO. 6, 1911)

"My No Hit Game, Oct. 2, 1908"

Of course, I was tickled half to death when I realized I had pitched a no-run, no-hit, no-man-reach-first-base game. I had never pitched a no-hit game before and to think that I should equal the world's record when I did manage to hold the opposition hitless made me feel pretty good.

However, I had no mean rival in Ed. Walsh, and his pitching would win nine games out of ten; yes, 99 out of every 100.

Why, Walsh had us all breaking our backs going after his spitters. He fanned 15, a world's record for eight innings, while I struck out but three. Had it not been for the grand support accorded me, I think the Sox would have won. We got our one run only through the daring of Joe Birmingham and a couple of bad pegs.

For the record, the standard for strikeouts in a single game—regardless of innings pitched—was established and equaled within one month in 1884, when Charlie Sweeney (59-game-winner Hoss Radbourn's teammate) and Hugh Daily struck out 19 batters. In that Season of the Pitcher, Dupee Shaw and

Henry Porter both fanned 18 batters in games, and Boston's Charlie Buffinton set down eight Cleveland Spiders in a row, 17 overall, on September 2. Addie's brief account of his perfect game appeared posthumously. This fragment by the newly fallen hero, used as a filler for completing the bottom of page 64, gives the odd effect of an afterthought—much like the reputation of Adrian Joss, ace twirler of the Cleveland Naps.

Chapter Notes

Preface

1. Letter to R.F. Paine, April 13, 1907.

2. One other baseball player published non-ghosted articles during the time of Addie's sports writing career. Fred Tenney, a graduate of Brown University, wrote syndicated pieces that were carried in popular periodicals like *The Baseball Magazine* and *Everybody's Magazine* and newspapers, including the Boston *Sunday Post* and the New York *Times*. The long-time first baseman and manager for the Boston Nationals and the New York Giants was conspicuous for another reason: He broke in as a left-handed catcher. Fred Tenney continued to write for publication after his retirement from baseball. Eddie Collins, after the 1909 season, wrote columns for the Philadelphia *Evening Bulletin* on various subjects.

3. Biographer Scott Longert recalls that Addie was offered an off-season job to write for a Brooklyn newspaper, in 1907.

4. American journalism's old distinctions between local, regional, and national were being challenged: 1907 also happens to be the first year of operations for the United Press wire service.

5. It's possible that nine-year-old Harold Crane saw Joss play, before he became the poet Hart Crane.

6. On the difficulties of confirming the so-called facts of history, I recommend Louis Turco's "The Mutable Past," collected in *Fantaseers*. In the story, the writer questions his childhood "memory" of working for Ed Walsh in his hometown of Meriden, Connecticut.

A Brief Biography

1. The *Reach Guide for 1903*, on the transformation of the Cleveland team, enthuses that "the acquisition of Lajoie, Flick, Bernhard and Hickman ... converted a probable cemetery into a blooming financial garden."

2. Period umpires used hand-held "indicators" to keep track of balls, strikes, and outs.

Chapter 1

1. In the championship summer of 1896, all of the Spiders' players were arrested for "disorderly conduct" on the field against the Louisville Colonels.

2. John Husman determined that "Garry Herrmann bought the [Toledo] club (undercover) in 1905 and Armour came in 1907 as front man for Charles Somers of Cleveland" (e-mail

to editor). The era's Mud Hens enjoyed a long-term close relationship with the Naps: Toledo played "at home" in Cleveland for the 1914 and 1915 seasons, Somers' move to block the Federal League from moving to the city.

3. Addie had the experience of playing right field. In two games, in 1906, he handled eight chances without an error, and even contributed an assist.

4. Pen names were a common feature of the sports pages of the day: e.g., the Cleveland *Press* ran a column of opinionated commentary by "The Little Old Man."

5. For the record: It was 1897 when Lajoie, then the Athletics' regular first baseman, played 19 games in the outfield with Ed Delahanty, a fixture in left. The following season, Lajoie was moved permanently to second base. Roy Thomas comes into the picture later, in 1899, when the speedster was signed right off the Penn campus to play center, in a quick-to-the-ball A's' outfield, between Delahanty and right fielder Elmer Flick.

6. The New York *Times*' obituary (January 14, 1903) reasons that Mercer had recently grown despondent owing to his "pulmonary troubles," which "refused to yield to treatment," and summarily reports that "He left a statement of his financial accounts, showing that he owed no money."

7. The Cleveland *Press* offered the following perspective on players' salaries to its readers on April 2, 1907: "[Cy] Young used to draw $18 a week as a machinist. His salary as a pitcher [with the Boston Americans] this year will be $100 a week."

8. Russell Ford, the original Ford who pitched for New York in the American League, perfected the sandpapered "shine ball" about 1910.

9. Mud Hens' historian John Husman agrees that, since Addie had no assets, Charles Somers was probably his silent partner in the offer (e-mail to editor).

10. Named after Admiral Shays, a hero of the recent Spanish-American War.

Chapter 2

1. Hurst wasn't laughing the day he was banned from baseball for spitting at Eddie Collins in an August 1909 game. It's sobering to know that irrepressible Tim Hurst was dead by 1915.

2. After Addie decided to give up journalism, he was engaged one winter as a celebrity singer in "Doc" White's vaudeville act. The quartet opened in November 1910, in Milwaukee.

3. The newly formed American Association brought Sunday baseball to Cleveland in 1882. Three years later, Cleveland's Western League Cardinals scheduled games on Sundays, at Brooklyn Park on the city's West Side. After their first Sunday game, versus Toledo, Cleveland catcher Moses Fleetwood Walker was arrested for playing baseball on the Sabbath. (Walker is most remembered for his career with Toledo.) In 1887, the A.A. Spiders hosted a Sunday contest at the Cedar Avenue Driving Park, a horse track. The 1888 Cleveland Blues played on Sundays outside the city limits, beginning on July 22, at the Geauga Lake picnic grounds.

4. According to the *Reach Guide for 1903*, the only "inter-league" postseason series following Addie's rookie season was between Cleveland and Pittsburgh.

5. E.g., see "Take Him Out!," Chapter II in *Pitching in a Pinch*.

6. A young Cleveland *News* reporter, a southerner, got married at the Naps' spring training, in 1906. His name was Grantland Rice.

7. As far back as 1870, the National Association's Cincinnati and Chicago clubs had trained

in New Orleans, but most organizations held spring training locally until about 1890. The Cleveland Spiders made their camp at Hot Springs, Arkansas, in March 1889. And the first Grapefruit League game to be played in Florida matched the Spiders (training in Jacksonville) against the Pirates (St. Augustine), on April 3, 1891. By 1910, teams broke camp in the south or southwest and played a schedule of exhibition games all the way north for the regular season.

Chapter 3

1. It was easy for reporters to interview the two star pitchers in the lobby of the Euclid, the hotel where both teams stayed.

2. Cleveland notable Pete Hotaling played center field, beside a left fielder improbably named "Buttercup" Dickerson, the season Richmond tossed his perfect game against the Cleveland Blues.

3. Addie's teammates on the Naps included three brothers of Major League players: Frank Delahanty, Josh Clarke, and Harry Hinchman.

4. On August 4, 1911, Lee Tannehill of the Chisox would become the only shortstop to execute *two* unassisted triple plays in a game. He's featured at third base, in Addie's following story (and Bill Bradley, in the present article, is flip-flopped between third base and short).

5. "Heinie" Reitz was baseball's first auto fatality, in 1914.

Chapter 4

1. The term is also spelled "crank." I take my spelling from Boston businessman Thomas William Lawson's glossary, *The Krank: His Language and What It Means*, 1888.

2. The Brooklyn club was named the Trolley Dodgers in view of the dangers to fans who had to brave the streetcar traffic to attend old Eastern Park. But some organizations lived in both the old and modern worlds of mass transportation. McGraw's Giants were still carried to road-game parks in horse-drawn "tally-hos," although they traveled to the Polo Grounds via the new subway system.

3. Frank Robison built League Park at the intersection of two streetcar lines, at East 66th Street and Lexington Avenue: the long ride east was good business for his Cleveland City Railway Company.

4. In the lobby of another hotel, in Philadelphia in 1907, George Stovall broke an oak chair over his manager Napoleon Lajoie's head during an argument.

Chapter 5

1. Hanlon, who broke in as a Cleveland outfielder in 1880, is the only Blues player in Cooperstown.

2. McGraw, reminiscing in *My Thirty Years of Baseball*, declares: "So-called inside baseball is mostly bunk. It is merely working out of definite plans that the public does not observe." Of course, his annual guide and rule book was named *Scientific Baseball*, and his 1912 vaudeville monolog was billed "Inside Baseball." His colleague, Christy Mathewson, uses the term "inside baseball" to indicate insider dope, in *Pitching in a Pinch*.

3. Elmer Horton, after being traded to Hanlon's Orioles, remarked: "They play more with their heads than their hands. It's like going to college to watch them work" (*The Sporting News*, 3 July 1897).

4. In his biography of John McGraw, Charles Alexander finds that "The foundation of [the Hanlon-led Baltimore] attack was the hit-and-run play."

5. Gilks signed Addie to his first professional contract. When he played beside McAleer, in the Cleveland Spiders' outfields, he popularized the trap play to force the base runner.

6. Bill James observes, in his *Guide to Baseball Managers*: "Of [the] sixteen managers who began the 1919 season, at least seven had played for Ned Hanlon, and at least three of the others had played for some other manager who had played for Ned Hanlon."

7. McGraw's game eschewed the sacrifice bunt, or "giving up an out" in an inning, in favor of base stealing and the hit and run.

8. Christy Mathewson defines luck, in *Pitching in a Pinch*, as "a combination of confidence and getting the breaks. Ball-players get no breaks without confidence in themselves, and lucky omens inspire this confidence. On the other hand, unlucky signs take it away."

9. Pete Dowling, who pitched for Cleveland the year before Addie's rookie season, was killed by a train in 1905.

10. He was around long enough to form, with catcher Jack Ryan, the oldest battery in baseball history (almost 89 combined years of age), on October 4, 1913.

11. Before we credit John McGraw with another innovation, it should be noted that Fred Snodgrass, for one, found the manager's buddy Latham to be a joke as a coach.

12. Addie recorded the first win, and first shutout, in new Sportsman's Park, on May 14, 1909, beating Jack Powell.

13. According to the May 1, 1915 *Scientific American*, the average baseball player weighed 174 pounds.

Chapter 7

1. "Larry" Lajoie is filmed in the act of bunting a ball, thrown by Reds pitcher Jack Suttoff, to shortstop Tommy Corcoran, scoring Harry Bay from third.

2. The Pittsburgh *Press*, which did print a Sunday paper, carried Addie's syndicated reports during the week of the World Series. But on Sunday, it printed a United Press wire article and a story by Paul H. Bruske, and nothing by Joss.

3. Addie's figures don't always match the statistics we have in *Total Baseball*. For example, Frank Chance is on record with eight hits, and an average of .421; Joe Tinker's five base hits earn him a .238 BA.

4. In 1954, Bobby Avila and Willie Mays met in the Indians–Giants series.

5. The first Triple-Crown winner in the American League was Napoleon Lajoie (1901), with the Athletics.

Chapter 8

1. Addie may have voted a Democratic ticket. A box in the November 9, 1908, Cleveland *Press* has him declaring that William Jennings Bryan would win the presidential election over Ohioan William Howard Taft.

2. The first billboards in a Cleveland ball park were erected, in 1883, at the Kennard field. Norman Macht has discovered that, by the 1893 season, the Baltimore Orioles had painted their center field wall white to help batters see the discolored game ball (only one ball was used per game at that time).

3. For example, Billy Evans wrote: "All players want to win all the time. That's why the game cannot be dishonest" ("Is Baseball Honest?" in *Pearson's*, in 1912). Addie's column may be his reaction to Gen. Charles H. Taylor's article, "Is Baseball on the Level?" in *The Baseball Magazine*, Vol. 2, no. 1 (1908): pp. 10–12.

Bibliography

Archives

Cleveland Public Library, Charles W. Mears Baseball Collection.
Cleveland State University, Michael Schwartz Library, Special Collections.
David Stalker, Addie Joss Collection, Watertown, Wisconsin.
Toledo-Lucas County Public Library, Local History and Genealogy Department, and the Negley Cochran Collection.
University of Pittsburgh, Hillman Library, Special Collections.

Web Sites

www.andrewclem.com/Baseball/LeaguePark.html
www.baseball-almanac.com
www.baseballfever.com
www.baseballguru.com
www.thebaseballpage.com
www.baseball-reference.com
www.baseball-statistics.com
www.bioproj.sabr.org
www.clevelandmemory.org
www.csudigitalhumanities.org
www.ech.case.edu
www.hardballtimes.com
www.leaguepark.org
www.minorleaguebaseball.com
www.ohiohistory.org
www.paperofrecord.com
www.retrosheet.com
www.sabr.org
www.thedeadballera.com
www.totalbaseball.com
www.watertownhistory.org

E-Mail Correspondence

Eckhouse, Morris
Fleitz, David
Husman, John
Kryss, Tom
Liscio, Stephanie
Longert, Scott
Stalker, David

Articles

Fleitz, David. "Addie Joss: One of Toledo's Winners." Toledo *Blade* Sunday magazine, May 1982.

_____. "Baseball's First All-Star Game." Toledo *Blade* Sunday magazine, 29 May 1988.

Husman, John R. "The Business of Baseball in Nineteenth Century Toledo." *The Muddy Times* 1, 2010: 64–66.

_____. "Professional Baseball in Toledo, Ohio, 1883–1955." Unpublished manuscript.

Reach Guide for 1903: 27.

The Sporting News, 3 July 1897: 4.

Books

Alexander, Charles. *John McGraw.* New York: Viking, 1988.

_____. *Ty Cobb.* New York: Oxford University Press, 1984.

Blake, Mike. *The Minor Leagues.* New York: Wynwood, 1991.

Browning, Reed. *Cy Young: A Baseball Life.* Amherst: University of Massachusetts Press, 2000.

Casway, Jerrold. *Ed Delehanty in the Emerald Age of Baseball.* South Bend: University of Notre Dame Press, 2004.

Deford, Frank. *The Old Ball Game: How John McGraw, Christy Mathewson, and the New York Giants Created Modern Baseball.* New York: Grove, 2005.

DeValeria, Dennis, and Jeanne Burke DeValeria. *Honus Wagner.* Pittsburgh: University of Pittsburgh Press, 1998.

Dickson, Paul. *Baseball Dictionary*, 3d ed. New York: Norton, 2009.

Di Salvatore, Bryan. *A Clever Base-Ballist: The Life and Times of John Montgomery Ward.* New York: Pantheon, 1999.

Eckhouse, Morris, ed. *The Graney Generation.* Cleveland: October, 2003.

Egan, James M. *Base Ball on the Western Reserve: The Early Game in Cleveland and Northeast Ohio.* Jefferson, NC: McFarland, 2008.

Fleitz, David. *Shoeless: The Life and Times of Joe Jackson.* Jefferson, NC: McFarland, 2001.

Husman, John R. *Baseball in Toledo.* Charleston, SC: Arcadia, 2003.

James, Bill. *The Bill James Guide to Baseball Managers.* New York: Scribner, 1997.
_____. *The New Bill James Historical Abstract.* New York: Free, 2001.
_____. and Rob Neyer. *The Neyer/James Guide to Pitchers.* New York: Fireside, 2004.
Jones, David, ed. *Deadball Stars of the American League.* Dulles, VA: Potomac, 2006.
Krah, Steve. "Lou Criger." SABR BioProject.
Lawson, Thomas W. *The Krank: His Language and What It Means.* Boston: Rand Avery Co., 1888.
Lewis, Franklin. *The Cleveland Indians.* New York: Putnam, 1949.
Lin Weber, Ralph Elliott. *The Toledo Baseball Guide of the Mud Hens, 1883–1943.* Rossford, OH: Baseball Research Bureau, 1944.
Longert, Scott. *Addie Joss: King of the Pitchers.* Cleveland: SABR, 1998.
Lowry, Philip J. *Green Cathedrals.* New York: Addison-Wesley, 1992.
Macht, Norman L. *Connie Mack and the Early Years of Baseball.* Lincoln: University of Nebraska Press, 2007.
Masur, Louis. *Autumn Glory: Baseball's First World Series.* New York: Hill and Wang, 2003.
Mathewson, Christy [and John N. Wheeler]. *Pitching in a Pinch: Or, Baseball from the Inside.* New York: Grosset and Dunlap, 1912.
Murphy, Cait. *Crazy '08.* New York: Smithsonian, 2007.
Nemec, David. *The Great Encyclopedia of 19th-Century Major League Baseball.* New York: Donald L. Fine, 1997.
Neyer, Rob. *Rob Neyer's Big Book of Baseball Lineups.* New York: Fireside, 2003.
Okkonen, Marc. *Baseball Uniforms of the 20th Century.* New York: Sterling, 1993.
Peterson, Richard. *Extra Innings: Writing on Baseball.* Urbana: University of Illinois Press, 2001.
Phillips, John. *Bill Hinchman's Boner and the 1908 Naps.* Cabin John, MD Capital, 1990.
Pietrusza, David, Matthew Silverman and Michael Geshman, eds. *Baseball: The Biographical Encyclopedia.* New York: Total/Sports Illustrated, 2000.
Porter, David, ed. *The Biographical Dictionary of American Sports.* Westport, CT: Greenwood, 1987.
Ritter, Lawrence. *The Glory of Their Times.* New York: William Morrow, 1992.
Schneider, Russell. *The Cleveland Indians Encyclopedia*, 3d ed. Champaign, IL: Sports, 2004.
Seymour, Harold [and Dorothy Seymour Mills]. *Baseball: The Golden Age.* New York: Oxford University Press, 1971.
Simon, Tom, ed. *Deadball Stars of the National League.* Dulles, VA: Brassey's, 2004.
Snyder, John. *Indians Journal.* Cincinnati: Clerisy, 2008.
Spatz, Lyle, ed. *The SABR Baseball List and Record Book.* New York: Scribner, 2007.
Speck, William D. *Toledo: A History in Architecture, 1890–1914.* Charleston, SC: Arcadia, 2003.
Spink, Alfred H. *The National Game.* Rpt. Urbana: University of Illinois Press, 2000.
Thomas, G. Scott. *Leveling the Field.* New York: Black Dog, 2002.

Thorn, John, Pete Palmer and Michael Gershman, eds. *Total Baseball VII: The Official Encyclopedia of Major League Baseball.* Kingston, NY: Total Sports, 2001.

Thorn, John, Pete Palmer, Michael Gershman and David Pietrusza, eds. *Total Baseball V: The Official Encyclopedia of Major League Baseball.* New York: Viking, 1997.

Weisberger, Bernard A. *When Chicago Ruled Baseball.* New York: Harper, 2006.

White, G. Edward. *Creating the National Pastime.* Princeton: Princeton University Press, 1996.

Zappala, Tom, and Ellen Zappala. *The T206 Collection: The Players and Their Stories.* Portsmouth, NH: Peter E. Randall, 2010.

Index